*Service Learning
and Literary Studies in English*

Service Learning and Literary Studies in English

Edited by
Laurie Grobman and Roberta Rosenberg

The Modern Language Association of America
New York   2015

MLA and the MODERN LANGUAGE ASSOCIATION are trademarks owned by the Modern Language Association of America. For information about obtaining permission to reprint material from MLA book publications, send your request by mail (see address below) or e-mail (permissions@mla.org).

Library of Congress Cataloging-in-Publication Data

Service learning and literary studies in English / edited by Laurie Grobman and Roberta Rosenberg.

    pages cm

  Includes bibliographical references and index.

  ISBN 978-1-60329-201-6 (cloth : alk. paper) —
  ISBN 978-1-60329-202-3 (pbk. : alk. paper) —
  ISBN 978-1-60329-203-0 (EPUB) —
  ISBN 978-1-60329-204-7 (Kindle)

  1. Literature—Study and teaching. I. Grobman, Laurie, 1962– editor.
II. Rosenberg, Roberta, editor.

  PN59.S47 2014

  807—dc23   2014045263

Published by The Modern Language Association of America

26 Broadway, New York, NY 10004-1789

www.mla.org

Contents

Part III   Service Learning in Creative Nonfiction and Memoir

Part IV   Service Learning in Literature-Based Writing

Part V   Service Learning in Cross-Disciplinary Studies

Acknowledgments

We are grateful to the contributors, community members, and students who shared their stories with us.

We thank the anonymous peer reviewers; James Hatch, senior acquisitions editor; Sara Pastel, associate editor; the MLA Publications Committee; everyone at MLA who gave support and assistance to this project; and Terry Lee.

The projects described in this book have inspired us to think of new ways to read, teach, think, and write about literature. There is so much to be explored in the publicly engaged humanities, and we hope that this book will inspire others to imagine new possibilities for their students, research, and communities. We believe that faculty members and students in literary studies have unique opportunities to contribute to the work of social change.

Laurie Grobman and Roberta Rosenberg

Introduction: Literary Studies, Service Learning, and the Public Humanities

In her 2010 article for *Profession*, "The English Major as Social Action," Sidonie Smith, then MLA president, argues that the field of literary studies needs to "shift attention from the major as formal to the major as performative" in order to "facilitate the classroom as an intergenerational learning community, where everyone collaborates in setting questions, seeking answers, making claims" (199). She defines this new vision for English studies as "performative social action," based on the idea of knowledge building as social. Smith, citing her colleague Eric Rabkin, argues for "real work, not homework" (200); "real work" produces knowledge and involves students in meaningful writing, thinking, and reflection. Smith gives several examples of "real work," including undergraduate research, study abroad, and digital literacies (200–01).

In our view, service learning provides extraordinary opportunities to enact Smith's vision of literary study as both real work and performative social action—to alter the focus, as Smith suggests, from what literary study is to what it may do (205). Service learning is a teaching and learning strategy that integrates meaningful community service, in many and diverse forms, with classroom instruction, textual study, literary theory, student writing, and reflection.

As pedagogy, service learning both enhances and deepens the learning experience and meets community partners' needs. At its best, service learning is reciprocally beneficial for the community partners and the students. Collaborative and recursive, service learning opens up new ways for students to make sense of the dissonances, gaps, and similarities between real and imagined lives. And imaginative literature has the power to stimulate empathy, inspire civic action, and connect the people that service-learning pedagogy brings to literary study. We hope that *Service*

Learning and Literary Studies in English demonstrates that a pedagogy of community engagement can enrich the study of literature by grounding current critical literary texts and theory in a "real" public space to meet pressing community needs.

Service Learning in Higher Education: An Overview

Service learning was developed in the 1960s, in the era of the launch of the Peace Corps (1961) and Volunteers in Service to America (1965; now AmeriCorps VISTA), when college students' involvement in community service came to the national fore (Jacoby 10–11). Yet service learning is rooted in higher education's earliest focus, from the founding of Harvard College in 1636, to prepare citizens for active involvement in community life (10). Two centuries later, the Morrill Act of 1862, also known as the Land-Grant College Act, established institutions that linked public higher education with the betterment of communities in agriculture and industry. John Dewey's *Democracy and Education*, published in 1916, remains one of the strongest calls for linking higher education, and particularly the humanities, with responsible citizenship.

A renewed, vigorous call for civic engagement in higher education came about in the 1980s, prompted by the concern that Americans valued individualism over the common good. With support from the National Society for Experiential Education, Campus Compact, and the student-driven Campus Outreach Opportunity League, community service and service learning increased dramatically. A two-year collaborative process involving seventy-five national and regional organizations committed to community service and experiential education culminated in the 1989 Wingspread Conference, hosted by the Johnson Foundation. Conference participants created the *Principles of Good Practice for Combining Service and Learning* (Honnet and Poulsen), a set of principles that established a foundation for service-learning programs in higher education nationwide.

At the same time, Ernest Boyer argued in *Scholarship Reconsidered: Priorities of the Professoriate* that traditional scholarship, what he referred to as the "scholarship of discovery," should be expanded to include the scholarships of "integration," "application," and "teaching" (16–25). Boyer noted that "at no time in our history has the need been greater for connecting the work of the academy to the social and environmental challenges beyond the campus" (xii) and called for "a new vision of scholarship . . . dedicated not only to the renewal of the academy, but, ultimately, to the renewal of society itself" (81). In an article published after his death, he continued his call for scholarship connected to and integrated with community service, using the phrase "scholarship of engagement" instead of "scholarship of application": "The academy must become a more vigorous partner in the search for answers to our most pressing social, civic, economic, and moral problems, and must reaffirm its historic commitment to what I call the scholarship of engagement" ("Scholarship" 11). Many teacher-scholars regard service learning as the most significant pedagogical form of the scholarship of engagement.

Service learning is also one of the ten "high-impact" teaching and learning practices that "have been widely tested and have been shown to be beneficial for college students from many backgrounds" (Kuh 9). Service learning is a form of experiential learning in which "students have to both *apply* what they are learning in real-world settings and *reflect* in a classroom setting on their service experiences" (11). Internships, for example, are also a form of experiential learning, but service learning includes the vital element of "civic engagement," "working to make a difference in the civic life of our communities and developing the combination of knowledge, skills, values and motivation to make that difference" (T. Ehrlich vi). Service learning is also a form of what is called *engaged learning,* in which students are actively involved in their learning. Service learning adds to engaged learning a focus that benefits the community while fostering students' civic learning and engagement.

Efforts to institutionalize and expand service learning were bolstered with the passage of the National and Community Service Act in 1990 under President George H. W. Bush's administration and the National and Community Service Trust Act of 1993 under the Clinton administration. The later act created the Corporation for National and Community Service, which administers Learn and Serve America and its programs for higher education, including Senior Corps, AmeriCorps, and the National Service-Learning Clearinghouse. Service learning in American colleges and universities expanded in the 1990s as disciplines as varied as philosophy, biology, and business created forms of service-learning pedagogy (Jacoby 13).

Practitioners and theorists in a wide range of disciplines laud the potential of service learning to create good citizen-scholars who are capable of connecting the classroom to text-based learning and the issues in their world. By working in "real-world" contexts, students become more connected to the communities in which they live and go to school, learn about systemic inequalities, develop intellectual and citizenship skills, explore values, and may even develop an ethic of caring and commitment. As Edward Zlotkowski argues, service learning "allows induction to complement deduction, personal discovery to challenge received truths, immediate experience to balance generalizations and abstract theory" (qtd. in Fallon xvi). Service learning is circular and recursive; as students apply the theoretical knowledge acquired in the classroom to a public activity, they contribute to community needs and enrich their learning of course content. Janet Eyler, Dwight Giles, Jr., Christine Stenson, and Charlene Gray, in their thorough study of the pedagogical effectiveness of service learning, illustrate that the skills acquired have "an impact on such academic outcomes as demonstrated complexity of understanding, problem analysis, critical thinking, and cognitive development" (4). Moreover, service learning intersects with many of the learning styles of twenty-first-century students. Arthur Levine and Jeanette Cureton argue that service-learning pedagogy may bridge the "widening gap between the ways in which students learn best and the ways faculty teach" (qtd. in Cooper 18). Service learning—with its recursive style; direct, high-impact method; and emphasis on abstraction embedded in practice—meets some of the learning needs of the current generation of students.

Despite its demonstrated learning benefits, service learning has its critics. Some argue that service learning may reinforce us-versus-them attitudes among privileged students who might see themselves as there to rescue the poor and minorities from their "plights." From this "savior" perspective, students may ignore the community as a valuable partner and resource in knowledge making and problem solving and, as a consequence, may perpetuate oppression and exploitation. Other criticisms of service learning are leveled at its "hit it and quit it" nature—students have short-term, superficial contact with individuals at a service site and then disappear when the course requirement ends. Thus the focus seems to be on student learning and not on community organization needs. Further, while students may develop a greater awareness of social issues, their service may have minimal impact on the underlying factors that contribute to those issues. In trying to shield themselves from charges of imposing political views on students, service-learning practitioners may focus on the universalist idea that service learning promotes respect for and reciprocity with diverse and underserved populations. As a result, some critics argue that this nonideological stance neglects the underlying needs of communities.

Attempts to address these potential problems have led to efforts to rename and revise the term *service learning* by replacing it with *community-based research, community-based learning, public scholarship,* and *community literacy.* In *community-based research,* the service activity is "research with and for the community" (Strand 85). Research activities include conducting surveys, interviews, or focus groups; recording oral histories; developing asset maps; conducting policy research; writing grants; and participating in education and outreach programs that arguably have long-term effects on communities and community organizations (Welch 180). *Community-based learning,* the term favored by some critics of service learning, refocuses the pedagogy away from service to and instead emphasizes mutual learning (see Cooper; Fallon; Zlotkowski and Duffy). Community-based learning is generally used as a "big tent" concept that includes many forms of academic and volunteer activities, including service trips and participant observation, as well as service learning. Thus community-based learning does not always involve academic pedagogy and, therefore, does not sufficiently encapsulate the intellectual rigor of service learning. *Public scholarship* is defined as scholarly and creative work, including teaching, research, artistic performance, and service that contributes to informed knowledge about and participation in the democratic process. Its advocates seek to remove the service component from engaged research and teaching (Cohen and Eberly). However, because public scholarship encompasses a broad array of nonpedagogical work, the term does not adequately substitute for *service learning.* Likewise, *community literacy* projects are increasingly common in English studies and refer to inquiry and interventions in public communicative practices. Across the nation, book clubs and other literary reading and writing groups meet in prisons, domestic abuse shelters, low-income elementary schools, and other places where underserved groups can be found. For example, Michael Bérubé, Hester Blum, Christopher Castiglia, and Julia Spicher Kasdorf note that Community Reads, the program they lead near Penn State University, centers on "reading and writing beyond the boundaries of the university," selections that pertain to conceptions of imagination, citizenship, and community in and beyond the academy (418–19). Again, however, *community literacy* is a broad term that does not focus exclusively on pedagogy.

Thus our use of the term *service learning* is deliberate and informed.[1] By using the term, we do not elide the very substantive concerns raised by critics. Many service-learning proponents, including us, would likely agree on an ideal service-learning pedagogy: it is activist and ideological, it involves reciprocal engagement and collaboration with a community partner, and it has long-term impact. Yet we believe that even when service learning does not meet this ideal, it is often nonetheless beneficial for both students and communities if it incorporates best practices as set forth by many service-learning scholar-practitioners.

The Genesis of Service Learning in Literary Studies and the Uses of Literature

In 2007, Edward Zlotkowski, professor of English and editor of the American Association for Higher Education's (AAHE) twenty-one-volume series on service learning and the academic disciplines (1997–2005), expressed his frustration about his field's reluctance to embrace service-learning pedagogy. Although the first volume in the AAHE series focused on composition, literary studies lagged far behind. "I was acutely aware of my fellow literary scholars' lack of interest in academy-community connections," Zlotkowski lamented. "Indeed, in the hundreds of service-learning workshops I led between 1995 and 2005, no group was less well represented" (xii).

Although teachers of literature seemed hesitant to incorporate service in their literature classes, service learning as both pedagogy and research emerged in composition and rhetoric in the mid to late 1990s. Some of these courses in rhetoric and composition included the reading and teaching of literature, though there was disagreement over literature's role in composition classes by scholars in the field. Indeed, service learning was arguably an effective way to turn away from literature in composition and to focus on such issues as literacy, academic discourse, and public writing. In our view, composition and rhetoric's continued focus on community literacy carves out an opening for the particular service-learning work that can be accomplished through literary courses.

Among the most influential early writings is Bruce Herzberg's 1994 theorizing of his first-year writing students' work as literacy tutors, drawing on their experiences studying and writing about the politics of education. Three years later, *Writing the Community: Concepts and Models for Service Learning in Composition* became the first volume in the AAHE series on service learning in the disciplines. In their introductory chapter, the volume's editors, Linda Adler-Kassner, Robert Crooks, and Ann Watters, wrote, "The past five years have seen a microrevolution in college-level Composition through service-learning" ("Service-Learning" 1). They use the term "microrevolution" to point to both the significant and meaningful work and learning in these classes as well as the limited number of instructors using service learning pedagogy. In 2000, Thomas Deans proposed three models for connecting writing courses to communities — writing for, about, and with the community. The peer-reviewed journal *Reflections: Writing, Service-Learning, and Community Literacy*, founded in 2000, attested to the discipline's commitment to service learning. Its recent name change to *Reflections: Public Rhetoric, Civic Writing, and Service Learning* indicates the journal's and the discipline's ongoing inquiry in the past two decades on substantial issues such as race, ethnicity, and other categories of difference; reciprocity and collaboration in community-university relationships; civic engagement, advocacy, and social justice as goals of service learning; and, of course, students' multiple and multilayered learning. *Writing and Community Engagement: A Critical Sourcebook*, by Deans, Barbara Roswell, and Adrian Wurr, is also an excellent resource for the groundbreaking practical and theoretical work in service learning, community and public writing, and rhetoric that informs literary studies and service learning.

Yet literary scholars intentionally distanced themselves from service learning until much later. This reluctance to embrace service learning has its earliest roots in traditional academic debates about the uses of literature. Whether literature should be read for its moral, ethical, or public uses or for its aesthetic, personal, or academic experiences has been part of an ongoing controversy that predates the twentieth century. This debate intensified in the 1960s as students demanded relevancy during the Vietnam War and reached its apex in the economic crisis of the 1990s as the study of literature in the academy was questioned from both economic and philosophical perspectives by college administrators, legislators, students, and even literary specialists.

In 1968, as the MLA considered an antiwar resolution on the Vietnam draft, O. B. Hardison, the MLA's president at the time, addressed committee members at the 28 March plenary meeting, characterizing the political proposal as "irrelevant" because, he argued, literature scholars "have no special qualifications to justify stands on the foreign and domestic problems" (985). In language that echoed age-old debates about the uses of literature, Hardison viewed the 1960s controversy as part of the "same tired drama" that had asked the humanities and literary study to be politically and morally accountable: "Again we are being told that our enterprise is trivial, that we live in ivory towers, that we are fiddling while Rome (or Detroit) burns, that our curriculum is anachronistic, and that our scholarship is pointless if not downright offensive" (986). Yet Hardison defended "humanistic study" by quoting from Allen Tate's "To Whom Is the Poet Responsible?," asserting that "as scholars we are not responsible for saving society but for preserving and enriching civilization that results from social organization" (987). However, the debate over art/life, academic/public, and scholar/activist clearly drawn by Hardison was surely not settled.

For many faculty members, the controversies that followed at the December 1968 MLA convention signaled a change in both their teaching and scholarly practice. In many respects, the publication of Louis Kampf and Paul Lauter's edited collection *The Politics of Literature: Dissenting Essays on the Teaching of English* (1972) was a direct response to what Kampf and Lauter described as the "Little Bourgeois Cultural Revolution of MLA 1968" (Introduction 34). Kampf and Lauter saw the arrests of professors and the failed attempts at convention resolutions as the beginning of a change in the uses of literary study in the classroom from a "passive consumption of culture to an active engagement with the emotions, ideas, politics, and sensibilities of writers and of others" (44). Kampf and Lauter were nonetheless unsure of how to turn their ideology into practice. But Florence Howe, in her contribution to the collection, "Why Teach Poetry?—An Experiment," introduced what would become an excellent example of service learning in literary studies. In collaboration with her undergraduate students at Goucher College, Howe created a poetry reading and writing project in Baltimore inner-city schools over a four-year period, offering thirty-nine undergraduates the opportunity to teach and learn from four hundred high school students. Howe's 1960s "experiment" is one of the earliest service-learning success stories in literary studies.

Years later, in 1983, the controversy over the uses of literary study was still a subject for discussion in Terry Eagleton's *Literary Theory: An Introduction*. After analyzing and illustrating an entire history of contemporary literary theory, Eagleton posited, ironically, the following question to his readers in the concluding chapter, "Political Criticism": "What is the point of literary theory? Why this perverse insistence on dragging politics into the argument?" Eagleton concluded that politics in literary theory "has been there from the beginning" (194). He then characterized the body of literary theory he had explained so succinctly as a "flight from real history" and worried that literary studies and theory were moribund (196). In describing his book, Eagleton paradoxically conceded that it was "less an introduction than an obituary" and that he had "ended by burying the object we sought to unearth" (204).

Like many literary theorists and service-learning practitioners, Eagleton sought a solution to the posited academic demise of literary study by calling for a new "humanism" that emphasized rhetoric, empathy for the public good, and literature's return to public accountability. Eagleton's stated goal was "to recall literary criticism from certain fashionable, newfangled ways of thinking . . . and return it to the ancient paths which it has abandoned." He then defined this traditional path as "rhetoric" (206). Like Robert Scholes twenty years later in his Presidential Address at the 2004 MLA convention, "The Humanities in a Posthumanist World," Eagleton sought the convergence of contemporary literary theory with a public use to justify literature's public role in the modern world.

Eagleton's modern version of rhetoric shared with liberal humanism a goal to "be a better person" (208), but it was superior to its predecessor because contemporary rhetoric would benefit from modern literary theories such as deconstruction, postcolonialism, and new historicism and, thereby, move beyond the personal and prescriptive to a critique of political power and social injustice. Although Eagleton acknowledged that his focus during the "theory moment" of the 1980s would alienate colleagues who might disagree "that literature has a *use*," he nonetheless maintained his position, despite his concession that "[f]ew words are more offensive to literary ears than 'use'" (208).

Eagleton's foray into political criticism, as predicted, was not warmly received, but nearly fifteen years later it remained relevant. A number of leading literary scholars were asked to respond to an ongoing debate about the public intellectual and the academy in a series of brief essays in the October 1997 issue of *PMLA* (Graff et al.; Perloff et al.; Todorov et al.). The impassioned essays described just this tension between the aesthetic/academic and public/political uses of literature and literary study. Although only one scholar offered a concrete solution to the impasse, all the contributors placed an importance on public and civic engagement, rejecting Hardison's 1968 claim for a disinterested literary study.

Significantly, several of these scholars historicized the debate. Tzvetan Todorov argued that, since the Enlightenment, there had been a historical precedent for literature's moral or ethical role: "until 1848, writers hoped to occupy the place vacated by priests . . . following the church's loss of power in the eighteenth century" (Todorov et al. 1122). Patrick Saveau also looked back to Enlightenment engagement and praised Voltaire's attack on "scholastic obscurantism" as a model. Saveau contended that "the future of intellectuals in the twenty-first century depends on their ability and willingness to be [like Voltaire] 'bidimensional,' equally devoted to engagement and autonomy, the academy and the public" (Todorov et al. 1127). J. Hillis Miller focused on nineteenth-century Romanticism and Coleridge as a literary model for the civically engaged literary artist who "used periodicals and books to promulgate social and literary ideas" (1138). Miller praised Coleridge as the ideal "distinguished spectator . . . who also wrote for a broad educated public that shared a common culture" (1138).

Although these preeminent literary scholars desired a public usefulness for the literary intellectual, they anticipated skepticism, criticism, and pushback. For instance, Stephen Greenblatt described an incident with an East German colleague that turned their discussion of Shakespeare, Brueghel, and Montaigne into a political argument about Cold War censorship and repression. Greenblatt's attempt to bridge the gap between literature and politics was met by his colleague's unexpected hostility, a reaction that made Greenblatt feel "naive and ridiculous." Although Greenblatt desired "a more secure link between the love of art and human decency," he asserted that "there is no easy passage between a cultivated aesthetic sensibility and a set of political choices in a difficult world" (Perloff et al. 1131).

The one concrete solution presented in the *PMLA* 1997 forum was offered by Dominick LaCapra, who suggested a professional, not pedagogical, solution to the lack of public work in the academy. He created what he termed a "fourth category" for the evaluation of scholarly professional work that went beyond the usual teaching, research, and service:

"critical intellectual citizenship," he argued, "would legitimate forms of reflection and writing that are not confined to specialized research." This hybrid "intellectual citizenship" combined the public and academic and included activities and research on public values and issues. Like Boyer seven years earlier, LaCapra imagined that these scholarly activities would "include 'outreach' in which the academy could be brought into more vital contact with the larger society" (Graff et al. 1134). Three years later, in the 2000 edition of *Profession*, Pierre Bourdieu's "For a Scholarship with Commitment" echoed LaCapra's call for civic engagement by formulating another hybrid—the "collective intellectual"—who would "invent an improbable combination: scholarship with commitment, that is, a collective politics of intervention" (44–45). Bourdieu, given his background in sociology, believed that intellectual autonomy and social commitment to the public good were compatible ideals in the academy.

At the same moment as the *PMLA* debate, other literary theorists were writing about the public value of literary study on moral and ethical grounds: literature allowed readers to access important private emotions like empathy and compassion that could stimulate them to do good work in the world. The philosopher and literary theorist Martha Nussbaum characterized "the literary imagination as a public imagination, an imagination that will steer judges in their judging, legislators in the legislating, policy makers in measuring the quality of life near and far" (*Poetic Justice* 3). Anticipating that some readers in the 1990s would find her analysis of the personal and private imagination as "idle and unhelpful," Nussbaum nonetheless argued that "literary forms have a unique contribution to make" to social and political policy making and analysis (3). Nussbaum extended the work of the established literary scholar Wayne Booth, who had developed a link between reading and ethics nearly ten years earlier in his book *The Company We Keep: An Ethics of Fiction*. Nussbaum concurred with Booth's major premise: "[T]he act of reading and assessing what one has read is ethically valuable precisely because it is constructed in a manner that demands both immersion and critical conversation. . . . We can already begin to see why we might find in it an activity well suited to public reasoning in a democratic society" (qtd. in Nussbaum, *Poetic Justice* 9).

Likewise, William Paulson saw the irony in literary theory's emphasis on "cultural constructivism" and political consciousness and its inability to do anything concrete about social and moral injustice: "It thus seems less and less plausible to suppose that the humanities can comfortably focus on society, culture and discourse while leaving aside the conditions of the material world on which they depend" (x). However, Paulson, like Hardison, flatly rejected "a call for direct commitment to causes" and offered no alternative beyond an interdisciplinary, idealistic strategy that would encourage students to think about "the social, historical, economic, and ecological contexts in which they live and about which, as citizens, they're called upon to make decisions" (14, 24). In 2001, Paulson's well-intentioned literary treatise was a strategy without a plan, a public mission for literary study without a praxis—but Nussbaum's, Booth's, and Paulson's analyses of the relation of reading and civic engagement would be used by service-learning theorists in the future.

This renewed call for engaged public intellectuals in literary studies, however, has been criticized by some members of the literary establishment. Among the most vocal is Stanley Fish. In the essay "Aim Low" (2003) and the book *Save the World on Your Own Time* (2008), Fish eschewed the uses of literature for public or political purposes. In "Aim Low," he contended that instructors should not attempt to make students into "better" or more moral or civically engaged or politically activist individuals. Instead, he argued that literature specialists were solely responsible for the transmission of objective knowledge: "selection of texts, the preparation of a syllabus, the sequence of assignments and exams. . . . What they [the students] do with what you have done is their business and not anything you should be either held to account for or praised for." He cautioned, "You might just make them into good researchers. You can't make them into good people, and you shouldn't try."

Other literary scholars simultaneously began to formulate strategies for bridging the chasm between the discipline and the public by theorizing forms of publicly engaged literary study. Scholes linked literary texts and theory to public welfare through grammar, rhetoric, and textual analysis when he argued that literature was "not merely beautiful objects from some lost past but tools for thinking and feeling, ways of understanding the world and its people" (732). Further, two essays published in the 2005 issue of *Profession* spoke directly about the need to bridge the gap between the public and literary education through service learning. About her pedagogical project linking community service with the study of multicultural American literature, Laurie Grobman argued that "literary texts and community service can work reciprocally to heighten (and in some cases introduce) [student] awareness of the complexities of race, gender, and class as they intersect in people's lives" ("Is There" 133). Grobman acknowledged that despite the fact that "the pairing of service learning and literature is in its infancy," the pedagogy possessed the promise to develop "Northrop Frye's notion of the 'educated imagination'" and provide a real benefit to the community (137). Invoking the Jeffersonian goal of education in a democracy, Amy Koritz responded to those, like Fish, who sought a singular, academic mission for literary studies. Koritz cautioned against such a one-dimensional approach and warned that "the future vitality of literary studies is not well served" by isolating literature from the public realm (83). While setting forth a philosophical and academic rationale for the public use of literary studies, she also acknowledged the ongoing debate about the economic "crisis" in the academy that sought practical, skill-set-driven purposes for literary studies. Koritz hoped that the scarcity of jobs, faculty lines, and research funding would yield more than "a public rationale for our discipline that goes beyond workforce development" and argued that aesthetics and economics could work together to produce an ideal strategy that would "embrace literature's power—through language, narrative, and imagination—to engage the world" (83).

Similarly, Bérubé attempted to find a public use for literary studies in *The Employment of English: Theory, Jobs, and the Future of Literary Studies* (1998). Bérubé surveyed the bleak prospects at century's end and advised the discipline to "rethink how English—and English teachers—can best be employed" (ix). Likewise, Ellen Cushman described the "dire" situation as "a time when the field of English studies grapples to redefine itself in the face of employment cutback, over-reliance on part-time labor, and pressure for accountability from students, administrators, and legislators" ("Service Learning" 204). Cushman argued that the "crisis of English studies as seen in the current job market is *an identity crisis* as much as an economic one" (206; emphasis added) that may have its roots in Matthew Arnold's conception of the literary critic as "disinterested," a position she characterized as "a coping mechanism against political [Victorian] impotence" (208). Significantly, Cushman asked that scholars both instruct and interact with their communities to "overcome the ivory tower isolation that marks so much current intellectual work" ("Opinion" 330). Cushman called on the public intellectual to "create knowledge with those whom the knowledge serves" (330). Not surprisingly, Cushman was among the first literary scholars to theorize the value of service learning as pedagogy for literature students.

In 2013, Julie Ellison, a founding member of Imagining America: Artists and Scholars in Public Life and professor of American culture and English at the University of Michigan, argued in *PMLA* that "a new sort of public humanities is finding traction in American colleges and universities," but she also noted that "[a]pplied public humanities degree programs did not take hold in literary and language studies" (290, 291). After praising some exemplary, time-ended public humanities projects like *Harriet Wilson's New England* (Boggis, Raimon, and White) and *Civic Engagement in the Wake of Katrina* (Koritz and Sanchez), Ellison discussed the importance of what she terms "reliable curricular links." She cited the need for a long-term pedagogical plan for community engagement when she argued that "public humanists need the curricular connection for reasons beyond mere sustainability"—that is, "to build publicly active learning communities that nurture critical practice by both students and faculty members" (297n12). As the existing research on service learning and literary studies and the essays in this volume attest, service learning is one such effective response to the complex problem of the public role for literary studies in a world that seeks public accountability for the humanities and education and a social and political role for the literary intellectual.

Service Learning and Literary Studies: Emerging Theory and Practice

Responding to disciplinary and educational calls for reform, a handful of literary scholars formulated strategies for rethinking the enterprise and uses of literary study by linking it with service learning—a concrete practice for social change. Koritz, Cathy Comstock, Cushman, Gerald Graff, Grobman, Gregory Jay, Susan Danielson, and Ann Marie Fallon, among others, have begun to theorize and apply service learning in literature classes. Graff argues that service learning enables students to discover what their education in literature "can do in the world outside the classroom" (Foreword ix). Julia Garbus identified a service-learning tradition in letters by researching the work of the turn-of-the-century service-learning "foremother" Vita Scudder. In 1999, Imagining America: Artists and Scholars in Public Life was founded by a consortium of colleges and the White House Millennium Council, in the hope of establishing a new identity for literature in the public realm. Its contributors continue to generate significant critical work. From this collective scholarship, we argue that service learning in literary studies has three distinct goals:

Students will develop a genuine understanding and sense of social responsibility and civic commitment.

Work performed by students will positively affect the community and fulfill an important need as identified by the community partner.

Courses will offer new questions and answers about the language, structure, and meaning of literature, criticism, and theory.

Social Responsibility and Civic Commitment

Among the most anticipated goals of service learning is to "produce critically, civically, and globally minded college graduates who possess problem-solving and leadership abilities for more socially equitable and sustainable communities as part of healthy, functioning democratic societies" (Cress and Donahue 2). That is, service learning helps students see themselves as part of a collective whole and value both their own well-being and that of others. Like Johnnella E. Butler, we view the "common good" as "inclusive of all members of society" and "the betterment of humankind" as a goal for all of us in higher education (54). Several studies on service-learning pedagogies demonstrate positive student-learning outcomes such as the reduction of negative stereotypes, citizenship development, greater commitment to community service, expanded and multifaceted understandings of difference, and the acquisition of social responsibility and citizenship skills (e.g., Cooper; Eyler, Giles, Stenson, and Gray; Grobman, "Is There," "Service-Learning," "Thinking"; Koritz). These are the skills and attitudes that may lead graduates to practice "responsible political engagement" (Cress and Donahue 7).

Helping students explore and become aware of systemic injustices provides the foundation for action and commitment. For some service-learning advocates, laying the groundwork for later social-justice work is a laudable goal. For others, however, service learning should involve social activism. In this sense, students' service-learning work in and with community organizations must change the community, organization, or members in some discernible, positive way. Students not only learn about systemic issues, they work to change them, by researching and writing policy briefs, engaging in consciousness-raising activities, teaching English to adults learning it as a second language, or conducting community-based research.

The emerging body of scholarship in literary studies and service learning suggests a similar focus on social justice. In their introduction to *The Ethics in Literature*, Andrew Hadford, Dominic Rainsford, and Tim Woods observe the recent renewed attention to ethics in literature and argue that the "famous question on which Aristotle based his ethical philosophy, how shall we live life, has been transformed into the question, how can we respect the other? What responsibilities do we owe to our fellows?" (9). We see this last question—"What responsibilities do we owe to our fellows?"—as the most compelling ethical and political motivation for service-learning students in literature classes. Like David D. Cooper, we believe that service learning within the study of literature helps students develop a set of "public skills" that involves recognizing and negotiating difference, understanding how power works in diverse social spaces and institutions, and negotiating self-interests and larger public issues (17). In this way, students develop the knowledge and tools to enact change.

One good illustration of this pedagogy is Koritz's course Narrative and Community, which combines service learning and multicultural literature to "help students gain the skills to become effective citizens in their communities" (87). The course goes beyond teaching tolerance, to expose students to "the class, racial, and ethnic differences and regional cultures that their partners bring to the table" (87). Koritz's courses include collaborative community projects that have as their goal the amelioration of prejudice and injustice, but more importantly a change in the structure of literary pedagogy. "Making civic purposes central to literary studies," argues Koritz, "entails recognizing that undergraduate education is a public good that carries with it obligations to the larger society" (86).

Like Nussbaum, Booth, and others, we believe literature retains a unique ability to foster compassion and ethics. Bringing service learning to the study of literature may intensify the experiences of moral concern, the moral imagination, and commitment to the public good and social change. In 2007, in his contribution to Danielson and Fallon's collection, Daniel S. Malachuk balances cultural studies' emphasis on ideology with literary traditionalists' emphasis on aesthetics, arguing that community-based learning involves the promise of teaching compassion through literature (27–31). Citing several political theorists, Malachuk argues that there is a perdurable human essence despite the richness of difference; citing Nussbaum, he further argues that this human essence is accessible in most literature and has the ability to inspire readers' compassion (32–33).[2] Malachuk asserts, "Literature, in bringing the lives of others before us in a way that no other kind of writing can, teaches us to care about others," and "this is what makes compassion and progressive politics possible" (34). Referring to his courses combining service learning and nineteenth-century American literature, Malachuk argues that the students were determined to delve deeply to understand the texts' calls for compassion and to respond to these texts in new ways to make them valuable to the community audiences (41).

These questions of difference and shared humanity are explored by several literary scholars who practice and theorize service learning. Grobman asserts that both multiculturalism and service learning emerged out of the recognition of oppression and privilege and the need for social and political change and that both service-learning scholars and multicultural education scholars see change as an integral part of their mission, seeking to challenge, deconstruct, resist, and replace dominant paradigms and structures ("Service-Learning" 80). She demonstrates that combining service learning with multicultural literature study in a general education first-year course can encourage students to theorize difference from many perspectives ("Thinking" 348). Likewise, Jay's service-learning and literature projects engage students in reflective "close readings" of their experiences off-campus as well as of their course texts, "bringing together their theorizing about race, class, nation, and gender on the page with their analyses of how these social constructions operate in our schools, neighborhoods, businesses, and other sites of public life" ("Service Learning" 258). Jay argues for including "multicultural awareness" as a primary learning outcome in a service-learning pedagogy that he refers to as "dialogue across differences" (258). Through cross-cultural and collaborative communication, students engage both multicultural texts and diverse community members, thereby learning about structural inequities, the social construction of difference, their own subject positions, and their effects on others (260). Multicultural awareness is an essential component of service-learning pedagogy and positions literary studies as exceptionally poised to "address common social justice issues" by "giving [students] the intellectual, emotional, and practical skills that they will need in trying to make a difference" (264, 279).

The essays in *Service Learning and Literary Studies in English* illustrate many examples of students' attitudinal change and understanding through their literature and service-learning courses. Stereotypes of all kinds are challenged: race, class, gender, and sexuality, as well as mental illness and age. Students' compassion for individuals in need is heightened, such as increased understanding about sexual violence victimization or ageist stereotyping. Students realize how they can enrich the lives of seniors through intellectual stimulation and creative expression. They come to understand their roles as citizens in tackling environmental issues, advocating food justice, and spreading cultural capital through art and literature. Finally, pairing service learning and literary studies powerfully teaches students about the effects of voice, especially for those long silenced.

Community Impact

Also critical to effective service learning and literary studies is that the students' service work will meet the community needs identified by community partners. The goal is for all entities—students, faculty members, higher education institutions, and community partners—to benefit from the experience. The essays in *Service Learning and Literary Studies in English* provide evidence of the potential for service-learning pedagogy in literature classes to benefit communities along what we see as a public good–social justice continuum. That is, many service-learning projects are oriented toward the public good. Although the term *public good* resists easy definition (Chambers and Gopaul 60–63), Tony Chambers's definition captures the spirit of community betterment evident in this volume: "The Public Good is an aspiration, a vision and destination of a 'better state' that we can know in common that we cannot know alone" (qtd. in Chambers and Gopaul 61; see also Kezar, Chambers, and Burkhardt for a comprehensive study of the meaning of *public good*). In her 2012 article in *PMLA*, "Public Stakes, Public Stories: Service Learning in Literary Studies," Marcy Schwartz uses the Spanish word *convivencia*, or "living together with others," to demonstrate the movement's respect for the community as equal partner and to reject the notion of community as a "problem community" (988). Jay reinforces this perspective, arguing that "the community is a set of assets, not an amalgam of deficits" ("Engaged Humanities" 59).

For many of this volume's authors, the goal is oriented toward the public good, an orientation that Jay refers to as "community cultural development" ("Engaged Humanities" 55). Examples include Emily Van-Dette's work with the National Endowment for the Arts (NEA) Big Read program and Fallon's collaboration with the local library's Everybody Reads program, the local version of the nationwide One City, One Book project. Enriching lives through literature and the arts is an important goal of Kathleen Béres Rogers's program in which first-year students work collaboratively with senior citizens to produce narratives of healing. Kristina Lucenko's students partner with the Osher Lifelong Learning Institute.

Moving along the continuum, some authors orient their goals toward advocacy, activism, and social justice. Lisa Rabin and Jennifer Leeman's students facilitate bilingual literacy education programs with bilingual speakers in elementary schools, book clubs, and adult ESL classes; students come to understand the ways that literature encapsulates multiple discourses and reveals that non-English languages in the United States have been deliberately erased. Sarah D. Wald's students address food justice and representations of poverty and the poor by working with Spanish-speaking farmworkers and with El Comité de Apoyo a los Trabajadores Agrícolas (CATA; The Farmworker Support Committee).

Of course, the categories along the continuum often overlap, as in Matthew C. Hansen's project in which college students bring Shakespeare to elementary students in Title IX schools, providing these children with "cultural capital." Further, Carol Tyx and Mary Vermillion's reading program with their students and prisoners at Anamosa State Penitentiary facilitates understandings of literature's significance in the public realm and readers' ethically engaged thinking.

Thus students in the service-learning and literary-studies projects in this collection are engaged in diverse work experiences with diverse community partners. Students work in homeless shelters, food pantries, senior centers, afterschool programs, ESL tutoring programs, prisons, homes for runaway youths, museums, rehabilitation centers, nursing care facilities, underfunded public schools, transitional housing for homeless and mentally ill adults, and housing for victims of domestic violence. They tutor, mentor, create safe-sex kits, facilitate reading groups, lead creative writing workshops, record and craft life narratives, support the NEA's Big Read initiatives, and stage theater productions. Some of these activities fulfill immediate needs of not-for-profit organizations seeking extra hands to advance their mission. Others have significant potential for long-term community impact and sustainability.

Measuring that impact is the next important step in this work. In general, research on community benefits through service learning is limited, but service-learning teacher-scholars are starting to pay attention to this need. Existing research on community impact through service learning is generally positive. Eyler, Giles, Stenson, and Gray found that communities report that students provide useful service in communities and that service learning enhances community-university relations (10). Marie Sandy and Barbara Holland's 2006 study of community partner perspectives of ninety-nine agencies working with eight California colleges and universities demonstrated that partners saw the additional workforce benefit as crucially important to the agency (36). Many respondents also described the benefits to their permanent staff as either enrichment or "transformational learning," and over half of those interviewed cited "the common struggle for social justice and equity" as central to the partnership (36). The community partners also reported the education of college students as central to the partnership. Sandy and Holland's study revealed community members' "unanimous" desire for long-term service-learning assignments, especially for clients who come from "sensitive populations such as refugee children" (39). This desire for long-term assignments was also among the most important found by Randy Stoecker and Elizabeth Tryon, who argue that their study demonstrates an urgent need for research to assess the community impact of service learning ("Unheard" 1–5).

Some of the essays in this volume have begun to assess and evaluate the community impact of their service-learning projects. Many of our authors provide supporting evidence of community impact through the community partners' and participants' voices. For example, Scott Hicks presents community children's poems and other fiction writing published in his students' literary magazine. Claudia Monpere McIsaac's essay about first-year students who read and write poetry with community members in a transitional housing project, a residential treatment program, and a youth community center illustrates that community members feel empowered through their poetic voices. In other projects, to bring awareness to their organizations, community partners use college-student-produced documents, such as the activist magazine *The Sky Is Wicked Huge*, created by Elizabeth Parfitt's students and requested by Boston Cares, an organization that manages service projects for hundreds of citywide not-for-profits with volunteer needs. Yet the assessment of community impact begun in this volume only lays the foundation for systematic and sustained evaluation of community impact in the integration of service learning and literary studies.

New Questions and Answers about Literature and Literary Theory

Despite the significance of the political, social, and ethical outcomes of combining service learning and literary studies, we must remain mindful of literature as literature; otherwise, service learning in literature becomes boilerplate service learning, and literary studies loses its specific functions in a comprehensive undergraduate curriculum. It is surely a wonderful paradox, however, that connecting literature to the "real world" through service learning gives rise to substantive attentiveness to literature and literary theory. Grounding literary theory in the actual provides inexperienced and advanced literature students with concrete ways of comprehending abstract concepts. The dialogue resulting from engagement with community partners and the work of literature yields new questions and answers about the language, structure, and meaning of literature and literary theory.

The interaction between community and literary text answers Bourdieu's call to "writers, artists, and especially researchers . . . [to] transcend the sacred boundary . . . between scholarship and commitment, in order to break out of the academic microcosm, to enter into sustained and vigorous exchange with the outside world" (44). Service learning is one such response to Bourdieu, bringing contemporary literary theory together with civic engagement to foster a public, activist role for literature. As many of the essays in this volume suggest, contemporary literary theory and service learning are complementary, not antagonistic. We disagree with Cooper's claims that contemporary literature classrooms are places where the "lived and affective impact of moral questions . . . [are] sacrificed to the clinical purity of theory," a site where students are "never invited or challenged by their professor to become intellectually, publicly, or socially engaged in these [public] issues as they were lived out and suffered through in their own community" (6–7). Postmodern theories do not by necessity mitigate against action in the real world. Rather, we argue that, while theory apart from practice has an important place in literary studies, service learning finds spaces in curricula to apply theory to real lives without losing sight of literature's artfulness. Cooper argues that postmodern theorists and instructors discourage students' sense of individual or community activism through cynicism about "power and social predation" (7), but we believe that postmodernism's skepticism about received knowledge may open students' understandings of systemic and historical injustices and stimulate them to search for meaningful, not temporary or superficial, solutions. Further, we argue that postmodern theory may facilitate Cooper's call for literary studies to "shift the ethical center of gravity in our teaching and scholarship from 'the other' to one another" (10).

Like literary theory, service learning provides new lenses through which students may approach literary texts because service learning grounds theory in social realities and provides students who are often concrete thinkers with living examples of theory's philosophical concepts. Service learning, like many postmodern theories, challenges students' previously held assumptions and thus opens literary texts to competing narratives. Aaron Schutz and Anne Ruggles Gere claim that, like cultural studies, service learning complicates the experience of "consuming and producing texts" (129–30). Citing Hannah Arendt's notion of the public, they assert, "Individuals participating in 'public' practices are focused not on the unique perspectives of specific 'others,' but on the common effort located between multiple individuals" (143). Schutz and Gere focus on service learning in writing studies, but their assertions about how the "multiple public and private spaces, operating at multiple levels, allow myriad kinds of difference to emerge into dialogue" point to literary texts as public spaces of contestation, negotiation, and cooperation (146). When students engage with both literary and community public spheres through service learning, they explore the ways in which these "fluid and fragmented spaces" interact with and inform one another (146). As Fallon argues in the preface to *Community-Based Learning and the Work of Literature*, "Literature trains students to become better and more compassionate readers of the world" (xvi).

Cushman likewise connects the spheres of literary texts and communities, theorizing that "[l]iterature itself can be powerfully instructive when it comes time to understand the conflicts taking place in students' and community residents' daily lives. Literary works themselves still hold significant cultural currency because they illustrate how characters and players negotiate the social world" ("Service Learning" 210). Positing textual study as a lens through which students explore complex social meanings both in the classroom and in the community, Cushman theorizes that service learning complements rigorous literary analysis.

Kate Crassons and Kara Mollis analyze their concrete experiences with service learning in literature classes. Crassons reflects on a class in literature and poverty with a service-learning component:

> [T]he combination of community service and literary study transforms the classroom experience, making the conventional work of reading and writing—the skills fostered by an English major—into a crucial civic practice. . . . Poverty, when viewed from a literary perspective in conjunction with community service, allows students to see the complexity of class as an immediate reality that has bearing on their own lives and intellectual concerns.   (95)

Crassons asserts that the voices of the poor are rarely present in the poetry of poverty; thus the community voices just outside the boundaries of Bethlehem, Pennsylvania, a city with a high poverty rate, contribute both to her students' knowledge about poverty and to the limitations of poetry in representing it (97–98). At the same time, reading poetry provides students with a window into interpreting the stories community residents tell about their lives in poverty (98). Both the literary and social public spheres involve interpretation and representation, and each informs the other.

Mollis, likewise, contends that community-service assignments in her course on the American women's novel are "equally effective tools," as are critical approaches for illuminating literature's sociopolitical ends (46). Mollis cites Eyler and Giles, who, in *Where's the Learning in Service-Learning?*, argue that service learning encourages "transformational learning," the questioning of one's fundamental assumptions and adoption of new ones (qtd. in Mollis 48). Eyler and Giles use the phrase "put on new glasses" to refer to students' looking at phenomena in new ways (qtd. in Mollis 48). Referring to literary studies specifically, Mollis argues that the community-service work facilitated students' understanding that literature is both socially relevant and limited in its capacity to solve social problems (51). What it can do, however, is "demonstrate how insights gained through literary interpretation can breed positive interactions with communities outside the classroom" and illuminate the "communal value of literary interpretation" (50, 51).

Grobman's work with literature students who led reading sessions with minority children demonstrates that students' examination of difference through literature and service involved four main elements: explicit

efforts to ascertain difference in value systems; movement toward identifying difference within difference; engagement with the constructed
nature of stereotypes, behaviors, and belief systems; and experience with
"othered" subject positions ("Thinking" 351–55). While the college students read and studied multicultural literature and issues of canonization,
they chose books for the children, considering issues of race, class, and
gender; as such, the college students were immersed in the social construction of literary value.

Without a service-learning structure, students must apply postmodern theory to literary texts without a concrete example or illustrative
experience. For instance, in *Texts and Contexts: Writing about Literature
with Critical Theory*, Steven Lynn provides the hypothetical example of
a literature student who is "startled" or "surprised" by the discontinui-
ties and dissonances of different stories, one told from the perspective of
"high culture" and one from the point of view of a disenfranchised community. Yet Lynn views this moment of frustration as important to learning because the student's "confusion" may precipitate a "New Historical" moment, enabling the student to "explore how different versions of
history are motivated and constructed . . . [how] history is somehow up
for grabs—that there are competing versions of what has happened, and
these stories might be put to different uses" (146). However, Lynn has no
pedagogical strategy beyond reading and class discussion to provide the
student with this understanding. Service learning, in our view, can provide that crucial context and instigating moment.

In another project, Comstock implements service learning to ground
theoretical issues that illuminate literary texts in her class on literature
and social violence. She teaches discursive analysis through Derrida and
deconstruction to encourage her students to see the multiplicity of interpretations in literature and community spaces: "rather than aiming
at 'the' truth, a discursive analysis examines the ways that meanings are
made possible or excluded according to one's frame of reference" (84).
In this way, students interpreting texts and working in the community
see how culturally inscribed and situated their experiences may be and,
therefore, develop a more complex ability to interpret texts, whether in
the community or the classroom. Comstock argues that students' community work makes them "more receptive to attentive reading and critical
theory" (85). If, as Lynn argues, "deconstruction reveals the arbitrariness
of language most strikingly by exposing the contradictions in a discourse,

thereby showing how a text undermines itself" (112), then the service-learning student negotiating dissonances in both literary and community texts will also see meaning and cultural assumptions called into question. The deconstructive moment can be an empowering one for both a reader and an activist. Although it is fashionable to critique deconstruction as an endless "game," Lynn sees it as stimulating for the literary critic, who can now "open up" the text "to multiply meanings" (112). Deconstruction thus encourages students "to resist a complacent acceptance of anything and to question our positions and statements in a particularly rigorous way" (112). This ability to question socially ordained assumptions aids both the literary critic and the activist.

Studying literature and doing relevant service highlight art's ability (or lack thereof) to capture the human experience in all its many perspectives and competing interpretations. Service learning complements and enriches the study of literature by helping students challenge cultural norms and stereotypes and see the arbitrariness of narratives and explanations, thereby providing a concrete basis for understanding the social construction of art and culture. For example, when service-learning students create a community member's life narrative, they must pay careful attention to literary and rhetorical choices and to the complexities of representation and cultural truth.

These are just a sampling of the many ways the study of literature and literary theory complement service learning. The critical and theoretical approaches in *Service Learning and Literary Studies in English* vary widely and illustrate how this pedagogy opens the field to new literary-critical approaches. Several essays focus on the interpretive process: in some, students examine assumptions they bring to texts as they confront readers with differing values and worldviews; in others, students learn to be more empathic readers of literature, informed by theories of reader empathy developed by Booth, Nussbaum, and Suzanne Keen. Paolo Freire's notion of dialogue as the human exchange at the base of all democracy and ethics is central to one course on performance, while another course situates food justice as a window into the literature of the United States. Another essay uses Bruno Latour's work on actor-network theory to argue that students and community members are agents in a social network whose influence extends well beyond classrooms. The service-based projects in another course situate the autobiographical act as both symbolic interaction and as identity and community construction. In a creative writing course, the poetry and fiction function as both social and cultural texts, raising issues of justice and aesthetics that guide the students' work.

Literature, Service Learning, and Technology

Technological advances, service learning, and literature involve two main categories: online courses and the digital humanities. Online courses, or what Jean Strait and Tim Sauer refer to as "E-service," a term they coined in 2004, "is an ideal method to create a bridge between academic learning and community service" (64). In 2010, Leora S. Waldner, Sue Y. McGorry, and Murray C. Widener asserted, "Service learning is beginning to transition online, often in a hybrid format where either the service or the instruction is partially online" ("Extreme E-service Learning" 840). They defined "extreme e-service learning (XE-SL)" as "service learning where both the instruction and service occur 100% online" (849). In addition to these articles, a small body of literature, none in literary studies or composition and rhetoric, describes both the effectiveness of and challenges to service learning in online courses (Guthrie and McCracken, "Making," "Teaching"; Poindexter, Arnold, and Osterhout; Waldner, McGorry, and Widener, "E-Service-Learning"). As distance education expands in literary studies, we anticipate that service learning will be integrated into these courses. Because it is reciprocal and collaborative, service learning is a good fit for the digital humanities, defined by William Pannapacker as the "many kinds of technologically enhanced scholarly work." Cathy Davidson, in a 2008 contribution to *PMLA*'s "The Changing Profession," writes, "we need to acknowledge" how much technologies have "changed our field in ways large and small and hold possibilities for far greater transformation in the three areas—research, writing, and teaching—that matter most" (708). Addressing the "crisis" in the humanities and its possible solutions, Jay argues that "the future of the humanities depends upon two interrelated innovations": increased and systematic engaged learning and scholarship, including service learning, and expansion and continued development of digital and new media learning and scholarship ("Engaged Humanities" 52).

According to Geoffrey Rockwell, most common types of current digital scholarship include online peer-reviewed publication, scholarly electronic editions, specifications, research tools, research blogs, Web 2.0 activity (social media, such as blogs and *Twitter*), hypermedia, and new media (155–62). Digital scholarship is "highly collaborative" (Schreibman, Mandell, and Olsen 132) and, therefore, holds great potential for further democratizing community-university partnerships. And unlike traditional scholarship, digital work often reaches a wide academic and nonacademic audience, expanding service learning's potential community benefits, outcomes, and activist work. Davidson suggests that Web 2.0 English courses may enable students to participate in "knowledge-sharing enterprise[s]" (711). Service learning using digital technologies may expand knowledge sharing among more and diverse producers and consumers of knowledge, and social media in particular may provide another path for service learning's civic action and democratizing functions (Lynch, Henry, Bardwell, and Richter).

A handful of contributors to this volume are tapping into the potential of digital work in service-learning literary studies. Lucenko describes how her students collaborate with retired community members in the Osher Lifelong Learning Institute to create digital stories for them. Digital storytelling, a genre that emerged in the 1990s by the Center for Digital Storytelling in Berkeley, California, "tell[s] stories with digital technologies" and facilitates voice, creativity, synthesis of knowledge, collaborative learning, and problem solving (Bryan Alexander 4, 214–17; see also Misook; Hull and Katz). Students in VanDette's senior seminar contributed to the public Big Read blog with descriptions and reflections on their Big Read discussion events; the blog facilitated students' literary engagement in the public sphere. Rabin and Leeman use blogs and wikis both for students' course work—discussions of course content and lesson plans for the on-site language and literacy classes—and to share their reflections and teaching and classroom management strategies with a public audience.

Four contributors describe digital products produced by students and given to community partners. Elizabeth K. Goodhue's students worked with the Studio for Southern California History, collecting and indexing oral histories of local residents and also contributing photo essays to the studio's digital archive. Robin J. Barrow's students worked with the Knox County, Tennessee, health department's rape and violence prevention health educator to produce videos that may ultimately become part of an online, viral media campaign. Another of Barrow's student groups used social media to advertise their 5K fund-raiser and the candlelight ceremony for the Court Appointed Special Advocates community organization.

Parfitt's students created an online magazine for their work exploring and defining civic engagement, which aligned with the mission of Boston Cares, an organization that puts the service experience at the forefront of community action. Boston Cares will use the magazine to raise funds and promote community awareness. One of Diana C. Archibald's students worked with a job-training program in media for high school dropouts; he created a script of Dickens's travel narrative *American Notes* that will be used as a public relations tool to promote Lowell as a famous destination. Rabin and Leeman's students who do an optional service-learning internship in conjunction with their Spanish literature course use blogs and wikis to discuss readings as well as teaching and course management strategies with other interns (for further information about digital technology and Spanish classes, see Leeman, Rabin, and Román-Mendoza, "Web 2.0").

Best Practices for Service Learning and Literary Studies

The ten principles outlined in *Principles of Good Practice for Combining Service and Learning: A Wingspread Special Report* (Honnet and Poulsen), published in 1989 by the Johnson Foundation, are regarded as the foundation for effective, meaningful service-learning practice in higher education; therefore, we benefit from a generation of best practices in service learning.[3] However, best practices for service learning and literary studies have yet to be articulated in a systematic way. In formulating these principles for literary study, we both build on the Wingspread principles and pay careful attention to the three distinct goals for service learning in literary studies we have articulated: students will develop a genuine understanding and sense of civic responsibility and commitment; work performed by students will positively impact the community and fulfill an important need as identified by the community partner; and courses will offer new questions and answers about literature, criticism, and theory.

In our view, each discipline has something unique to offer to students and communities through service learning. Toward that end, we add the following principles of good practice to service learning in literary studies. We are suggesting not that each principle be met in every service-learning course project but that each principle be considered.

Expose students to critical issues in service-learning scholarship, including the importance of public engagement, citizenship, and social justice.

Provide students with an awareness of current social problems and systemic injustice as well as the confidence to address these situations through community activism.

Expose students to critical multiculturalism and the concepts that emanate from it: mainstream and margins, the importance of listening as well as of speaking, respect for difference and diversity.

Integrate the literary and theoretical content of the course with service-learning placements and activities by providing significant time in class for students to make connections between their reading and civic engagement experiences. Group discussion and dialogue through classroom conversation, journal writing, and online discussion boards are vital components of the learning experience.

Encourage students to "read" both literary and life experiences as part of their textual study and course work, analyzing the ways in which literature does and does not reflect their actual experiences, including the ability of literature to imagine possibilities for bettering human lives.

Require reflective writing and other critical-thinking assignments that articulate both connections and dissonances between the reading of literature and service-learning experiences.

Allow for interdisciplinary research that helps students clarify and make sense of their experiences as literary readers and civic participants.

Assign course projects or papers that benefit community partners and may include the production of, for example, public writing, research and oral presentations, performances, oral histories, fund-raising letters, grants, Web sites, blogs, and social media contributions.

The "Resources" section of this volume lists online tool kits, workshops, and academic and not-for-profit organizations that can guide the new practitioner as well as the scholar interested in research opportunities. Among the most useful Web sites is the one for the National Service-Learning Clearinghouse (NSLC), which makes available *Faculty Toolkit for Service-Learning in Higher Education*, edited by Sarena Seifer and Kara Conners. Campus Compact, a national higher education association dedicated to campus-based civic engagement, provides access to sample syllabi and news of national and regional conferences. Many states have Campus Compact affiliate organizations that provide leadership at the local, state, and regional levels and offer myriad kinds of support for member campuses. The *MLA Commons* group Service Learning in Literature,

Language and Composition is helpful, as is the *Service-Learning Research Primer*, by Kathryn Steinberg, Robert Bringle, and Matthew Williams, also available online at the NSLC site.

Organization of the Collection and Essay Summaries

Service Learning and Literary Studies in English is divided into five parts by literary field, to make it easy for researchers to access essays directly relevant to their teaching and research. Teachers of American literature, for example, can go directly to part 1, "Service Learning in American Literature," but will also find projects in other sections helpful, such as cross-disciplinary classes and literature-based writing classes. The essays are sometimes overlapping rather than discrete: part 2, "Service Learning in English and World Literature," includes Archibald's essay on service learning in an upper-level Victorian literature class, and Rogers's essay in part 3, "Service Learning in Creative Nonfiction and Memoir," also focuses on some British texts in a first-year writing course. Some of the essays involve courses connected to national or regional projects such as the NEA's Big Read, whereas others describe and analyze courses developed and taught by a particular instructor. Part 5 specifically focuses on cross-disciplinary courses, yet many of the other essays ask students to think about literature in a sociological, psychological, or historical context that brings together content knowledge and research in other fields.

Although most of the essays in this volume describe courses taught in the United States with an emphasis on American and British literature (with the exception of Rabin and Leeman's essay on Latin American literature courses in a Spanish department), many include some non-English languages and literatures and texts that involve issues from around the world. For example, Fallon's essay includes Ishmael Beah's *Long Way Gone*, a memoir of a child soldier from Sierra Leone, and Khaled Hosseini's *The Kite Runner*, a fictional account of two families profoundly affected by the history, political turmoil, and violence in Afghanistan; Lucenko, in her course Life Writing and Storytelling, includes Edwidge Danticat's *Brother, I'm Dying*, a Haitian American immigrant family's story, and Jean-Dominique Bauby's *The Diving Bell and the Butterfly*, translated from the French. McIsaac's course depicts the oppression of women and girls in Asia and Africa, and Wald's students come to appreciate the disparities and expectations of what she calls "a multi-lingual space" when their conversations with Spanish-speaking farmworkers must be translated into English by Spanish majors.

Despite the discussion of world issues mentioned above, we view this collection's emphasis on British and American literature and English-language literature as symptomatic of the early stages of service learning in literary studies. However, much service learning is done in non-English languages in the United States, in study-abroad programs, and in countries around the globe, and there is a burgeoning body of scholarship on this work (see, e.g., Graham and Crawford; Prins and Webster; Woolf). Leeman and Rabin, Schwartz, and Kevin Guerrieri are among the most published scholars on service learning with literature in Spanish (see Leeman, Rabin, and Román-Mendoza, "Critical Pedagogy" and "Web 2.0"; Schwartz, "Public" and "Right"). Guerrieri describes the course Introduction to Hispanic Literature, taught in Spanish, analyzing the "interwoven threads of language, literatura, and community" (155). In Isolde Mueller's upper-division German culture course, students practiced German by working with German-speaking senior citizens and Alzheimer's patients; according to Mueller, the texts and service learning worked reciprocally: "While the content of the literature created a metacognitive framework for the community-based learning, the community-based learning provided an interpretive tool for the literature" (181).

As service learning and other forms of curricular community engagement expand in literary studies, we expect to see an increase in courses involving texts and languages from around the globe. We believe the work explored and analyzed in this collection serves as a model for many service-learning and literary pedagogies yet to be imagined, bearing in mind the importance of cultural difference in creating sound pedagogies.

While service learning in literary studies has a long way to go in terms of national and linguistic diversity, it is already witnessing increasingly diverse student participants. Many essays describe courses with a fairly homogenous group of students, but others describe service-learning projects that involve relatively diverse student populations, in terms of race or ethnicity, sexuality, religion, class, educational background, and socioeconomic status. Hicks's course was the most racially and socio-economically diverse and included students from working and lower-middle-class families; many of his students were the first in their families to attend college. Ivy Schweitzer's class at Dartmouth included African American students, international students (from China, Myanmar, and

Eastern Europe), gay students, and feminists. More than half the projects include adult students, including veterans, farmworkers, adult rape survivors, and adult ESL learners.[4]

Part 1, "Service Learning in American Literature," opens with "Everybody Reads: Public Literature Programs as Agents of Social Exchange and Connection," by Fallon, who begins with the premise that we understand books as nonhuman agents of social change. This theoretical perspective is based in Latour's work in actor-network theory and applies this lens to a humanistic context. Making the humanities relevant and engaging to the general public is one of the most pressing issues in the academy today. The collaboration between Multnomah County Library and Portland State University around the One City, One Book project Everybody Reads exemplifies the benefits of civic collaboration for the community at large and for the university. But for literary critics, this project also suggests a powerful way to imagine and reframe why and how books matter to individual readers and to a larger reading public.

Integrating service learning with another nationwide public reading program, the NEA's Big Read, is described in VanDette's essay, "The Literature Classroom, College Library, and Reading Publics." While Fallon's essay describes a university-wide collaboration with Everybody Reads, VanDette's focuses on one course, an English senior seminar capstone at the State University of New York, Fredonia. VanDette's students read literature and design programs and exhibits for several public library audiences while confronting issues of literary reception, canonicity, and debates about the relevance of specialized literary studies. The project also enhances students' professional communication and research and literary skills, creates a rich reading environment for the general public, and fulfills the historic public mission of American universities.

Schweitzer's essay, "Completing the Circle: Teaching Literature as Community-Based Learning," discusses undergraduate and graduate students in a Dartmouth graduate-level memoir course who collaborate with local prisoners to create personal narratives that are performed before public audiences. Students' and prisoners' collaborations result in "transformational" learning experiences that affect students' social and ethical values while altering their ideas about the purposes of literary study. Students are challenged to integrate Freire's abstract theories of dialogue into an actual life narrative. As students move dialectally between theory and practice, they develop an important understanding of the unique immersive power of literature. At the same time, "prisoners feel recognized and heard in new healing ways."

In his essay, "Reliving and Remaking the Harlem Renaissance," Hicks's undergraduate students at the University of North Carolina, Pembroke, read important texts of the Harlem Renaissance and develop a firsthand understanding of the issues of representation, audience, and social justice surrounding the period. The students organize community writing workshops and publish a literary magazine of the creative writing of the local Lumbee community. The workshops offer mentoring and tutoring for community youth, and the literary magazine provides them with a venue for creative expression. Hicks's students also benefit as they experience the challenges of cross-cultural representation and "a revolutionary consciousness worthy of the spirit that animated the [Harlem Renaissance's] writers and artists."

Part 2, "Service Learning in English and World Literature," commences with Goodhue's "Satire, Sentimentalism, and Civic Engagement: From Eighteenth-Century Britain to the Twenty-First-Century Writing Course." Students examine literature about urban life from various historical eras while working with not-for-profit organizations to document previously untold stories of Los Angeles residents. Reading eighteenth-century texts in a community-based context, Goodhue argues, heightens student awareness of how literary form shapes meaning and simultaneously prompts deep reflection on power and privilege in civil society. Students pay close attention to literary and social concerns as they analyze published texts, collaborate with local residents, and generate their own stories. Goodhue further asserts that including both analytic and creative writing projects in service-learning literature courses "encourage[s] undergraduates to see their academic work as part and parcel of their collaboration with and service to the local community."

In "Shake It Up After-School: Service Learning, Shakespeare, and Performance as Interpretation," Hansen relates how his college students adapt, direct, and produce a Shakespeare play with elementary students in Title IX schools requiring mastery of plot, character analysis, and performance fundamentals. Reflections from his students demonstrate how the service-learning experience deepens their skills as critics of dramatic literature, fostering their literary and critical-thinking skills as well as communication and administrative capabilities; the college students also "acquire a profound and deep understanding of Shakespeare's language and dramaturgy." Hansen argues that the collaboration on a Shakespeare play benefits all constituencies: "we all learn and we all teach, together."

Archibald's "Learning across 'Different Zones': Bridging the Gap between 'Two Nations' through Community Engagement" describes an upper-level English course at the University of Massachusetts, Lowell, in which students consider the similarities and differences between contemporary and Victorian social and class tensions. The course was informed by new historicist theories of the referentiality and subjectivity of history, highlighting the ways that the Victorian novelists were influenced by, and in turn influenced, history and culture. Students work in local soup kitchens, shelters, libraries, and recycling centers, and this engagement "led back to a better understanding of the text and to a commitment to collaborative problem solving and community engagement." The reading and service experiences, Archibald argues, are helpful for students, "deepening understanding of the time periods and spurring them to action."

In an effort to transform their George Mason University Latin American literatures courses from a "classroom study of language ideologies to hands-on language activism," Rabin and Leeman invite students through an optional credit-bearing internship to facilitate bilingual literacy education programs with bilingual speakers in elementary schools, book clubs, and adult ESL classes. In their essay, "Critical Service Learning and Literary Study in Spanish," Rabin and Leeman argue that by engaging in activist work and analyzing Latin American texts from the seventeenth century to the present, students come to understand "literature's role as a purveyor of multiple discourses" as well as the "historical erasure of non-English languages in the United States." Rabin and Leeman demonstrate students' enthusiasm for both contributing to social change and reading and studying literature.

Part 3, "Service Learning in Creative Nonfiction and Memoir," includes three essays describing students' work with elders, providing three effective models for this work. Lucenko's essay, "Generation(s) of Narratives: Life Writing and Digital Storytelling," describes her seminar Life Writing and Storytelling, at Stony Brook University. In this course, students partner with the university's chapter of the Osher Lifelong Learning Institute (OLLI), an enrichment program for retired community members, and collaboratively create a digital storytelling project of the seniors' life stories. Both students and seniors experience the complexities of self-reflexive narrative, including subjective memory, provisional truths, enduring themes, and the transformation of knowledge into art through language. In this intergenerational writing workshop, students and seniors collectively develop interpretive skills, make meaning, and build relationships.

In the next essay, "'The Boldness of Imagination': Illness Narratives outside the Classroom," Rogers's first-year students listen to, document, and produce texts narrated and coedited by community elders with chronic illnesses. Simultaneously, they read published illness narratives. This reciprocal work expands Anis Bawarshi's concept of generic action and invention (*Genre*; "Genres"), allowing students to make important connections between elders' stories and canonized literary narratives. Through this experience, students develop an increased understanding of genre and better understand the experience of illness, ideas of subjectivity, and the power of storytelling as social action.

Joan Wagner's "Care, Compassion, and the Examined Life: Combining Creative Nonfiction and Community Engagement in a First-Year Seminar" connects her Saint Michael's College students with members of the senior community at PACE VT (Program of All-Inclusive Care for the Elderly in Vermont). Students gain an intergenerational perspective on aging and a firsthand experience in creative nonfiction by assisting their senior partners in writing life narratives. By reading literary texts and collaborating with PACE elders, students learn about complex and fluid identities. On completion, the writing projects are given to the seniors, their families, and the PACE staff, to further PACE's mission to "preserv[e] the dignity of the elderly in the community."

Part 4, "Service Learning in Literature-Based Writing," pays special attention to the intersection of literature, writing, civic engagement, and the first year of college. Parfitt's "Teaching Literature to Raise a Voice in the First-Year Writing Course" describes her course at Emerson College that uses the Boston cityscape as a literary text. Parfitt links students' service-learning knowledge of the city and its culture to literary narratives of social activism and community empowerment. After working with community partners, studying literature, and honing their writing skills, students create a public magazine that "echoes the aims of activist literature: it initiates a conversation that raises consciousness and, ideally, inspires a community of readers to act."

"'Beneath Thatched Shelters, We Paint Wide-Brimmed Straw Hats': Creative Writing and Social Justice" is McIsaac's essay about Santa Clara

University's upper-division students who read and write poetry with community members in transitional housing, a residential treatment program, and a youth community center. Students analyze poetry through both formalist and multicultural critical approaches, and they write poetry that both addresses social justice issues and pays careful attention to aesthetics and poetic elements. Community members feel empowered through their poetic voices, and students develop an awareness of poetry as a catalyst for human growth and social change. Both groups develop a deeper ability to enjoy reading and writing poetry.

Part 5, "Service Learning in Cross-Disciplinary Studies," begins with Tyx and Vermillion's "Literature Goes to Prison: A Reciprocal Service-Learning Project." With the help of English majors in a variety of courses at Mount Mercy University, Tyx and Vermillion created a reading program for prisoners at Anamosa State Penitentiary. Their students of American literature and Shakespeare surveys engage in a sustained reading and reflection experience with prisoners to understand "why literature matters beyond the academy" and "to foster self-reflection, ethical thinking, empathy, and a more inclusive community."

Barrow's "Building Empathy through Service Learning and Narratives of Sexual Violence" describes an interdisciplinary service-learning seminar, Sexual Violence in Western Culture, at the University of Tennessee. Linking the vital role of empathy in rape survivors' recovery processes with empathic theories of literature, Barrow illustrates that service learning and literary study function recursively to build students' empathy with both literary characters and real people, fostering students' desire for social change. Reading literary texts informs students' understanding of victims' lives, and service experiences enrich students' empathic readings of literary texts.

The final essay of the volume, Wald's "Sustainable Harvests: Food Justice, Service Learning, and Environmental Justice Pedagogy," turns attention to food justice and representations of poverty and the poor by linking literature with service learning. With the help of translators, Drew University students work with Spanish-speaking farmworkers and with El Comité de Apoyo a los Trabajadores Agrícolas (CATA; The Farmworker Support Committee), an organization advocating on behalf of and organizing farmworkers across the mid-Atlantic region of the United States. The course encourages students to interrogate well-known literary representations of farmworkers and to consider "the interpretive act of literary analysis alongside the interpretive act of translation." Students "learned to see both established literary texts and their own writing as public work with a social impact."

The final section, "Selected Resources," extends the reach of this volume by listing opportunities for further research and collaboration, as well as sources for publication and funding of new projects. Readers who wish to contact the editors of this volume or other scholars interested in service learning may also join the group Service Learning in Literature, Language and Composition on *MLA Commons* (http://commons.mla.org/groups/service-learning-in-literature-language-and-composition/).

Conclusion: The Future of Service Learning and Literary Studies

We began this introduction by citing Sidonie Smith's reference to "real work"; students' "real work," Smith asserts, "has an afterlife" (200). Service learning in literature courses, we argue, has an afterlife as well. Literature teachers' contributions to the discipline, the academy, and the field of service learning, as well as students' work in their communities, live on past any given semester. Community work in literature classes may also initiate a lifetime of civic commitment for students who carry this practice into their adult lives. We also see service learning as one definition of the *public humanities* and the *public intellectual*—a new role for literary studies that reflects its origins and initiates its future potential.

"The experience of the imagination is a human right, and literature invites and enhances this right," proclaims Schwartz ("Right" 746). We can think of fewer more meaningful uses of literature than this, and through service learning, literature faculty members are able to connect the imagination and human rights, widening and deepening literature's reach. Relatedly, implicit in this book are the ways that literary teacher-scholars are integrating research, teaching, and service and transforming their academic experiences. As Schwartz claims, "Working with local community initiatives through teaching and on my own has transformed my research as well as my teaching" ("Public Stakes" 988). Schwartz's transformative experiences mirror our own and may be a model that others in our field will choose to follow.

Literature, with its strong link to moral, ethical, and social imagination, has the ability to energize the next generation of service-learning practitioners and their students, providing them with a new space to reimagine literary study and its importance. In *Where's the Learning in Service-Learning?*, a comprehensive empirical study, Eyler and Giles document the learning outcomes and personal and civic development of our nation's students. They conclude with a quote from part 5 of T. S. Eliot's "Little Gidding" in *Four Quartets*:

> We shall not cease from exploration
> And the end of all our exploring
> Will be to arrive where we started
> And know the place for the first time.   (qtd. in Eyler and Giles 208)

By "exploring," Eliot's travelers journey forth and return significantly changed by their actions: they "know the place for the first time." Service-learning pedagogy in literary studies asks students to explore simultaneously and intensely real and imagined people and communities; in so doing, students and communities may change for the better. Although Eliot wrote his words during a particularly bleak time in history—the Blitz—the present has its own challenges and dangers. We hope that, given its commitment to the humanities, social justice, and the public good, service learning in literary studies will provide the imaginative space for renewal in our time that Eliot imagined in his own.

NOTES

1. In this collection, two authors, Ivy Schweitzer and Joan Wagner, choose to use different terms, *community-based learning* and *community-engaged learning*, respectively, to emphasize reciprocal, socially just, college-community relationships.

2. Unlike Malachuk, we do not believe that cultural studies is necessarily "politically *regressive*" (28). While Malachuk begins by stating that cultural studies is not easily defined, he nonetheless simplifies it as only and always about power and as unable to "support compassion" (29–30). In our view, cultural studies opens interpretive possibilities for literary texts that include aesthetics, compassion, and politics.

3. Successful service learning follows these ten principles: (1) engages people in responsible and challenging actions for the common good; (2) provides structured opportunities for people to reflect critically on their service experience; (3) articulates clear service and learning goals for everyone involved; (4) allows for those with needs to clarify those needs; (5) clarifies the responsibilities of each person and organization involved; (6) matches service

providers and service needs through a process that recognizes changing circumstances; (7) expects genuine, active, and sustained organizational commitment; (8) includes training, supervision, monitoring, support, recognition, and evaluation to meet service and learning goals; (9) ensures that the time commitment for service and learning is flexible, appropriate, and in the best interests of all involved; (10) is committed to program participation by and with diverse populations (Honnet and Poulsen).

4. Recent research in service learning has begun to explore the ways in which learning outcomes may differ by students' racial identifications and other categories of social difference and privilege. As Scott Seider, James Huguley, and Sarah Novick assert, most studies on service-learning outcomes "have focused on the effects of White and affluent college students, and few have considered whether there are differential effects for participants depending on their racial and ethnic backgrounds" (2). Stephanie Y. Evans, Colette M. Taylor, Michelle R. Dunlap, and DeMond S. Miller's *African Americans and Community Engagement in Higher Education Community Service, Service-Learning, and Community-Based Research* brings dialogues about race into multiple facets and constituencies of community-engagement, including student participants (Evans). Also important in service-learning assessment are its outcomes for adult students, as M. Cecil Smith notes: "there are few investigations of service learning that have involved older, nontraditional adult students or other adults" (5).

Part I

Service Learning
in American Literature

Ann Marie Fallon

Everybody Reads: Public Literature Programs as Agents of Social Exchange and Connection

"I'm a story," says the main character, Rachel, in Heidi Durrow's 2010 novel *The Girl Who Fell from the Sky* (264). Rachel, a biracial orphan coming of age in Portland, Oregon, during the 1980s, is referring to her ability to construct her identity and sense of self amid family tragedy. Her declaration of narrative personification at the novel's end serves as the centerpiece of a public discussion led by three literature faculty members from Portland State University (PSU) for the 2012 Everybody Reads season. Since 2005 PSU has brought together a variety of departments across campus to reengage the humanities in a civic project in the Portland metro area. Working with Multnomah County Library's Everybody Reads program, the local version of the project One City, One Book, PSU has established a productive collaboration that has significantly increased public participation in the community project, helped solidify a sense of campus community, and notably raised the profile of the humanities on campus and in the city.

Rachel's declaration shapes our public discussion and offers readers an entrée into the themes of the novel. Her framing of identity as a story opens the door to a community-wide conversation on close reading as a method for carefully examining small details of literary structure. But Rachel's declaration also invites readers and audience members (students, faculty members, Portlanders) to see themselves as a story and to share these stories with one another. Rachel's story, like most of the Everybody Reads selections, prompts difficult conversations about race, gender, and gentrification. These topics, addressed in all the programs over the years, are consequently framed by readers' experiences during the act of reading and their personal identification with the characters. Affective responses are key to creating the interpretive communities that arise around the texts during the roundtables and book discussions traversing the city over the six weeks of programming each year.[1] At PSU, this program presents a unique opportunity for the community and the university to come together and to be transformed by books, themselves agents of social exchange and connection.

Here I argue that service learning in the public humanities offers a unique opportunity to combat the public's apparent disengagement with literature in particular and the humanities more broadly. Moreover, incorporating community projects in literature-specific courses broadens the theoretical understanding of literature for literary critics. Finally, having students involved in community reading programs deepens their learning and understanding of literature and modes of reading.

Books as Nonhuman Actors

Everybody Reads demonstrates literature's power to move individual readers. If we as critics take seriously this affective power instead of being suspicious of it as naive reading, we might experiment with new approaches to criticism and use this personal investment in the text to understand how books as works of art, as "non-human actors," to borrow a phrase from Bruno Latour, function as agents in social exchange (148). Service learning conceived in this way allows us to see that books are part of a network of social dialogue that brings together individual readers (students and community participants), the broad public, and literary critics.

Multnomah County Library frames its project with the question, "What if everyone read the same book?" ("Everybody"). The question challenges our work as literary critics in important ways. After all, we in literary criticism no longer merely see books as aesthetic objects, "the best that has been thought or said" (Arnold viii), or as mere sociological commentaries. Books are both constructions of reality and reflections of it. When we read, our job is sometimes to point to the shortcomings of a text, to provide or engage in historical contextualization, to ponder the formal structures of the work in question. But the question posed by Multnomah County Library seems to invite a sociological response. The question isn't how or why a specific book evokes a particular kind of reaction or even how the book works as a piece of fiction. Instead, literature here is both a conduit and an invitation to discussion.

Broadening the audience for fiction implies that the selected books—and, by extension, literature more generally—matter because of their affective power to draw out individual stories and to provide moments of empathy both between the reader and the writer and, in this instance, among community readers, during a discrete period of time. The questions prompted by the program imagine literature as powerful: How might literature remake a community? How might literature provide us with an opportunity to converse and connect? The act of choosing a text to facilitate community change is a far cry from the work we usually do in classes or in our research, where we might choose texts to illustrate a point, to make an argument on historical context, period, style, voice, or poetics. The selection for Everybody Reads presupposes a different way of approaching the work that literary texts can do in the world.

Everybody Reads privileges texts as agents of social change, imbuing them with a power not often accorded to them in literary criticism, where they are objects of study. When the character Rachel makes her declaration, "I'm a story," the book is making a statement and has become a non-human agent inviting readers to engage in the same project of making social change. Certainly, some readers might conflate the author Heidi with the character Rachel, but in the moment of reading and in public conversations, Rachel is a powerful entity in her own right. This exceptional privileging of the text as an active agent in community exchange extends Martha Nussbaum's thesis on the importance of novels to a thriving democracy. In *Poetic Justice*, Nussbaum offers a treatise on the subversiveness of the novel and its ability to allow us readers to confront uncomfortable truths about ourselves and our society:

> Novels present persistent forms of human need and desire realized in specific social situations. These situations frequently, indeed usually, differ a good deal from the reader's own. Novels, recognizing this, in general construct and speak to an implicit reader who shares with the characters certain hopes, fears, and general human concerns, and who for that reason is able to form bonds of identification and sympathy with them, but who is also situated elsewhere and needs to be informed about the concrete situation of the characters. In this way, the very structure of the interaction between the text and its imagined reader invites the reader to see how the mutable features of society and circumstances bear on the realization of shared hopes and desires.   (7)

Nussbaum emphasizes the importance of the realist novel in her work on why literature matters and how it works politically. The Everybody Reads selections tend to be either recent realist novels written in the first-person or memoirs. The librarians who select the texts emphasize their particular interest in books that can facilitate a community conversation. While the library has chosen two Oregon writers in recent years, location is almost incidental. Instead, librarians look for themes and experiences that will speak to a wide range of readers. We can hear in the responses to these texts, both from students and community members, that the affective experiences participants bring to the reading process are those that most deeply connect them to the texts and, in turn, become the foundation from which community conversation emerges.

Borrowing from and developing on Latour's work on actor-network theory, Rita Felski argues that books and works of art might be considered agents in a network, entities creating attachments and provoking emotions rather than simply objects to be studied or that reflect aesthetic or social trends:

> The significance of a text is not exhausted by what it reveals or conceals about the social conditions that surround it. Rather, it is also a matter of what it makes possible in the viewer or reader—what kind of emotions it elicits, what perceptual changes it triggers, what affective bonds it calls into being. What would it mean to do justice to these responses rather than treating them as naïve, rudimentary, or defective? ("'Context'"585)

Likewise, Everybody Reads takes seriously the affective bonds readers need to be successful and authentic. Readers are community members and equal participants in a conversation that takes books seriously. In embracing the transformative power of literature, Everybody Reads provocatively expands Stanley Fish's notion of an interpretive community (*Is There*). The meaning or the interpretation of the book isn't simply shaped by the communities that form around it—the reading groups, the roundtables, and the lectures on history or art. Instead, the book itself shapes those conversations; the book creates different kinds of attachments and connections and evokes different emotions and conversations.

Literature in the Public Sphere

Everybody Reads began as the brainchild of librarians invested in public literacy programming. Portland's version of the project One City, One Book came out of the Seattle Center for the Book in 1998. Since 2002, Multno-mah County Library has been sponsoring this annual event, inviting peo-ple from throughout the metropolitan area to read a common book. And beginning in 2005, Portland State University began partnering with the library to provide in-depth academic and cultural programming designed to support the project. The partnership has allowed the library system to offer diverse types of programming, including bringing in national and regional experts, and simultaneously has presented PSU with an opportu-nity to reach out to the local community. Overall, an average of thirteen thousand people participate in the Everybody Reads events each year, and the project offers an average of almost forty programs throughout the city (on campus and throughout the county's libraries) over the course of the six-week project (T. Chun). A common sense of purpose between the two public institutions—the library and the university—to provide opportu-nities for people to read, learn, and connect has inspired both partners to work together in a resource-poor environment.

Everybody Reads offers a compelling space for the humanities in the local public sphere. The exciting challenge of the project has been to find multiple ways for people to engage with the programs around the city, in-spired by the issues raised by any given book in a single year. People must feel personally compelled or encouraged to embark on a reading project and interested to find a shared sense of community beyond the book.

Since the English professor Maude Hines initiated the partnership with Multnomah County Library, we have experimented with a variety of programs, events, and other ways to involve faculty members, students, and community members. As a faculty member at Portland State, I serve on the organizing committee for Everybody Reads, and over the course of the partnership, I have led community book discussion groups, taught seminars featuring the Everybody Read's selection, and offered classes in which students created community programming for the selection. As a campus partner, I have encouraged other faculty members to use the Everybody Reads selection in their courses, from first-year seminars to graduate-level literature courses.

Collaboration

Everybody Reads has enabled PSU students and faculty members to learn to be literary entrepreneurs. This entrepreneurial spirit is evident in our faculty panels. From *The Kite Runner*, by Khalid Hosseini, the novel from the first year of the collaboration, to our most recent selection, set in Portland, we have been able to marshal faculty expertise on topics as diverse as Afghanistan, Chinese-exclusion laws, the Japanese American internment, and gentrification in Portland. In taking a broad interpretive approach to each book, we have built connections to diverse groups throughout the community and with one another on campus. We have included faculty members from the Middle East Studies Center; from Judaic studies, urban studies, history and literature; and from other departments to give presentations and lead panel discussions. Faculty members continue to learn from librarians about public programming and entrepreneurship to market our work to the public, and librarians learn more about scholarship and the culture of professional literary criticism and research. We also connected with faculty members we had only tangentially met and were able to engage and read their scholarship, often for the first time.

Common Experiences

The common book brings a sense of shared experience to campus, as well as a sense of connection to the city, since the book is also common to the community. As interest across campus has continued to grow, faculty members from different departments and disciplines — including history, international studies, and women's studies — have required the book in their courses. Making the book and the related programming more closely interwoven brings a sense of community to the book, simultaneously broadening and deepening the discussion around one novel and drawing connections between the Chinese Canadian literary experience, for example, and the history of immigration across the North American hemisphere. In an anonymous faculty feedback form, one instructor reported:

> The students got an enormous amount out of the experience. From the simple delighted response of a few students who admitted to having read and enjoyed their first book "all the way through" to the students who report having been "transformed" by the experience of reading and talking about a book with all kinds of people they might otherwise never have imagined speaking to.

What we learned was that just as students in writing classes appreciate having real-world audiences for their work, students in all kinds of college classes appreciate knowing that our conversations extend beyond the classroom walls. Something as simple as having freshmen participate in community book groups at coffee shops down the street from campus changed their perspectives about how books work.

The Benefits of Partnership

Students also gained experience packaging and promoting humanistic study. In the third year of the collaborative project, having had freshmen previously participate as discussants and readers, I decided to try to bring in seniors to the behind-the-scenes organization and programming. In the summer before the public project began (Everybody Reads always runs from late January through early March), I designed a capstone seminar in which seniors worked with a faculty member to develop a series of programs for the book. The book for 2008 was Ishmael Beah's *Long Way Gone*, a memoir of a child soldier from Sierra Leone. Of the fifteen course participants, only two were English majors. The others represented social sciences, other humanities programs, and professional degree programs. The most striking thing about the group and their approach to creating programming was the tremendous creative freedom they took. Since they were unconstrained by a sense of obligation to form or even to history, although that was clearly part of the course as well, they were able to think broadly about what constitutes art and what might be paired with a text. Their events included a hip-hop lyrics workshop, a memoir workshop, film screenings of documentaries on Sierra Leone with follow-up discussions with film directors or other local experts, panels with recent immigrants from Sierra Leone and Peace Corps volunteers, food tastings, storytelling, puppet shows, zoo visits to local libraries with related animals, and dancing. Students brought an additional perspective to this complicated collaboration, finding new resources in the community and bringing in new ideas, energy, and programming for an even broader and more diverse audience. Students were able to create partnerships with local puppet companies, storytellers, mask makers, anthropologists, linguists, and writers, connecting an ever more complex and interesting web of ideas.

The partnership with Everybody Reads is clearly good for students. The teaching evaluations are uniformly positive; the work students produce for portfolios is well-written and engaging since they seem genuinely invested in their projects and excited to have a wide audience for their ideas. For the 2012 winter term, students wrote a blog tracking the Everybody Reads events and went into the community to lead book groups. One student, Marty Botts, read the selected book aloud to nursing home residents. He wrote about the novel in his final reflection:

> I saw the unique transformational power of a literary artifact. . . . One care resident held the book within two inches of her face, her voice began to modulate as she rekindled the bond with her childhood neighbor. . . . [F]or the first time I could discuss the race issue with a black person who I did not know.

The novel mediates the relationship between these two readers; from the student perspective, it creates a bond and an opportunity for exchange and connection. Through creating an affective bond with the characters in the story, two people were able to delve into an otherwise taboo discussion.

Everybody Reads is also a great project for faculty members. We get to connect across departments, meet new community partners, and promote our work in the public sphere. Moreover, the benefit to PSU also seems evident. Despite tight budgets, PSU is able to become a major sponsor through the in-kind donations of faculty time and university space. Our logo appeared on books and even on bus advertisements.

Community Engagement

Equally important, the community benefits of Everybody Reads and of the partnership with PSU are evident in statistics on participation and through interviews. In library surveys, ninety-seven percent of the participants in the library's public literacy programs find them to be good or excellent. Eighty percent of participants say they learned something from the programming, and fifty percent say that the programming helped them feel more connected to their communities ("FY 2012"). These numbers tell us something about investment and participation in the reading project.

Furthermore, video interviews with Everybody Reads community participants and students about *The Girl Who Fell from the Sky* help us better understand the qualitative impact of reading literature as a community. The interviews demonstrate individual readers' powerful affective responses and connections to the novels as they see their own stories reflected in literary texts. Readers connect to Rachel's pronouncement, "I'm a story." Said Lisa McCall:

> I felt a real connection to the story because my nine-year old, he is biracial. He's a product of me, an African-American mother, and a white

father. And I'll never forget two years ago I was driving him to day care, and out of the blue my son said, "Mom, am I a black person?"

McCall created an affective connection between the deep anguish over identity expressed in the novel and her own thoughtful reflection as a mother thinking about how identity is imbued in her son.

Patricia Hudson, in an interview with her daughter, notes:

> As the mother of biracial children I was especially interested to read her story. . . . I'm very proud of my children, and I think they're beautiful, but I think people need to know that they aren't just exotic creatures, that they're real people with real feelings and experiences and they're more than just something to look at, you know, they're deep.
>
> (Hudson and Hudson)

This response demonstrates how readers connect to the anguish of motherhood and loss in the novel, and their connection to the fictional story is marked by an emphasis on their own "real feelings."

Rachel Porter, a PSU student who was in the Everybody Reads seminar in 2012, gave an interview explaining how the novel helped her: "Reading *The Girl Who Fell from the Sky* helped me come to terms with my 'not-completely-whiteness.' I realized it is okay to acknowledge myself."

As a scholar, I am struck by how these strongly affective reading practices are reflected not only in these interviews but also in the book discussions and in questions that arise in the roundtables. Audience members almost always preface their question with a personal story about a connection they found in the text. The story affirms readers' individual experience, opens a doorway into their children's lives, or gives them permission to share their own connected story. This thread has become so noticeable that in the 2012 programming, Oregon Public Broadcasting invited listeners to share their own experiences growing up biracial, like the protagonist of the novel from that year.

Literature functions as a public good because it facilitates this deeply individual sense of personal and emotional attachment to which other people can in turn relate. While the act of reading a novel or memoir remains private, the public work of discussing that connection across a community deepens a sense of shared experience. The reader's experience is consequently individual and emotionally communal. To use Felski's provocations, the book becomes an agent in creating attachments and connections. For many readers of *The Girl Who Fell from the Sky*, for example, the intimacy of the fictional story provides an entrée into a conversation about topics that are important and even controversial in our community. As readers connect to those whose experiences and cultures might differ from their own, they develop that ability to empathize mentioned by Nussbaum and other literary critics. By consciously drawing on this sense of shared empathy and shared experience, we are able to critically create a public experience of the community good through conversation about literature.

Implications for Professional Literary Criticism

This goal affects how we practice literary criticism. Even for most of the students participating in the various iterations of these projects, the initial book discussions are more of an introduction to literary criticism and theory. When we teach the book, largely in our interdisciplinary general education courses, we always introduce concepts of genre, structure, literary devices, and reader-response criticism. But Everybody Reads also challenges us to take seriously the affective responses of readers. Everybody Reads makes apparent the power of emotional connections to books and the power of books to function as social agents that organize and create connection.

I propose that we use the question posed by Multnomah County Library, "What if everyone read the same book?," as an opportunity to consider how we as critics understand the function and functionality of literature. These shared texts, as nonhuman actors, provoke reactions, emotions, and connection and offer us a glimpse into alternative modes of thinking about literature. If we think of the book as one of the actors at play in this complex public network among university, city, library, student, teacher, critic, and reader, we might reimagine our work as not just an attempt to model close reading for the general public but also an opportunity to reconsider our reading and writing practices both in the classroom and in the greater society.

Everybody Reads is inspiring for scholars in the humanities because it allows us to invite other people to share in the experience and importance of reading literary texts. It also suggests research agendas extending beyond problems of periodization or critical readings that attempt to objectify or simply take apart the text to reveal ideological bias or hidden meaning. Public reading projects offer scholars in the humanities an opportunity to reframe the types of research questions they engage in and invite us to make our work deeply engaged with the big questions that continue to resonate with the American public at large: How do stories of race connect and divide us? How can literature facilitate difficult conversations and issues? Why do we organize our lives around stories? What is it about the first-person experience or voice that resonates with so many types of readers? How does fiction shape the way we understand our life's work? The public reading experience underlines the need for research on how reading influences how people think, both about literature and about their community. Everybody Reads provides an important forum to demonstrate that humanities do matter today, that books continue to change our lives and shape the stories we tell our communities and ourselves.

NOTE

1. Fish's evocative phrase "interpretive communities" is useful for defining the communities of readers that get established during the period of Everybody Reads (*Is There*). This community becomes a lose affiliation of readers that bond over the common reading experience.

Emily VanDette

The Literature Classroom, College Library, and Reading Publics: Building Collaborative Critical Reading Networks

With their shared value for reading, literature classrooms and libraries are natural partners. Libraries have a long history of building literary collections and hosting book discussions, literature exhibits, and readings. While libraries have contributed to an engaged and literate society for well over a century, such recent cultural shifts as the growing presence of coffee shops and electronic books, combined with decreasing budgets, have led to challenges to the traditional functions of libraries. In response, over the past two decades public librarians have increasingly sought to restore the role of the library as a civic and cultural center, as signaled by two consecutive themes selected by recent American Library Association presidents: "Libraries Build Community" and "Libraries: The Cornerstone of Democracy" (McCabe xiv). The pedagogy of civic librarianship, as Ronald B. McCabe defines it, "seeks to strengthen communities through developmental strategies that renew the public library's mission of education for a democratic society" (77). This community-centered initiative is paralleled on college campuses in the movement to restore the civic mission of higher education through innovations like service-learning pedagogy. Uniquely poised to link the service-learning environments of college classrooms with public libraries seeking to build their community focus, academic libraries have the capacity to bring together students, faculty members, and library communities and to enrich the mutual benefits to both college student learners and the publics they serve.

Several successful experiments involving students in the creation of exhibits, literary readings, book discussions, and civic initiatives at the campus library at the State University of New York, Fredonia, affirmed the exciting potential of a strong collaboration between the college library and literature classrooms. It only seemed natural to extend the benefits of these relationships to our public library partners when the campus library took a lead role in the Big Read, a community-wide reading initiative. A program funded by the National Endowment for the Arts (NEA) with the ambitious and noble goal of "restoring reading to the center of American culture" (*Big Read*), the Big Read presents an ideal opportunity for students to collaborate with public libraries to inspire individuals in local communities to read classic works of literature.

With their fresh perspectives, academic training, and passion for reading, college literature students have much to offer community literary programs. In turn, the library members and community readers act as coeducators, enriching the students' learning about rhetorical situations, professionalization, and literary relevance in the real world. The main learning outcomes for this capstone course include professional communication skills, advanced literary research methods, and the application of scholarly discoveries in real-world settings, as well as key topics related to canonicity and rhetorical studies. The enhanced capacity for empathy and moral consciousness, an outcome shared by both students and their public audiences, invokes Martha Nussbaum's concept of the "narrative imagination" essential for a successful democracy (*Not for Profit* 95).

Fostering Human Development through Literature in Classrooms and Communities

The idea to feature this public literary project in Senior Seminar, a capstone course for English majors, grew out of a more modest effort during the previous year: a three-week service-learning unit in the undergraduate course American Literary Landmarks. In place of a traditional research project, students worked in teams to design library exhibits to enhance the local communities' appreciation of the Big Read selection, Harper Lee's *To Kill a Mockingbird*, which fit perfectly with the canonical scope of the course. This assignment challenged students to practice literary research methods, study critical interpretations of the novel, and learn about American literary history, three central objectives of the course. Given the complex rhetorical scenario of their exhibits, which required them to consider the library directors and their patrons, the NEA's stated goals, and the novel's reception history, the project yielded fodder for much more substantial debates than the interpretation of a novel, including such enduring questions in the field as how literature is assessed and by whom and with what consequences. The students' learning ventured into surprising depths, and the library directors and their patrons appreciated the students' contributions. Given the mutual impact of that modest assignment, for the next Big Read I turned to a Senior Seminar class for more extensive service with the public literacy initiative, as well as with a more significant learning focus on the theoretical and literary methods that such a collaboration would enhance.

The most compelling intellectual outcomes of the American Literary Landmarks public literary project involved literary reception, canonicity, and debates about the relevance of specialized literary studies—all topics that have special significance to students on the cusp of graduating with English degrees. Senior Seminar afforded a full semester and three credit hours to devote to the pertinent questions that arise as a result of a collaboration between a college English classroom and a public reading initiative, questions about canonicity, authority, and the role of the profession, such as the following: Does the study of literature have any relevance in the world outside the academy? What role do students, teachers, readers, library patrons, and citizens play in the shaping of the canon? Does the interpreting of literature belong to the specialist or to the common reader? In the process of contributing to a public reading program, graduating English majors realize firsthand the complex dynamics between the humanities and society, and they become more conscious about their roles as citizens and intellectuals.

For this service-learning project, students research a major novel in order to design programs and exhibits tailored for distinct library communities. The assignment transcends students' learning of literature, since it invokes a history of controversy within the field of literary studies—a history that the pedagogy of service learning seeks to disrupt. While the detachment of humanistic studies from the public sphere may seem puzzling, the perception of the humanities as irrelevant to people outside academic settings is rooted in anxieties that have long plagued the field. The pedagogy of service learning has the potential to invite practitioners—scholars, students, and public participants—to interrogate and challenge the sites of authority in the consumption, generation, and dissemination of ideas, which perhaps represents for the field the ultimate enactment of John Guillory's call, now twenty years ago, for the broadening of access to knowledge and resources (339–40).

While the field of literary studies has grappled with the notion of the college classroom's role in regulating and perpetuating the containment of knowledge and power—a paradigm shift Stanley Fish famously dubbed "Fear and Self-Loathing in Literary Studies" ("Profession")—the growing public distrust and devaluing of the humanities provokes continued protectiveness of specialized academic knowledge. But with the humanities continuing to lose ground in the battle for the cultural capital it once commanded in higher education, the pedagogy of service learning offers a potential resolution to the seemingly conflicting aims of economic progress and civic responsibility. As Nussbaum cautions, higher education increasingly prioritizes "applied skills suited to profit making" over "humanistic aspects of science and social science—the imaginative and creative aspect, and the aspect of rigorous critical thought" (*Not for Profit* 2). This prioritization sacrifices critical thinking and argumentation skills, which Nussbaum asserts as "abilities crucial to the health of any democracy" (7). Given this trend toward the narrowing of educational goals to the agenda of preparing students to compete in a global economy, the humanities, instead of losing their worth, are more crucial than ever to the preservation of critical analysis, logical thinking, and creativity.

Service-learning pedagogy restores the relevance of the humanities and preserves the stalwart mission of nurturing the skills crucial for civically responsible world citizens. The collaboration between an English capstone course and a public reading program performs the sort of intervention that enhances the "human development" that Nussbaum urges as a counterforce to the new mission of economic development in higher education (*Not for Profit* 24), and it also offers a host of specific outcomes for both students and their public-sphere partners. While the libraries benefit from the resources needed to strengthen their participation in the Big Read and thereby enhance the program's impact for local citizens, the students' experience providing those services offers a unique text for their theoretical engagement; moreover, by collaborating with librarians and community readers, students learn valuable professional and civic skills.

Collaborative Dialogues and the Protopublic Classroom

During the first half of the semester, students worked in pairs as Big Read coordinators, developing public programs and materials for their assigned libraries. Several built-in measures of support reinforced both the course goals and the public-service objectives, facilitating the students' capacity for scholarly research and their rhetorical awareness and, in turn, improving the effectiveness of their contributions to the public literary program. Early in the semester we invited campus and public librarians to spend a class period explaining the program to the students, which established their roles as coeducators in the learning process. The public library directors shared their visions for how the student collaborations could help shape the programming at their institutions, providing the students with valuable information about their communities. Students were able to make an initial contact with their partner librarians, which created a great opportunity for initiating a productive dialogue. The course design supported and sustained this dialogue throughout the semester by carving out several class periods for students to meet with their community partners. In addition, several class sessions were dedicated to the university librarian's instruction in research methods, effective exhibit design, and program planning and development, providing a further opportunity for support and collaboration. Allocating time to these types of activities helps develop the students' professional, technical, and communication skills, and the university and public librarians play central roles in shaping those important practical experiences. These logistical concessions proved to be crucial to overcoming the biggest challenge posed by a real-world setting—namely, finding time for busy college students to connect with busy community partners.

Establishing the library partners' collaborative roles at the onset of the project not only served the practical purpose of defining the scope and goals of the assignment but also contributed to the shaping of what Rosa Eberly calls the "protopublic classroom," in which students' engagement with real audiences creates a "place for individual experience, memory, and identity to find—through arguments about literary or cultural texts . . . a collective voice" (171). The community partnership was essential to the balance of rhetoric and literary study that was designed to make this project an opportunity for advanced academic research as well as an exercise in civic development, an opportunity for "producing discourses that form or sustain literary public spheres" (170). As Eberly explains, this new classroom "can help create a public-oriented agency or subjectivity in students that transcends the limits of liberal democratic citizenship as well as formalist criteria for ethos—'good sense, good will, and good moral character'" (170). As the students worked closely with their cooperating libraries to understand their patrons' needs and interests, learning valuable nonprofit marketing skills from their library partners, they integrated their audience awareness with their own critical ideas to design Big Read events.

While students researched the Big Read selection, Willa Cather's *My Ántonia*, they also researched their target audiences. The assignment asked students to prepare a professional proposal to share their critical research about the novel, their discoveries about their assigned library communities, and their plans for public programs and materials that would enhance the communities' reading of Cather's novel. To prepare their proposals, students met with their library directors to brainstorm ideas and logistics; they also conducted archival and secondary research about *My Antonia*, in accordance with goals they developed with their partner library directors. Because the proposals were intended to persuade both the course instructor and the cooperating library director to approve the students' programming plans, the stakes were high for the students to research carefully, write effectively, and appeal to their target audiences. This experience gave the students direct practice with understanding the rhetorical situation, which we would theorize later in our class discussions, and it gave valuable professional writing practice to English majors, who typically have fewer opportunities for real-world professional training than their peers outside the humanities. There was no need to create a separate unit for workplace writing with hypothetical scenarios and documents. Integrating instruction about professional writing style into the service-learning project offered a built-in, authentic audience and purpose, streamlining learning outcomes and giving them more immediate significance for the students. Offering support and feedback, campus and public librarians played a vital role as coeducators.

In their formal proposals, informal reflective writing, discussions, and classroom presentations, students shared their plans for balancing their critical ideas about the novel with their audience's expectations. When the members of a book club at one of our partner libraries recommended a local retired English teacher as a guest speaker, the students cheerfully obliged. That group of students rounded out the library program with engaging discussion questions that stemmed from their research about feminist perspectives on the novel, asking the participants to consider such possibilities as Cather's revisionist record of the roles that women played in the settlement of the prairies.

Logistical factors shaped the rhetorical situation, too, as when a student pair avoided including mature materials about sexuality themes in an exhibit for a library that shared its space with the town's preschool and instead chose to highlight prairie life as an exhibit topic appropriate for all ages. In contrast, the students who were assigned to our campus library seized on the opportunity to reach an adult audience, applying their research about queer theory and feminist approaches to Cather's life and works in a display titled *Willa Cather, Gender and Sexuality Exhibit*. To complement their exhibit, the campus library team drew on the university's rich resources with an interdisciplinary series that featured faculty members and students from history, creative writing, women's studies, theater performance, and costume design.

The libraries off campus had their own resources and networks for student coordinators to tap into, and their community settings enhanced the social experience of reading literature. When one of our partner library directors introduced her Big Read student coordinators to the director of a local senior citizen home where her most active library participants lived, the students were able to reach out to learn about the residents; as a result, they designed discussion events and exhibit materials that focused on the novel's immigration and international themes that connected with their partnering readers' personal histories and literary interests. For a library director who wanted to use the Big Read to bring youth back into the library, the student coordinators tied Patricia MacLachlan's popular children's novel *Sarah, Plain and Tall* into the discussion series; for another community, for whom Cather's representation of folk customs had immediate appeal, the coordinators planned a series that included a quilting demonstration, a theatrical skit, and a square dance with menus that were inspired by the novel's domestic scenes.

The programs the students led revealed the power of the novel to connect with the lives of readers with widely ranging backgrounds and experiences—some with little formal education, others with advanced degrees; some having hardly ever left their Western New York rural hometowns, others world travelers; some teens and many senior citizens; readers of various ethnic, religious, and family backgrounds. Together, the college English students, library staff members, and community readers connected with the narrative of the title character's compelling life story, Cather's masculine narrative point of view, and the memories of the American frontier.

Intergenerational discussions provided especially rich contexts for mutual reading enhancement. As one blog posting by a librarian shared,

"The vision of some of the town's most youthful and most senior citizens coming together to take in Cather's novel was especially meaningful in light of the novel's emphasis on the dynamics and connections between the generations" ("Big Read-ing"). Senior citizen readers who reflected personally on their own or their parents' immigration experiences identified with the title character's conflicted feelings of nostalgia for her native land and desire to adapt to her adopted region, and their perspectives enriched the reading experience of the college students, for most of whom immigration is a more distant part of their personal histories. Meanwhile, items that students discovered in their archival research and included in their exhibits and presentations, such as photographs depicting newly arrived immigrant families, inspired and jogged the memories of senior community readers.

In our public blog, My Antonia—*The Big Read Program of Chautauqua and Cattaraugus Counties*, students reflected on the change of setting for literary analysis; they found community settings to be refreshingly "lively and fun, and far more laid back than the classroom setting [they had] grown so accustomed to" ("Randolph Library"). In class discussions, students remarked on how much more diverse were their literary discussions in the community than in most of their classrooms; they noticed a higher threshold for disagreement in the public discussion, especially, for instance, in response to the relevance of Cather's sexuality to the critical interpretation of her novel. The varied and rich exchanges reminded us all of the power of literature to evoke empathy, imagination, and critical thought—crucial civic skills for a healthy democracy. By promoting literary reading in the public sphere, graduating English majors put to use their academic learning and boosted their civic competencies, while they enhanced for the local communities what Nussbaum calls "the narrative imagination," or "the ability to think what it might be like to be in the shoes of a person different from oneself, to be an intelligent reader of that person's story, and to understand the emotions and wishes and desires that someone so placed might have" (*Not for Profit* 95–96).

When a student, Ashley, recognized that her "program would not have been successful if we didn't step outside our comfort zones and look at the different perspectives," she attested to the power of such empathy building. She reflected:

> We planned a series of events in great detail, but until we started thinking about what the community members would like to do or talk about we

had difficulty getting our participants to open up. By our third book discussion, our participants were more interested in sharing life stories and
forming bonds with each other.   (Zengerski)

In addition, taking the literary discussion outside the classroom and autho-
rizing students to moderate it facilitates their intellectual self-awareness
and their reflections on how their academic knowledge functions in the
real world. Much of that self-discovery and enlightenment, important
outcomes for capstone pedagogy,[1] resulted from the theoretical engagement in the course in response to the Big Read programming project.

Literary Theory in the Public Sphere

The course concluded with a unit of relevant readings that extended the
public-service project's capacity to bring valuable theoretical debates to
life for students. Eberly's study of the connections among literature, rhetoric, and democracy helped students consider the potential for rational
discourse in the public sphere to shape the reception of literary works, as
well as the extent to which specialized literary study determines a text's
status. Eberly's explanation of the democratic capacity for literary public
spheres as "discursive spaces in which private people can come together
in public, bracket some of their differences, and invent common interests by arguing in speech or writing about literary and cultural texts" (9)
resonated with the actual experiences students had facilitating rational
exchanges about literature, including such potentially divisive issues as
gender, sexuality, religion, region, and immigration in the public sphere.
Giving students an opportunity to facilitate public-sphere literary reading
allowed them to, in the language of Edward Said, "reopen the blocked social processes ceding objective representation (hence power) of the world
to a small coterie of experts and their clients, to consider that the audience for literacy is not a closed circle of three thousand professional critics
but the community of human beings living in society" (25). Given the
opportunity, students were eager to expand the reaches of academic discourse and connect with real readers. As one student reflected in her blog
posting, "The atmosphere [of the library discussion] was tense at first, due
to many of them feeling as though I would wow them with some sort of
hoity-toity English jargon. After I told them to relax and just discuss what
they wanted to discuss, they became a wealth of knowledge" ("Randolph

Site"). This expanded space for reading literature brought new aspects of the reading experience to light for students, including humor, an unexpected response to such a serious novel. One student who worked with senior citizens in a small-town library noted, "Laughs were in no short supply; these women knew how to talk about a novel and have a good time doing it," and he reflected that he was "glad The Big Read [introduced him to] these six kind, intelligent, and downright hilarious older women" ("Randolph Library").

After engaging in their own public-sphere critical interventions, students were especially well prepared to consider the histories of contentious power struggles such as those over canonicity and institutionalized literary study, as well as to recognize the sites of those struggles in their personal experiences. Discussing Carey Kaplan and Ellen Cronan Rose's treatment of the historical divisions between academic English and "common readers" helped students come to terms with the barriers they sometimes experienced in their efforts to contribute to the Big Read, since the resistance they occasionally met reflected nonexpert readers' anxieties about the power and authority held by academic institutions.[2] In the most extreme instance of such resistance, a book club affiliated with one of our partner libraries declined our students' contributions because the library wanted complete ownership over their programming; as an alternative to shaping the events in person, the students contributed with a virtual alternative, posting thought-provoking discussion prompts and critical perspectives on the public blog.[3] While that occasional hostility toward the students' academic identities posed a challenge for us, it ended up providing an invaluable "text" to reflect on and theorize in the classroom and in writing exercises, as we considered the historical factors that shed light on such power struggles. Understanding that common readers may feel threatened by the presence of academics helped students develop sensitivity about their voices in community discussions. The historical tensions between academic and public contexts also shed light on their professor's transformation from vocal discussion leader in the classroom to quiet listener in the background of a library meeting room, as I shared with the class my consciousness that the presence of a college English professor may have a dampening effect on a public literary discussion.

Invoking Kaplan and Rose's classic criticism of the role that the authors of American Memory, a project funded by the National Endowment for the Humanities, played in reinforcing "timeless, eternal 'classics' that institutionalize and ossify the world they already control" (3), the class analyzed the public assertions and resources on the Big Read Web site and the implications of the NEA's short list of candidates for Big Read texts.[4] Students who wondered how the list of books was determined were baffled at the nebulous response they found on the Web site, that the books were chosen by a "Readers Circle—a distinguished group of writers, scholars, librarians, critics, and publishing professionals" (*Big Read*). Students realized firsthand the institutional power asserted by the gesture of withholding the identities of the "Readers Circle" and of highlighting only their "distinguished" expertise.

We asked whether our participation in the program makes us complicit with reinscribing a "great texts" history of literature, and we concluded together that participating allows us to disrupt that potential consequence. We considered the role that such academic material as historical contexts, archival sources, contemporary connections, and intertextual readings may play in complicating a public-sphere focus on classic literature. Carving out space in the class for theoretical engagement enabled students to consider how to support the more laudable goals of initiatives like the Big Read, especially the restoring of literary reading to enhance civic competency, while also consciously disrupting any tendency such classic literature programs may have to reinstate the canon and homogenize the American experience.

The capstone course—beginning with rigorous literary research applied to nonacademic rhetorical settings and developing into theoretical analysis of authority, canon, representation, and the public sphere— culminated with a critical essay assignment that affirmed the impact of the students' work in the public sphere. Our work with rhetorical studies prompted one student to evaluate discourse about literacy in local bookstores and another to assess our college library's recent acquisition of extensive graphic novel collections. The course's engagement pedagogy led one student to study the presence and impact of service learning in our campus and community and a student majoring in art and English to compose an editorial response to recent controversies in the local media about arts programming on our campus. A student bound for a master's of fine arts after graduation blogged about the debates surrounding creative writing workshops in academic and public settings. "Authors and professors of literature," she explained, "stand toe to toe on issues of what is the right atmosphere for creative writing workshops to take place or whether they can take place at all" (Ziemianski, "Criticisms"). Her treatment of the complex power dynamics surrounding writing in the public and academic realms revealed her growing consciousness as a professional creative writer and soon-to-be teacher, as captured in her concluding remarks: "With the guidance of a watchful teacher, the rewards of an environment so honest can have a huge impact on the beginning stages of a writer's career, whether they end up in the field of creative writing or elsewhere" (Ziemianski, "Exploring"). Our consideration of public-sphere history and theory influenced a senior bound for a master's of library science to theorize the relation of the public sphere to Internet identity dynamics in an impressive essay that compared Richard Sennett's powerful *The Fall of Public Man* to the phenomenon of identity posturing on social networking Web sites, a topic with important relevance to today's scholars of library and media sciences.

Revising the Role of Institutionalized Literary Study; or, Building Access, Not Roadblocks

The frequent recurrence of aesthetic evaluations and queries in the public literary discussions brought to life for students the famous conclusion of *Cultural Capital*, in which Guillory suggests the potential for a revised canon formation to "become a much larger part of social life, because not restricted to the institutions of the materially advantaged" (339). Inviting nonacademic readers to analyze Cather's treatment of domesticity and gender or to resurrect and enjoy a part of that domestic culture in the form of a traditional culinary recipe realizes Guillory's utopian vision, where, "[i]n a culture of such universal access, canonical works could not be experienced as they so often are, as lifeless monuments, or as proofs of class distinction" (340). That such access was made possible not in spite of but because of the resources from a college classroom suggests an important revision for the role that institutions may play in facilitating that vision instead of obstructing it with roadblocks.

Involving students as facilitators in building literary appreciation in the public sphere makes visible the legitimacy and power of literary studies in the social world. As a sure sign of the potential for students to support public literacy, one hundred percent of the library directors said they would work with our students on similar initiatives again, and the positive networks we have established have led to other rich service-learning opportunities for our English students beyond the Big Read, including public relations work, community programming, book clubs, afterschool enrichment clubs, and programming for senior citizen homes. Even these modest gestures suggest the potential for the discipline to institute such change more radically—to, as Amy Koritz has suggested, "eschew the self-referential structure of the research university that became dominant after World War II and that has served the humanities so poorly" (81) and to restore the role of the university in developing responsible citizens. Service learning, especially when it encourages students' public intellectual engagement and when it involves students in working thoughtfully with community partners, has the capacity to restore the social and civic relevance and power of literature, both within and beyond the academy.

NOTES

Special thanks to Dawn Eckenrode, whose collaboration was essential to the success of this service-learning project.

1. As Gary Goldstein and Peter Fernald note, "students' learning and experiences, rather than course content and subject matter, are critical" for well-rounded capstone pedagogy (27).

2. The reading assignment is from Kaplan and Rose's chapter 4, "Academic English and the Common Reader" (47–65).

3. See, e.g., "Lakewood Library—Discussion: On Individuality."

4. The list features thirty-six titles as of July 2014.

Ivy *Schweitzer*

Completing the Circle: Teaching Literature as Community-Based Learning

As we attempt to analyze dialogue as a human phenomenon, we discover something which is the essence of dialogue itself: *the word*. But the word is more than just an instrument which makes dialogue possible; accordingly, we must seek its constitutive elements. Within the word we find two dimensions, reflection and action, in such radical interaction that if one is sacrificed—even in part—the other immediately suffers. There is no true word that is not at the same time a praxis. Thus, to speak a true word is to transform the world.   (Freire, *Pedagogy* 87)

The anxious student I will call Kirsten wriggles in my office chair as if being attacked by fire ants.[1] "But I'm an English major and art history minor," she wails, on the verge of tears. "I don't know how to write these kinds of papers." Despite extensive in-class discussion about our first "reflection" paper, this usually cheerful young woman feels lost and shaken. It takes all my willpower not to tell her that her previous academic training and success are not fully transferable to this course. Nor do I mention that according to research on improving cognitive development, discomfort and cognitive dissonance, within a structure that allows for exploration and—dare I use the academic f-word—*failure*, are crucial parts of the process of experiential learning (Eyler and Giles 17).

The course is Transforming Narratives, a mid-level, community-based learning (CBL) English class, cross-listed with women's and gender studies, that brings undergraduate majors and minors as well as graduate students from Dartmouth College's two small humanities graduate programs to local prisons and jails.[2] Students spend one of two weekly class meetings at the facility, where they participate with prisoners in Telling My Story (see Hernandez), a not-for-profit program created and directed by my coteacher, Pati Hernandez, a theater artist who emigrated here from Chile in the 1980s. For the other weekly class meeting, students convene on campus with me and prisoners gather with Pati at the facility to read and reflect on literature, history, and theory focused on visible and invisible walls and the structural violence and social abandonment that disproportionately afflict people in our nation's bloated prison system.

This course, which Pati and I have team-taught since 2007, is an unconventional version of prison education because students do not teach, tutor, or mentor at the facility, nor do we offer courses to prisoners for academic credit. Rather, students participate as "equals" with inmates (I put this word in quotation marks, because "equality" is only ever a utopic horizon). Because my training is in American literature and women's and gender studies, our course focuses on contemporary literature and film and the history and theory that contextualize them. Furthermore, CBL is not a component of the course, as it is at many other institutions, but instead its raison d'être.

At the facility, students and prisoners work in groups of four to six to create a set of skits focused on eight words chosen by the prisoners and based on their experiences. At the end of the term, everyone performs these skits and offers short testimonials combining personal and social reflections for their families, the facility, and the Dartmouth and local communities. Audience members frequently respond that they couldn't tell who was who—and that is just the point.

The assignment for the first reflection paper asks students to work with at least one of the class readings, which include Paolo Freire's indispensable *Pedagogy of the Oppressed*; Buzz Alexander on teaching the arts behind bars; Dorothy Allison's essay "A Question of Class" and her memoir, *Two or Three Things I Know for Sure*; excerpts from Michel Foucault's *Discipline and Punish: The Birth of the Prison*; and Barbara Ehrenreich's *Nickel and Dimed: On (Not) Getting By in America*. I ask students first to describe a specific incident that happened at the facility, then to discuss how they felt about it, and finally to analyze it in the light of an idea or theory from our class readings. I suggest they focus on how the ideas or theories help them understand their experiences at the facility or don't fit and vice versa. Finally, I suggest that if they find incongruence between theory and experience, they should speculate on why it exists and how they can adapt the theory in the light of their practice, addressing a more advanced set of questions.

This assignment challenges students to complete what I am calling, after Freire's definition of *dialogue,* in the quotation that begins my essay, the circle of theory and practice, to bring into "radical interaction" the two dimensions of "the word," action and reflection (87). For many faculty members who champion CBL, this interaction is its very heart: a "fundamentally embodied process" that attempts to move us "from an intellectual analysis of moral and ethical social issues to a socially responsible life" (Butin 101; Grobman, "Is There" 132). Not just experiential and student-centered, the learning that occurs, according to a study of service learning by Janet Eyler and Dwight Giles, can be "transformational" (9), affecting us at the level of our core beliefs precisely because it operates at the intersection of cognitive and affective modes of comprehension (17). Consequently, CBL is important for promoting social awareness, but it also serves as the intersection where imaginative literature operates: grabbing us by the head and the heart, a novel, play, or poem can renovate our view of the world.

Such learning also produces an existential or academic discomfort that disrupts what we accept as natural and commonsensical and involves more failure, uncertainty, and improvisation than my accomplished Dartmouth students are used to. In an astute comparison of what she terms "community service learning" with feminist ethnography, Margaret Himley uses Sara Ahmed's postcolonial theory of encounter with the stranger to describe the problems in ethics and representation that arise when we move from the complex contexts of working with community organizations serving people in crisis to our theory-informed reflections, or, in Himley's neat phrase, "from fieldwork to deskwork" (419). Presumably, much "deskwork" has to occur before we can move to fieldwork and back again, but the depiction Himley offers of this process is disturbingly unidirectional—perhaps because she is describing a graduate-level course where the professional expectations for students' written work are very high.

According to educational theorists like John Dewey, whose principles underlie experiential learning, "Learning occurs through a cycle of action and reflection, not simply through being able to recount what has been learned through reading and lecture" (Eyler and Giles 7–8). This cycle, or dialectic, that sparks when we close the circle of theory and practice moves us from an intellectual to an affective awareness, promoting social responsibility, and then runs back again to enrich our intellectual apprehension. Thus, it has specific relevance to academic literary study. Students experience directly the power of narrative and story to affect people at their core. They practice the foundational interpretive skill of close reading, and, most important, they test those readings against the theories they have read in the context of concrete experiences. Through the process of written reflection, they revise their ideas and theories and take them back out into the world again.

That Kirsten felt consternation at the prospect of writing a reflection paper suggests that she had little or no experience or training in writing essays that bring theory and practice into a dynamic and "radical interaction." English professors often ask students to read a critical essay, even a theoretical one from another discipline, and apply its method or approach to a specific text. The notion of play in Jacques Derrida's "Structure, Sign, and Play in the Discourse of the Human Sciences," for example, has little to do with literature directly but sheds revelatory light on Poe's classic story "The Purloined Letter." We may even prompt students to discuss how Derrida's theory fails to address certain aspects of the story and ask them to apply other theories or approaches that produce different readings. However, we don't usually invite students to adapt or modify existing theories in the light of the limitations they discover, much less modify Poe's famous story based on its incongruence with a postmodern theory.

The best literary criticism does just that; it does not accept the text or theory as inviolable or static. Rather, it puts critical, contextual, and creative texts in dialogue, moving back and forth among them, applying and adapting literary or other kinds of theory to specific texts and contexts. CBL enriches this process by introducing fieldwork into literature courses, providing opportunities for students to escape the classroom, the solipsism of conventional teaching and learning, and "the Dartmouth bubble," as my students call it, to test theories and reading practices in a world of differences and divergent readers. This is the realm of popular culture where Judith (Jack) Halberstam locates "low theory," an idea derived in part from the "'open' pedagogy" of Freire that "detaches itself from prescriptive methods, fixed logics, and epistemes, and . . . orients us towards problem-solving knowledge or social visions of radical justice" (16–17). Off campus, students experience the false though pervasive opposition that Gerald Graff identifies between "book smarts" and "street smarts" ("Hidden Intellectualism" 21–22), another way of describing Freireian dialogue that rightly apportions "smarts" to both the haves at Ivy League institutions and the have-nots incarcerated at county jailhouses and state prisons. Both Graff and Halberstam argue that we are missing opportunities for critical engagement when we "overlook moments when the one is a vehicle for the other" (Graff, "Hidden Intellectualism" 21).

The prospect of bringing these disparate worlds to bear on each other, however, sends my student into a panic. Like her fellow classmates, Kirsten has no trouble distilling salient ideas from our readings, but she cannot see the relevance of these abstract theories to her work with women prisoners in rural New Hampshire. "Describe an incident at the facility," I prompt. "Pati asked the groups to create a skit about playing a sport," Kirsten says, and her group chose baseball. She describes how they assigned roles and decided on a set of dramatic incidents. "What did you notice about this process?" I ask. "The one weird thing," she remarks, "was how the women prisoners in the group insisted that I and the other Dartmouth student play the role of the umpires."

We talk about what might be behind this insistence, the role of umpires in the game, rehearsing many general points we have discussed in class that Kirsten had not been ready to process because, I suspect, they were merely abstract: the prisoners' preconceptions about Dartmouth students and vice versa and the structural relation of students to prisoners— positioned as smart, wealthy, privileged, and trained for leadership, decision making, and power. Although the Dartmouth students confess to feeling deficient in street smarts compared with the prisoners, Kirsten's detail suggests that the prisoners actively act out their disempowerment in relation to the students. When I ask her whether any of the theories in our reading describe this dynamic, she immediately cites Freire's theory of "internalized oppression," a situation where the oppressed have "internalized the image of the oppressor and adopted his guidelines" and values (*Pedagogy* 47). Although she is adapting theory derived from Freire's experience with illiterate Brazilian peasants, Kirsten writes an insightful reflection "reading" her experience in its light.

Strong claims have been made both for and against CBL in the literature classroom: it has been hailed as the savior of our benighted discipline for teaching compassion and thus social responsibility (Cooper; Malachuk) but also distrusted as politically ideological (liberal) and suspected of oversimplifying complex social issues and leaching the aesthetic and the specifically literary from literature (Grobman, "Is There" 130, 135). Approached as paternalism, it runs the risk of inculcating patronizing attitudes among students who want to help needy partners whom they see as having little or nothing to offer them, thus reifying hegemonic structures and invisible walls (Himley). But if we accept that "story [is] a foundational means of understanding the world and acting within it" (Bartel 98) and that, by sharing our stories, we tear down visible and invisible walls and turn them into bridges between us, then a literature-centered CBL course can benefit students and community partners. CBL in concert with the power of literature works through the imagination and ethical sense to produce not compassion, as many proponents argue, but something less sentimental—the power of stories to challenge stereotypes and preconceptions and produce recognition of our shared humanity. In other words, together they can recuperate our reading of the world.

There are challenges and benefits in CBL for teachers as well. When we shift the emphasis from *our teaching* to *student learning*, the classroom becomes more dynamic but less predictable. As several proponents point out, teaching a CBL literature course requires that instructors cede a portion of control to students and to the process itself and that we manage and facilitate rather than lecture and direct. In this reoriented classroom, our scholarly expertise may matter less than our ability to listen (Cooper 15; Bartel 93).

The goals of our course, Transforming Narratives, include the traditional acquisition of content (history, literature, and theory about social inequality, justice, and incarceration) integrated into the performance and the untraditional practice of the workshops that bring experience to bear directly on otherwise abstract content. In this process, we work together as people, learn from one another, improvise, and create something tangible—the performance, a time and space for the flowering of "equality." The prisoners feel recognized and heard in new and healing ways, not just by a small group of students but by various audiences who attend the performances. For example, after a recent performance attended by her parents, Trish shocked us when she revealed, "Ya know this is the first time my parents actually know my whole life. I used to hide everything."[3] Audience members literally see on the makeshift stage that Ivy League students and convicted criminals are, at the very least, visually indistinguishable. As David Cooper eloquently remarks, through CBL we are shifting "the ethical center of gravity in our teaching and scholarship from 'the Other' to *one another*" (10).

Perhaps the hardest concept for everyone to grasp is that the course's stated goal of facilitating the voices of the unheard is lofty but unattainable; any wording for this process is inaccurate and beset by power dynamics. The best we can do, as Pati keeps reminding me, is to create a platform for exchange and active listening. I was slow to fully comprehend Pati's version of Freire's dialogue and implement it through the class readings and reflection papers, to recognize that in creating a platform for active listening, our own voices are also facilitated in new and surprising ways. Because I came to this teaching from the perspective of prison studies and not CBL, I was fixated on content and coverage — offering students the history of prisons and driving home the injustices of the incarceration system through memoirs, films, critical essays, and narratives — and imagined these ends to be competitive with the workshop process. It was several years before I agreed that the assessment of the workshop should count equally with the classroom theory work in the final grade. I did not fully understand the salience of sparking the dialectic of theory and practice, and I certainly did not feel competent in assessing fieldwork that, according to Pati, requires a nonjudgmental attitude, active presence, flexibility, discipline, and commitment.

My resistance was largely overcome by seeing the increase in both critical consciousness and the ability to move dialectically between theory and practice demonstrated in my students' reflection papers. The two I share here are from the course Pati and I taught in summer 2010 in collaboration with a small women's unit within the male facility at Sullivan County House of Corrections, in Unity, New Hampshire. This course is also the subject of *Telling My Story*, a documentary filmed inside the jail and on campus (S. Taylor). Only thirty-five miles south of Dartmouth College, Unity, with a population of 1,671, felt like a world away. The small county jail welcomed our program because the superintendent and program director wanted to give inmates awaiting sentencing or serving short sentences resources like increased self-awareness, self-esteem, and self-expression to help them make a speedy transition to the outside. The women prisoners were a tough, world-weary group mostly from rural New England, some very young, many from dysfunctional backgrounds, and all wildly enthusiastic about the opportunity to tell their stories.

I chose the literary readings for the course to give students a window into the women's world and give the women prisoners a mirror, banking on what Daniel Malachuk contends is the unique ability of imaginative literature to "bring the lives of others before us in a way that no other kind of writing can" (34). In reading, we become, in Martha Nussbaum's resonant phrase, "immersed participants" in the highly textured realities of people and realms unfamiliar to us (*Poetic Justice* 8). In this respect, Allison's "A Question of Class" is possibly the most brilliant evocation of white people's feelings of class discrimination in the United States. The racial specificity is important because the prison population in rural New England is largely white. In fact, my Dartmouth classes are more racially and culturally diverse and more international than the groups who make up our community partners. Class issues, however, remain a particularly fraught territory at the college. Many students have trouble acknowledging and embracing class differences, while outsiders perceive all Dartmouth students as airbrushed to a privileged homogeneity.

Ashley, the student who chose Allison's essay for her theoretical application, is a tall, blond athlete with a carefully controlled demeanor and pointedly dry humor. In her reflection paper, she begins by illustrating the "external division society places between people of Allison's class and the rest of society" through Allison's memory of "a mother telling her child, 'Don't you play with her. I don't want you talking to them.' Me and my family, we had always been *they*." From a close reading of this initial split, Ashley argues that "Allison internalized this experience, and when given the opportunity to make her past a 'they' and her future an 'us,' she forced a schism in her identity that resulted in her internal compartmentalization of who she was throughout her late childhood and adulthood." Ashley inadvertently reveals her own internal division to the women at the jail during an exercise in which Pati asked the group to discuss their dreams for the future. Over the years, Pati has noted that in this exercise, the Dartmouth students understand "dreams" as aspirations, while the prisoners are dumbfounded by the idea, not only of futurity but of a positive vision of it. Ashley's reaction, as she reveals in her essay, runs counter to this trend:

> I don't like using the word dream to describe something I want to happen in the future. I have had vivid, persistent bad dreams and night terrors a few times a week since I was little. When people ask me what my dream is for my life I get upset because I think of my bad dreams and wonder if this will mean I'll have a bad future.

In the reflection session following the exercise, Ashley recounts:

> [O]ne of the women said to me that she could hear herself in me. She said that she now realized that Dartmouth students "are fucked up too." At this

moment I understood that I understand Allison's "temptation to lie," her temptation to hide her history and focus solely on the present. I realized, as I assume most in the room did as well, that I do not live up to the image of the mythical rich or mythical Dartmouth student who comes from a past of pure happiness and now has it all together all the time. In this instance I understood, as Allison also finally did, that I had forced myself to split internally. I realized that despite the fact that this woman and I have almost no common life circumstances, I relate to her much more than I do to many of the people I've chosen to surround myself with. When I have struggled for so long to hide my pain and have tried with all my strength to leave my past in my past, to finally find understanding and acceptance inside of a woman inside of a prison was overwhelming.

This is the moment of transformative learning that, through reading a literary text, produces a new self-awareness. Ashley concretizes her intellectual understanding of Allison's self-analysis by finally articulating and sharing her fears, which are recognized and shared by a prisoner Ashley previously felt she had nothing in common with and may have segregated herself from in order to take refuge in the image of the "mythical rich or mythical Dartmouth student" who leads a charmed life. Reciprocally, the woman prisoner glimpses the emotional vulnerability of the elite student she thought of as somehow untouched by fear, shame, or failure.

The repetition "understood . . . understand" and "inside . . . inside" points to the recursiveness of Ashley's recognitions: first, her inability to dream a futurity because her night dreams are terrifying; then, her revelation of this inability, which meets with unexpected identification ("she could hear herself in me"); then, the relief of shedding an image of perfection at odds with her internal sense of herself. Reading the essay motivates this process, yet Ashley reads it in a more embodied way through her experience at the facility. Allison's essay is not static: Ashley reads something new into it. Nor is it merely a vehicle for her personal insights; the reflection highlights its literariness, its power to create a reality and move her.

The second reflection is by Benjy, one of the two men in the class, a graduate student in the master of arts in liberal studies program who is originally from a small village in mainland China. As one might expect, this graduate student takes a more intellectual approach than Ashley did, but his essay is no less transformational. Benjy examines Freire's idea of dialogue, the theory at the very heart of the course, in the light of a brief interaction he had with one of the women prisoners forced to leave the program and facility because of drug use.

During one of the initial workshops, a young woman named Emily shared with the group what Benjy describes as "helpless and yet profound examinations about her life, father and child," signaling her desperation (and, he thinks, relapse into drug use) "when she gazed into the air with despair, her eyes wet, sighing, 'I feel so lonely!'" Later, Benjy says he and Emily "had moments of soulful connection through eye-contact, mere silence, plus a simple smile; approaching me voluntarily, at our departure, she gave me a hug, an unexpectedly tight one." Asking what this silent communication means, Benjy muses "on the communicative value of silence, and its relation to Freire's concept of dialogue," especially in the light of Freire's claim that "[h]uman existence cannot be silent" (*Pedagogy* 88). Considering the wordless exchange between such different people, Benjy finds "that silence means and communicates, and it can very well be a dialogical 'encounter between men, mediated by the world, in order to name the world.'" To support his argument, Benjy marshals a contending theory of intersubjectivity, Martin Buber's "I-Thou" relationship, and asserts boldly, "Speaking of *the word*, it seems to me Freire remains irrationally obsessed with it. . . . When a culture prefers verbalism," words separated from actions, "to meaningful silence, how dialogical does one expect our communal life to be?"

Although Benjy reads Freire's obsession with words (versus "the word") too literally, he struggles to turn what appears to him as a failure in communication through language—the basis of imaginative literature— into another form of speaking, a silent embodied form using eyes and arms, one practiced for centuries by Quakers. "As a lover of words myself," Benjy continues, "I don't intend to debunk Freire's overall concept of dialogue in words, but the overriding point of my paper is to show that in silence we equally name the world, and change it, so long as the moment is rejoiced in, with, according to Freire, love, humility, faith, hope and critical thinking." These are the steps in Freire's praxis of dialogue—moving through deep affection (love of humanity) to deep abstraction (critical thinking) and back again. Locked in a grubby cafeteria with a group of jailhouse inmates, Benjy has an experience he recognizes and processes through Freire's idea, but in reflecting on the experience, he sees its divergence from Freire's theory and argues for the necessity of expanding that theory: "'Dialogue is thus an existential necessity.' So is silence, I'd add."

In both reflection papers, transformative learning occurs through a dialectic of action and reflection mediated by literature. Ashley embodies Allison's account of social difference as the other or the stranger, a disavowed internal division that becomes bearable and legible when it is recognized by an "other," who turns out to be "another" like the damaged, imperfect, disguised self. Affected by his eloquent encounter with an "other" who shows herself through wordless communication to be "another" feeling person, Benjy expands our understanding of dialogue that underwrites the powerful empathetic effects of literature. Like the prisoners who have trouble imagining futurity, both students experience getting lost, learning from failure, learning as failure, the limits of language, and a different kind of achievement. Everyone's world is subtly shifted, as Emma, another prisoner, confirms about her experience in *Telling My Story*:

> I used to have this theory that with therapists or clinicians, what's the point of going to talk about all this trauma and abuse? It's not going to change it. And I definitely took that into every aspect of my life. Why talk about it, it's not going to change it? But I was definitely wrong. If enough people get together and, you know, use their voice, things can change, I hope. I'm hopeful. I was never hopeful. Now I'm a little bit hopeful.

These insights, of course, are among the most successful forays, but they suggest the surge in critical consciousness that can occur when students and community members complete the circle connecting theory to practice and literature to its imaginative power.

NOTES

1. I have changed the names of all the students and prisoners I mention. I want to thank them all profoundly, and especially my coteacher, Pati Hernandez, for walking this road with me.

2. CBL is what Freire calls "problem-posing education" because it combines experiential learning outside the classroom with academic study and guided reflection (*Pedagogy* 80). While the term is interchangeable with *service learning*, I prefer *CBL* because I want to stress the role of group collaboration with a community.

3. All quotations from prisoners are from transcriptions of interviews filmed by Signe Taylor in the documentary *Telling My Story*.

Scott Hicks

Reliving and Remaking the Harlem Renaissance

In their straightforward prose, the volume editors of *The Norton Anthology of African American Literature* claim that the years of the Harlem Renaissance "[u]nquestionably . . . marked an especially brilliant moment in the history of blacks in America," defined by "an outpouring of publications that was unprecedented in its variety and scope" (Gates and McKay, "Harlem Renaissance" 953). Thus I taught Harlem Renaissance literature, in 2007 and 2009, with all the conventional arrows in a literary scholar's quiver—class discussion, small group work, response essays, signification exams, and term papers—appreciating with my students each instance of historical brilliance and precedence. Yet the subject—with its dynamics of collaborative creation; confrontations of race, gender, and sexuality; and experiments in form and subject—invited intensity and demanded innovation. It insisted on unveiling the dynamics of canon creation and movement making, instead of simply reifying the anthology's sanctification of "great works" and periodization. It called for a revolutionary consciousness worthy of the spirit that animated the period's writers and artists, individuals who negotiated the epoch's capricious patrons, anxious arbiters, and volatile public before they saw their work published. As I collaborated with like-minded colleagues in institutionalizing service-learning pedagogies across my campus, I saw incisively how service learning could meet the challenges my subject presented.

In this chapter, I describe how service learning enriched my junior- and senior-level course on Harlem Renaissance literature at the University of North Carolina, Pembroke (UNCP). Thanks to service learning, students made profound connections between literature and context that reconceptualized canonical texts, brought to light understudied ones, and fostered a revisionary attitude toward literary study. Likewise, they worked through difficult, sometimes disquieting thesis statements and arguments because their community-based learning anchored their authority. Put simply, service learning helped me execute the demands of my program and discipline—to guide students in literary study—with the bonuses of deepening their appreciation of literature and social justice, linking their voices to those of disfranchised persons, and developing their skills of critical thinking, reading, and writing.

The Seeds of the Class

I began planning for the class by balancing Harlem Renaissance theory and context with my community's needs and self-understanding. Inspired by modern-day scholarship, I wanted students to wrestle with the notion that the Harlem Renaissance was not just about race but also about sexuality and to grapple with their power as collectors, editors, publishers, and critics to nurture or thwart a grassroots movement. I wanted students, with a heightened critical eye, to interrogate their reading: to look beyond race and sexuality to find the infinite perspectives and counterperspectives each text articulated; to see the works anew not simply as artifacts of talented individuals but as pieces imagined, shaped, reshaped, and disseminated by artists, marketers, and consumers working harmoniously and disharmoniously; and to evaluate the Harlem Renaissance on the basis of the success or failure not of its aesthetic but its community.

I wanted students to approach the subjects of their future seminar essays by becoming writers, advocates, editors, and publishers in a community with striking similarities to the Harlem of the Harlem Renaissance. Almost everyone living in Harlem was African American; almost everyone living in Pembroke is Lumbee. Just as this New York neighborhood, in Alain Locke's famous analysis, was the Negro's world capital, Pembroke is the Lumbee people's ancestral homeland. Each community, interwoven by a shared ethnic heritage, has long sought, and continues to seek, to preserve itself and celebrate its culture, and thus each maintains an uneasy relationship to white society. For the purposes of service learning in my class, Pembroke offered a real-world laboratory for learning how literature comes to be and to signify in a place where race matters. Moreover, the electric diversity of UNCP's student body and our community partners would augment students' learning, I believed, just as the ideological, geo-graphic, cultural, and national diversity of the Harlem Renaissance shaped the complexity of ideas, genres, and perspectives captured in the texts we read and study today. A historically Native American–serving nontribal institution, UNCP boasts a student body roughly thirty-one percent African American, sixteen percent American Indian, and forty-two percent white. Crisscrossed by the nearly twenty-seven percent of the student body who are nontraditional-age students, UNCP's diversity could approximate the complex diversity of 1920s Harlem and inspire a similar ideological foment. Because many of the leaders of our community partners were Lumbee and most of their clients were African American and American Indian, our partnerships would elicit even deeper complexities for consideration and analysis.

I decided that a literary magazine would be the service-learning activity that would best realize the outcomes I wanted students to achieve. My students, divided into small groups, worked with the clients of community partners through writing workshops culminating in the production of magazines featuring community members' creative writing. When students translated course content into community-minded, audience-appropriate writing workshops inspired by the Harlem Renaissance, I saw them explore the power of personal expression as a component of civic and cultural engagement and confront the challenge of influencing an interpersonal consciousness durable enough to transcend division and unite against injustice and oppression. In the peer-review elements of their workshops, students mentored and instructed the clients of community partners in writing skills; by writing prefaces for, editing, and proof-reading submissions, students practiced their editorial skills. When they submitted their manuscripts for printing, they left the class proud of their work and empowered with new skills and literary perspectives.

I also saw the project benefit our community partners, who serve a region suffering from high rates of poverty, violence, and unemployment. For organizations serving youth, the project offered tutoring in writing and reading (subjects tested on state exams) and mentoring by college-student role models. For organizations serving the elderly or infirm, we offered companionship, intellectual stimulation, and outlets for creative expression. Our community partners—Robeson County Guardian ad Litem, Methodist Home for Children, Pembroke Housing Authority, and Wesley Pines, a senior living community—appreciated the opportunity to publicize the creativity and worth of their clients in a society that otherwise would push them out of sight.

Our Syllabus, Assignments, and Classwork

When I first met my class, I underscored how different this course would be and that the difference was crucial to their understanding fully and deeply the content we would study. I also wanted them to know that, in participating in service learning, we would not sacrifice content or rigor. I adhered closely to departmental guidelines on reading assignments in upper-division courses, requiring a novel (they could choose from Nella Larsen's *Quicksand*, George S. Schuyler's *Black No More*, Jean Toomer's *Cane*, and Wallace Thurman's *Infants of the Spring*), several full-length plays (such as Angelina Grimké's *Rachel* and Langston Hughes's *Mulatto: A Tragedy of the Deep South*), and dozens of essays, poems, short plays, and short stories. Moreover, our guidelines stipulate including "relevant literary terminology, critical approaches, and scholarly methodology" ("Literature Course Guidelines"); given the course's service-learning pedagogy, I highlighted reader response, deconstruction, cultural studies, queer theory, and new historicism.

In addition, the department requires students to write source-based papers of eight pages or more, products that should assess "student comprehension of basic literary research methodology and mastery of course topic(s)." To my typical seminar-essay assignment that students write about a text (or texts) of their choosing, I added the wrinkle that they interweave published scholarship with what they saw and heard in their interactions with the community partners. With this addition, students would craft fresh interpretations of the texts, and so service learning would help them "develop independence, responsibility, and appreciation for literary studies," the department's final goal.

To ensure that the magazine project helped students apply their readings and write their essays, I scheduled our time thoughtfully. Early in the semester, we pored over archived copies of Harlem Renaissance magazines such as *Crisis*, *Fire!!*, and *Opportunity* for insight into the historical inspiration of their service-learning assignment and models for their own magazines.[1] We also watched *Brother to Brother*, a film that explores raced and sexed identity in 1920s Harlem alongside the trials and tribulations of creating a countermainstream journal. To help students connect their readings and community partner workshops, we grouped the texts by genre, discussing them over several class meetings while making time for workshop planning. Thus students visited their community partners armed with freewriting prompts, discussion questions, and role-playing activities they had prepared, inspired by Pat Schneider's principles for inclusive and empowering writers' workshops. When students returned to the classroom, we discussed what worked, what didn't, what they learned, and why. In this way we moved through the semester, crosshatching our discussion of literature with students' service-learning experiences and reflections.

Following the general introduction to the period, we tackled poetry. To help students limber up their interpretive muscles for the blurring of academic and community realms, I had them work in small groups to brainstorm readings and counterreadings of specific poems. On one half of a sheet of flip-chart paper, students recorded readings of the poem—conventional interpretations that would cohere with the concept of the Harlem Renaissance as a blossoming of a new spirit of African American consciousness and creativity. Then, on the other half of the sheet, they recorded counterreadings—unconventional interpretations of the same poem that would cohere with the equally present concept of the Harlem Renaissance as a blossoming of new ideas of art, aesthetics, subject matter, voice, sexuality, geography, and audience, irrespective of race. For instance, we considered Gwendolyn Bennett's "Hatred": students posited a reading of the poem as a statement of rage against white oppression and discrimination and a counterreading of it that saw the speaker as a jilted lover and the poem a forceful personal expression and a forceful refusal to speak for the race, a declaration of social and emotional autonomy. In this way, students prepared themselves to offer participants from their community partner models of social resistance that could be just as easily perceived and adapted as models of personal affirmation and self-articulation.

When we discussed the dramas of the period, we began with students' debriefing from their poetry workshops. In particular, students who worked with at-risk youth reported that their partners shared disconcerting narratives of domestic abuse, abandonment, and violence that made inescapable the pattern of domestic disharmony, insecurity, and terror that permeated the dramas we studied. Play after play fixated on a domestic space, we realized, only to depict a protagonist who, damned if she did, damned if she didn't, could not survive the domestic sphere and, for whatever reason, could not lean on a caring community for support. Why did these Harlem Renaissance plays devastate notions of domestic bliss, when the Great Migration propelled thousands of African Americans northward for security and protection? Why did these plays take a dim view of African American agency, especially in the heart of the Negro capital of the world? Students took such ideas back to their community partners, and then they brought their experiences and reflections back to our classroom. From campus to community and back again, we immersed ourselves in a cross-pollination that shaped the questions we asked, gave new urgency to why we read literature, and demanded that we put forth interpretations that took seriously social problems and marginalized voices.

With a semester's worth of community interactions behind us and animated by this rich ferment of ideas, we were struck, in our last unit, by eerie parallels between the concerns of the short stories and those of our community partners a century later. Some of our community partners expressed the hurt of colorism, the crux of Thurman's "Emma Lou," for example, or described their parents' abusive relationships, a central theme of Zora Neale Hurston's "Sweat." Others expressed feelings of distrust and betrayal, often inflected by classism, as seen in Rudolph Fisher's "The City of Refuge." Without the community experience, such themes might have gone unnoticed.

Indeed, service learning helped students see in these stories and the semester's other texts that personal experience (such as domestic abuse or feelings of inferiority, things some students described confronting) had literary, civic, and social dimensions and that their education and privilege as college students gave them power to take a stand and make a change. To my mind, two of my UNCP students, Patricia Taylor and Renae Eades, exemplify the power of this recognition. In her seminar essay, Taylor describes growing up poor and in a broken home yet finding in the works of the Harlem Renaissance an abiding sense of legacy, a positive force that undergirds her drive to "leave a legacy of success and the knowledge of how to overcome for [her] son to inherit."[2] Likewise, Eades made an announcement at the end-of-semester celebration of the project: sharing the literature of the Harlem Renaissance with her partners from Guardian ad Litem revealed to her a new career. Thanks to this project, she decided to go to graduate school to become a social worker. The Harlem Renaissance's animating ideas were alive even today, and we could help those best able to convey those ideas by giving them an opportunity to publish. At the semester's end, inspired by the needs of our community partners and the richness of the literature, students were ready to publish community members' voices and write their seminar essays.

A Celebration of Texts

The literary magazines students and community partners created were impressive in their forthrightness, urgency, and technique. The UNCP students Courtney Collins, Katherine Laws, Brittany Morales, and Meeko Simpson partnered with the housing authority's afterschool program to publish *I Dream*, whose poems and short prose centered on racism and self-affirmation. I observed this group teaching the program's participants how racism during the 1920s forced stars like Josephine Baker to immigrate to Europe, setting Hughes's poems to beats, and creating their own mixes. The program's predominantly African American and Lumbee participants likened performers like Baker to icons like Beyoncé, and they saw in poetry like Hughes's models for their own lyrics. One afterschool participant wrote in "My Interpretation of ME" that "Colored is great / And there is nothing wrong with your skin." Other student writers from the afterschool program articulated how racism diminished them, as Antoinette Floyd in "Back Then" writes of running away, changing her hairstyle, and renaming herself "Vanita." Participants expressed the racism they had experienced, communicated its insidious psychological impact, and asserted cultural pride. At the housing authority, what was originally merely a time for homework tutoring became a time of creative writing and mentoring.

Participants from the Methodist Home for Children, who created *Inspiration of Talented Youth*, likewise sought to express themselves and their relationship to racism, violence, and poverty. In their workshops, the UNCP students Sarah Heard, Desirée Manello, Keon Pacheco, and Stephanie Tillman asked the Methodist Home participants to rewrite Hughes's "Theme for English B" (1949), resulting in poems like this one:

> I am Rae'Kwon fourteen, native, born in Lumberton
> I went to school in Red Springs, then
> I went to the group home right across the road from
>   the prison

I can play ball better than anyone in the group home
The steps from the group home lead to the basketball
   court
How I got to the group home I hit a girl and I put a
   hole in the school wall
That girl made me mad so I hit the girl in the face
   then I hit the school wall.   (Rae'Kwon)

Other writers likewise spoke to being victims of structural violence: of being threatened and doing drugs, hearing voices and wanting war, feeling
hated and discriminated against, and worrying about their spiritual lives.
In class, we agreed that these writers heeded Hughes's admonition in "The
Negro Artist and the Racial Mountain" "to express our individual dark-
skinned selves without fear or shame" (1314)—precisely the goal of the
center's director for our partnership. Yet we could not help fearing that
this sense of transcendence was tenuous: the youths might be "free within
[them]selves," but their poems nonetheless reinscribed the threats they
sought to escape.

Such concerns arose in all student groups, and they influenced our
discussion of, and engagement with, the period's literature, bold as it
sought to be, tenuous as it might have been. Jovita Vereen, a UNCP student, captures this double bind in her seminar essay, juxtaposing acts of
dreams and wishes in Harlem Renaissance poetry and fiction: "the link-
age of the writers of the Harlem Renaissance to the self-expression of the
young students . . . gives the courage to write when others don't agree, or
draw when no one understands what is being created, and to wish, dream,
and take action even when no one fully believes." She continues, "I hope
that we did the [literature] of the Harlem Renaissance justice in bringing
the best out of these young people, and giving them an opportunity and
the knowledge to succeed beyond their wildest wishes or dreams, to create
actions that they will never regret."

To be sure, the "DARE" curriculum Vereen and her UNCP classmates
Katie Baker, Renae Eades, and Lewis Edwards created for Guardian ad
Litem sought to make a durable intervention in the young participants'
lives. Charged by the agency's director to help these tweens and early
teens begin imagining positive, independent lives for themselves once
they aged out of the agency's purview, my students, a mix of English, psychology, and social work majors, pooled their knowledge to lead students

in DARE: Dreams, Actions, Resolve, and Evolve. In the pages of their journal, *Dreams, Actions, Resolve, Evolve: Those Who Dare to Grow Become Leaders in Life's Undertow*, participants dream of being singers and helping their family run a five-star day care and outline actions like apologizing to others they had hurt. They resolve to improve their lives, for example, by ending negative friendships, and to evolve into role models like Mahatma Gandhi, Rosa Parks, and Martin Luther King, Jr.

Even when a collaboration collapsed, as happened in our partnership with Wesley Pines, students found a way to persevere. Taking the title *Crisis!* for their magazine, my students Ashley Allen, Sosha McAllister, Bernise Moody, and Taylor described meeting their senior citizen participants in February—and then not being able to meet again, thanks to rounds of illnesses that passed through the retirement and nursing home. So that they had something to publish, each student wrote a narrative and a poem of overcoming a personal crisis. Their work underscored their metaphor of the Harlem Renaissance as a moment of triumph despite all odds. As Moody, a nontraditional-aged student who graduated in May 2012, writes:

> Learning that you have a gift and trying to become that artist that you know down on the inside of you that you can be is a struggle within itself. When I read about how black artists such as Langston Hughes [and] Ann Petry . . . made their mark on the world . . . I have hope for my future, knowing that the words down on the inside of me can come to life and maybe one day be left on record for that next generation to learn from.

As they put it, "This is our artistic rendering of our journey in ENG 3100— The Harlem Renaissance" (Allen, McAllister, Moody, and Taylor 3)—a rendering that finds grand meaning even in ostensible disappointment.

Students' seminar essays give invaluable insight into the ways that service learning enhanced their mastery of our program's goals of critical textual knowledge, critical thinking, and literary appreciation. In "Where I'm From," one student grappled with her family's racial prejudice that she had internalized in her own psyche: "It is very common to hear the word 'nigger' in a typical conversation at a family get-together. This is not something I am proud of. Their ignorance is often embarrassing, and the fact that they find it so entertaining to degrade another culture is incredibly offensive to me. But what can I do? They are family." Her seminar essay grappled with how her background would affect her future as a language arts teacher responsible for individuals of all races. Narrating the ups and downs of the Wesley Pines partnership, this student described how Schneider's *Writing Alone and with Others* helped her break through personal inhibitions. After composing a poem for *Crisis!* and analyzing it through the lens of heritage expressed in Bennett's "Heritage," she came to a powerful conclusion: "I can create and shape my own identity, just as the African Americans did during the Harlem Renaissance. They wanted to express themselves individually, while keeping close ties with their cultural heritage." I not only appreciated this student's grappling with an important poem of the Harlem Renaissance and her usage of reader response but also applauded her forthright self-disclosure in her transformation of the academic essay.

In contrast, Manello focused outward on an incident that occurred during a writing workshop at the Methodist Home, a moment that, in her theorizing, came to expose the connection of silence and violence. After she and her teammates started the Methodist Home residents on a freewriting exercise, she saw "two of the boys . . . off in a corner, mad and in each other's faces, ready to fight. An adult broke that up before anything happened, and both boys were sent to their rooms for the rest of our visit." The reason, she came to understand, was that one young man would not permit another to read his work aloud. Like "the writers and artists of the Harlem Renaissance," Manello wrote, "[t]hey wanted their voices to be heard." Fighting might resolve the situation in the short term, but in the long term, "[f]ighting with words, like those of the Harlem Renaissance did, leaves a lasting impression." As a foil to the interpenetration of silence and violence, she pointed to Tamara, an African American resident of the home, whose voice and perspective Manello juxtaposes with the speaker and themes of Hurston's poem "Passion." The short story Tamara contributed to the literary magazine, Manello asserted, "showed . . . that even in her circumstances and even at her age, Tamara has quite the imagination and she wasn't going to let anyone take that from her." Tamara's story, Hurston's poem, and Manello's observations underscored for Manello the urgency of sharing one's voice and interrogating the forces that decide who speaks and who does not.

As a final example, Heard used her essay to reenvision Hughes's "Negro Artist" as a complication of the authority of the family, brought to light by the lack of family presence felt by the Methodist Home's young boys and girls. Her essay begins with a close counterreading of Hughes's essay resituated by the service-learning experience and inflected by family systems theory. Heard undertakes a compelling analysis of her own family history and sounds again the call for leveling the mountains that stand in the way of society's marginalized members: "In the case of the young poet in Hughes's essay, his mountain was his lack of faith in the richness and fulfillment that his Negro skin could provide for him," she writes. "For the boys at MHC, they must overcome the mountain of ignorance and indifference, and only then will they truly be able to appreciate the beauty of men who express their emotions." I valued Heard's essay for tackling such a canonical piece and for showing how even an oft-theorized text could be reimagined by a sensitive, nuanced perspective.

Reading all the students' essays and seeing their literary magazines published made the end of the semester both a pleasure and a sadness. When we hosted a celebration of the magazines at a nearby church, inviting every participant from all four community partners for cake, chips, and Coke, my students and their partners laughed and cried and laughed again as they reminisced about their workshops together and read anew their now published work. I thus was sad to see this semester, this class, end. Yet I am excited to do it again in future classes. I will continue what worked: giving students the chance to learn and practice professional skills like editing and publishing, exposing them to challenges that result in deeply thought and felt critical thinking, and sustaining the productive dialogue between service to the community and mastery of literary studies. I also will work to improve what I can: making successful a partnership with community elders, for example, and bringing not just poetry but drama and short fiction as well to the magazines. These challenges and visions drive me in my career, and, for sustaining my professional and intellectual curiosity and putting literature in service to the community, I am grateful to service learning.

NOTES

1. The leading civil rights organizations of the period—the National Association for the Advancement of Colored People and the National Urban League—published journals to promote their perspectives. These journals—*Crisis* and *Opportunity*, respectively—often included literature and art as a means of establishing an aesthetic that cohered to their political, social, and cultural agendas. *Fire!!* was created by Aaron Douglas, Langston Hughes, Zora

Neale Hurston, Richard Bruce Nugent, and Wallace Thurman in bombastic riposte to the two mainstream journals. The group published only one issue.

2. In this essay, I quote material from seminar essays students wrote for my class, from the literary magazines that contain the work of my students and their community partner participants, and from statements made in public gatherings. Students whose seminar essays I have cited have given written consent for the quotation of their work and its attribution. Because other material—literary magazines and statements made in public gatherings—are public documents, consent is not necessary for their reproduction.

Part II

Service Learning in English and World Literature

Elizabeth K. Goodhue

Satire, Sentimentalism, and Civic Engagement: From Eighteenth-Century Britain to the Twenty-First-Century Writing Course

When I was a PhD student at the University of California, Los Angeles (UCLA), where I completed my degree in 2011, I spent several quarters teaching literature-based writing courses, as do many PhD candidates studying English at large research universities. Such courses are typically part of the general education curriculum and as such require instructors to comply with many institutionally mandated guidelines. The thought of incorporating service-learning strategies can often seem overwhelming when instructors are already asked to introduce students who are not English majors to all the primary literary genres while simultaneously covering multiple historical periods, incorporating writers from diverse backgrounds, and meeting benchmarks for undergraduate writing competency. I argue here, however, that service learning is anything but an unwelcome burden for literature courses in the general education curriculum. Rather, pairing literary analysis with structured service in local communities encourages students who are not English majors to recognize the continuing relevance of texts written in the distant past and helps them see both scholarly and creative writing as forms of participation in public discourse about social issues.

In making this case for the value of service learning in general education, I draw primarily on my experience teaching a literature-based writing course using texts that document urban life from the eighteenth century to the present. Students in the class examined a wide variety of cultural artifacts, beginning with satiric and sentimental poetry, prose, and visual art from eighteenth-century Britain and then moving on to documents depicting modern Los Angeles and New York. During the ten-week quarter, the students also completed twenty hours of service learn-ing with one of three not-for-profit organizations dedicated to archiving untold stories of Los Angeles residents. Students working with a literacy not-for-profit organization called 826LA helped elementary and middle school students prepare autobiographical stories and fiction for publica-tion by the organization's in-house chapbook press. Students working with the Studio for Southern California History collected and indexed oral histories of local residents and also contributed photo essays to the studio's digital archive. Those working with the Museum of Tolerance sup-ported the Tools for Tolerance partnership with high schools and updated visitor guides to ensure that all patrons understood how to participate in the museum's interactive exhibits, many of which invite visitors to share stories of cross-cultural contact.[1]

Each of these service projects helped my undergraduates develop the types of personal and interpersonal skills that researchers have often iden-tified as positive outcomes of service learning. In reflection journals and class discussions, my students frequently noted that working alongside community partners deepened their understanding of controversial social issues such as economic and educational inequality by encouraging them to collaborate with people from diverse cultural backgrounds. Above and beyond those traditional sorts of perspective transformation, however, the service-learning projects for this course transformed how my students thought about literary form by urging them to think critically—and in very practical ways—about how people from various historical eras, in-cluding the present, use language and other media to shape stories about urban life.[2] By offering undergraduates unique opportunities to put their study of the mechanics and ethics of representation into practice, litera-ture courses that pair project-based writing in the classroom with struc-tured service off campus not only foster academic and civic skills but also link the undergraduate curriculum with ongoing efforts to reaffirm the public relevance of higher education in the humanities.[3]

When I tell colleagues that I have used service-learning pedagogy to teach eighteenth-century British literature—the area of specialization for my doctoral research—I have generally been met with quizzical stares at best, if not open expressions of disbelief.[4] This reaction mirrors a gap in the scholarship on service learning in literary studies, which has focused overwhelmingly on strategies for teaching the literature of the last hun-dred years and especially on teaching the multicultural literature of that era. As Matthew Hansen notes in "'O Brave New World': Service-Learning and Shakespeare," "As limited as the exploration is of the fruitful possibilities of incorporating service-learning as part of a literature course," such exploration is practically nonexistent for studies of early periods, such as the Renaissance or the eighteenth century (179).

In some ways, this focus on texts from the present and recent past is not surprising. In literature departments, as in other areas of the university, service learning frequently took hold through fields such as ethnic studies and feminist studies, which carved out their place in higher education on a platform of social justice. This alliance has been mutually beneficial in gaining traction for service learning in the academy, on the one hand, and in helping fields like ethnic studies make good on their commitment to promoting respect for cultural diversity, on the other.[5] But aligning service learning with the study of what often amounts to post-1960s liberal culture and its immediate history also severely limits how service learning is applied in literature departments. Indeed, although service learning is widely recognized as a highly effective way to help undergraduates see that what they learn in the college classroom applies outside it, literature instructors often fail to embrace civically engaged pedagogy in general education courses. We fail to do this even though general education is the area of the curriculum where undergraduates confront texts written many centuries before their birth for the first time and often struggle to see those texts as anything more than artifacts of an ancient and irrelevant past.

My experience in the classroom indicates that pairing eighteenth-century British literature with structured service in local communities not only helps undergraduates recognize the ongoing relevance of early texts but also helps address many of the challenges reported by service-learning instructors who specialize in later periods. Literature instructors who employ service learning to teach multicultural texts of the last century, such as Gregory Jay, often express frustration about the way that undergraduates in such courses readily "fall into the trap of a banal cultural liberalism . . . ignoring the specific differences that make up a culture's history" ("Service Learning" 264). In a related vein, Laurie Grobman contends that even when service learners do recognize cultural difference as difference, their interpretation of multicultural literature can often remain "narrow," treating the text as "a case study rather than a work of art [or] as if it corresponded in a one-to-one relation with life" ("Is There" 130, 135). I advocate teaching eighteenth-century texts in a community-based context precisely because many of the dominant literary forms in the early modern era refuse to be interpreted in a one-to-one correspondence with lived experiences of social injustice in the twenty-first century. Much of the period's most striking literature of social intervention calls attention to its artfulness by employing extravagant rhetoric—often satire or sentimentalism and sometimes both, as in William Blake's poetry. Instead of presenting social service as an abstract ethical good, the texts of such writers force modern readers to confront how language can be used to reinforce troubling hierarchies of class and race, elevating those in a position to serve others by defining them against communities assumed to be in need of assistance. These dynamics can make it very difficult for students to identify with authors and characters from earlier eras, but that discontinuity allows room for critical thinking about the present as well as the past.

Scrutinizing the uneven distribution of power and resources in eighteenth-century texts in particular helps undergraduates recognize how meaning is shaped by elements of literary form—such as point of view and tone—and simultaneously prompts them to engage in the sort of reflection on privilege that distinguishes engaged service learning from mere volunteerism.[6] I have taught Blake's *Songs of Innocence* many times, for instance, but until I taught the poems in a service-learning context, my students had never been so quick to debate the ethical implications of Blake's decision to fictionalize the voices of disenfranchised child laborers and slaves to make a political point. Even in courses for English majors, some students invariably miss the irony that turns lines like these from Blake's "The Chimney Sweeper" into parodic commentary on the danger of accepting religious paternalism at face value:

> And the Angel told Tom if he'd be a good boy,
> He'd have God for his father & never want joy.
> And so Tom awoke and we rose in the dark
> And got with our bags & our brushes to work.
> Tho' the morning was cold, Tom was happy & warm,
> So if all to their duty, they need not fear harm.   (10)

Blake takes an even more challenging rhetorical stance in "The Little Black Boy" (9), which critiques delays in the abolition of slavery by placing a parody of the rhetoric of amelioration in the mouth of the eponymous child slave. During class discussion, several of my service-learning students initially indicated that they found these poems and their speakers to be as innocent as the collection title suggests; but once the students began trying to connect the *Songs* to their service learning, the terms of the conversation shifted. Some students asked what it would mean if the Studio for Southern California History did not quote the farmworkers they interviewed and instead left their voices unattributed, as Blake does with the children. Other students noted that the success of 826LA's student publication program rests on the satisfaction a young child gains from seeing his or her name in print. Still others confessed that they struggled to know what to say when they witnessed poverty but believed they had a responsibility to speak up for those less fortunate than themselves. These students sympathized with Blake's activist difficulty and commended his efforts to expose the patronizing language and attitudes of his contemporaries—even if doing so required mimicking that behavior and co-opting the voices of children who had no access to the means of publishing their stories.

I was thrilled with these turns in the conversation because truly nuanced analysis of politics and poetics, and of Blakean parody, can only be achieved when students recognize how many different rhetorical strategies, with different ethical effects, are available for telling stories of social injustice. As my students examined the archival tactics and publication strategies of their community partners alongside published texts, they discovered the real-world relevance of representational strategies that take center stage in introductory literature courses. Through their collaboration with local not-for-profit organizations, my students gained more than merely the skills in textual analysis typically developed in writing courses; they gained perspective about the ethical quandaries that underlie decisions to speak or write on behalf of someone else.

This heightened awareness not only led to spirited classroom discussion that promoted self-reflection but also sharpened my students' analysis of point of view and tone in their papers. For instance, a student who initially struggled to make sense of the presence of racial stereotypes in "The Little Black Boy" ultimately wrote an incisive paper about how Blake blames parents and other authority figures for patronizing language in the *Songs* and, implicitly, for the suffering that such discourse justifies. Another student applied themes from our class discussion of Blake to analyze

Thomas Holcroft's "The Dying Prostitute: An Elegy," noting that the poem also takes up the voice of a disenfranchised minority but does so without Blake's irony and thus without acknowledging the ethical pitfalls raised by such appropriation. While papers like these still exhibited many of the challenges that often plague students pursuing their first college literature course—failure to cite enough evidence to back up claims, for one—the sophistication of these arguments demonstrates how collaborating with community partners implicitly enhances traditional areas of academic inquiry, such as textual analysis.

One of the biggest challenges I faced while developing this service-learning course, however, was devising writing assignments that would allow students to demonstrate explicit as well as implicit connections between their service learning and their study of literary form. Meeting this challenge required me to develop new types of assignments that went beyond the extended close-reading papers typically assigned in literature courses and beyond the reflection journals that hold such a prominent place in service-learning pedagogy.[7] In one of these new assignments, I asked my students to write a persuasive letter recommending why their service-learning sites should be profiled by an imaginary documentary film director. As students honed their skills in argumentation for this assignment, they simultaneously worked to demonstrate that they had thought critically about the genre of urban documentary and the medium of film, thus framing their reflections on service to fit cultural artifacts we were studying in the second half of the class. The letter also provided students with a chance to apply what they had learned about the rhetorical value—and limits—of first-person testimonials by asking them to incorporate at least two forms of evidence into their arguments: personal experience and research into the published missions of their community partners.

Like many instructors new to service learning, I was initially hesitant about departing from traditional close-reading papers, but this creative project yielded some of the best persuasive writing I have ever received from undergraduates. One particularly stellar student recommended the Museum of Tolerance to the fictional film director by providing a powerful account of attending a panel discussion entitled "From Hate to Hope," during which a gay museum employee and the former white supremacist who assaulted him reflect on their eventual reconciliation.[8] This student balanced his testimonial account of that particular day at the museum with research into its overall mission before closing the letter with a skillful rhetorical maneuver that flattered the fictional film director's chosen medium by arguing that his video would provide a valuable supplement to the visitors' guides revised and expanded by service-learning students. Earlier in the quarter, this student had written a solid paper about how Blake builds sympathy for chimney sweepers. But his attention to the ways point of view affects content grew even sharper when he had to make decisions about how to situate his personal experience with service as part of his community partner's story of civic engagement. Experiences like this one have shown me that the most effective writing assignments in service-learning courses are often those that depart from strict text-based analysis and encourage students to see themselves and their academic coursework as part of an ongoing conversation about the challenges of collaborating across diverse communities.

While many different types of assignments can foster this heightened engagement, another project I have found especially effective in general education courses asks students to use the representational strategies they have examined in published texts in two ways: to write production notes for an urban documentary in any of the media we studied and then to produce a paper analyzing their rhetorical decisions as they would any other text. On the final day of class, the students present their projects in a showcase and invite their community partners to attend.

Like the persuasive letter, this assignment has produced some of the sharpest analytic writing (and most effective public speaking) I have ever received from undergraduates. Students who may have had difficulty comparing William Wordsworth's use of first-person point of view in the London section of *The Prelude* with Mary Robinson's use of the third person in "London's Summer Morning" understood the significance of those formal differences once they started trying to tell their own stories about the local community. Inspired by 826LA's commitment to publishing the stories of young English language learners, one of my students composed a poem about his experience as the child of Latino immigrants, fusing the metrical forms we had studied in class with the beat of rap music. Other students explored the challenges of narrating a story from more than one point of view. Working in a group, they drew on the community-based research skills they developed with the Studio for Southern California History and the Museum of Tolerance to collect oral histories and other documents about Stevens House, one of the first cooperative residences near UCLA to welcome nonwhite female students in the 1940s. The young women in my class then carefully framed a presentation that honored the voices of earlier UCLA undergraduates while also reflecting their own experiences at the same multicultural campus six decades later.

Because of busy schedules, only one of our community partners was able to send a representative to the student showcase, but all the students shared revised versions of their recommendation letters with their partners, and several also shared their final projects independently after the term concluded. The students who developed a visual time line depicting the history of Stevens House gave their work to the organization's scholarship board, and one member of the group went on to contribute to the LA History Archive after she accepted a job with the Studio for Southern California History.

As I continue to develop service-learning courses as part of my duties as assistant director for UCLA's Center for Community Learning, I am exploring possibilities for increasing the extent to which my students support the missions of community partners through their academic work as well as through direct service. In particular, I have considered moving the student showcase from campus to one of our service-learning sites. In conversations, Sharon Sekhon, the director of the Studio for Southern California History, has already indicated that displaying student work at her pop-up gallery in Chinatown would enhance her scheduled programming, and 826LA staff members have also said that the students they serve could benefit greatly from participating in a joint public reading alongside their college-going mentors. The constraints of UCLA's ten-week quarter and the notoriously tight schedules of undergraduates and community partners have thwarted my efforts to organize events of this sort thus far, but I continue to try because I believe that a more public form of academic scholarship can and should stem from the ethos of reciprocity that undergirds service-learning pedagogy.[9]

Other service-learning instructors in literature programs have also begun working toward this goal by pairing traditional analytic essays with project-based writing assignments designed in collaboration with local communities. At Northern Oklahoma College, students in a language arts course taught by Tamera Davis not only study contributions to the nationwide This I Believe project but also write their own essays and partner with students at an alternative high school to publish a chapbook on the core values of their community. Undergraduates in an introductory English course created by Bridget Draxler at the University of Iowa hone their skills in literary analysis by adapting scenes from famous gothic texts for family-friendly live performances at the Old Capitol Museum during Iowa City's annual Halloween festivities. Community-based projects like these do more than simply help college students recognize that the texts they study in general education courses speak to much wider audiences; such projects also encourage undergraduates to see their academic work as part and parcel of their collaboration with and service to the local community.[10]

To my mind, the second of these outcomes is the most compelling because it indicates that service learning provides opportunities to infuse the undergraduate literature and writing curriculum with the same drive toward public engagement that is transforming how faculty members and graduate students pursue humanities scholarship. Kathleen Woodward, professor of English and director of the Simpson Center for the Humanities at the University of Washington, Seattle, offers a cogent assessment of the benefits that stem from this ongoing reconfiguration of the field:

> What is ultimately at stake in the public humanities is a form of scholarship and research, of teaching and learning, that honors commitment and concrete purpose, has a clear and present substance, reduces the distance between the university and life, and offers civic education for all involved, revealing the expansive future of the humanities—in the present and in public. (123)

I teach community-based courses about literature from the eighteenth century to the present because I want my students to recognize that we live in a world shaped by language and other forms of representation, a world in which the stories people tell about one another have tangible effects in communities. Literature students who are civically engaged learn to see both scholarly and creative writing as ways of representing the world and our relation to it—and thus as activities for which we are each individually responsible. For me, cultivating this responsibility to both self and community is the essence of what it means to practice the humanities.

NOTES

1. More information about these organizations is available online: for 826LA, visit www.826la.org; for the Museum of Tolerance, www.museum oftolerance.com; and for the Studio of Southern California History, www .socalstudio.org (a digital archive is located at www.lahistoryarchive.org).

2. For an extensive discussion of perspective transformation in relation to service learning, see the groundbreaking study by Janet Eyler and Dwight E. Giles, Jr., *Where's the Learning in Service-Learning?*

3. Debate about the public relevance of the humanities has intensified in recent years, in part thanks to increased budget pressures. Stanley Fish has led the charge that the humanities need not—and, more important, should not—serve utilitarian ends (*Save the World*). Organizations leading the effort to promote civically engaged humanities projects include Imagining America (www.imaginingamerica.org) and the Animating Democracy initiative of Americans for the Arts (www.animatingdemocracy.org).

4. The memorable exception to this norm took place at the 2010 Imagining America conference in Seattle when I met Bridget Draxler, who was then a PhD candidate specializing in eighteenth-century literature at the University of Iowa and is now an assistant professor at Monmouth College. I remain grateful for that meeting because talking with Draxler confirmed that I was alone neither in receiving these quizzical stares nor in believing they pointed to a persistent—and largely unacknowledged—assumption that service-learning pedagogy has little applicability in English departments beyond courses on contemporary literature.

5. Tania Mitchell rightly notes that service learning has not always featured the "social change orientation" associated with civil rights movements and allied academic fields, but her research also demonstrates that service learning frequently gains traction at universities when courses are structured around such themes (52).

6. Teresa Mangum has made similar observations about Victorian literature, arguing that civically engaged courses offset assumptions of "inconsequence" by reminding students "of the continuing power of earlier literatures to raise powerful questions about the present as well as the past" ("Many Lives").

7. Ellen Cushman has also called on service-learning instructors to develop assignments that push students beyond passive reflection into critical analysis of power dynamics in the community and in campus-community partnerships ("Sustainable Service Learning Programs").

8. "From Hate to Hope" is an ongoing monthly lecture at the Museum of Tolerance featuring a conversation between Matthew Boger and Tim Zaal. This student attended the lecture during the spring of 2007.

9. As part of my work at the Center for Community Learning, I am currently exploring ways to use digital media to foster public exchanges of the knowledge created through service-learning partnerships. To this end, I have

begun collaborating with UCLA's Center for Digital Humanities to develop a virtual map of service-learning sites that UCLA faculty members, students, and community partners will be able to augment with reflections and photos.

10. For an overview of community-based projects with similar aims at other institutions, see Mangum, "Going Public."

Matthew C. Hansen

Shake It Up After-School: Service Learning, Shakespeare, and Performance as Interpretation

> "Play out the play. I have much to say in the behalf of that."
> *1 Henry* IV 2.4.467–68

Since this essay collection demonstrates the viability of connecting service learning and literary studies, surely consideration must be given to how this innovative and enriching pedagogy applies to Shakespeare courses, a staple of nearly every university course catalog. The approach described and analyzed here emphasizes performance as interpretation and asks students to spend much of the semester focusing on one Shakespeare play, discussing it, performing scenes from it, writing about it, and teaching it to elementary students by helping them produce a one-hour performance version of that play. This exercise is part of my service-learning project, Shake It Up After-School (SIUAS), which is "fundamentally concerned with civic education and social justice because improving access for all to Shakespeare as cultural capital (not only of high or elite culture, but also of youth, popular, and even low culture) is an issue of social justice" (Hansen, "'O Brave New World'" 181).[1] This essay argues that the incorporation of a performance-focused service-learning project like the one I describe significantly improves students' literary-analytic and critical-thinking skills.

My approach is messy. A student in 2009 characterized the experience as "getting your hands dirty with Shakespeare."[2] It's complicated and demanding but also deeply rewarding. Asking students to work in teams on collaborative projects can yield both great and disastrous results. While my course focuses on the learning outcomes one would typically expect for an upper-division literature course—effective literary analysis and argumentation in written and oral form—by including a community-based project, I also enable students to connect the traditional work of literary studies with other transferable skills that will aid them in a wide variety of future endeavors. To complete assigned tasks, including in-class performances of scenes from Shakespeare's plays and the management of and teaching in the afterschool program, students must call on effective communication skills, be able to delegate responsibility and tasks, engage in conflict resolution, and learn time management. As Erica, one of my 2012 students, observed:

> I have done group work for classes, but it's not often for literature-related material. With Shake It Up, I've had the chance to work with my troupe, the directors, and the elementary students with the common goal of producing a play. For me, learning becomes easier and more in-depth when it is done with other people, and this project has been no exception.

This student's general claim about how her learning works is neither idiosyncratic nor unique. Students involved in SIUAS acquire a profound and deep understanding of Shakespeare's language and dramaturgy.

Shake It Up After-School: A Performance-Based Service-Learning Project

I began teaching an upper-division undergraduate Shakespeare course with service learning in 2006. All students collaborate on a single project—SIUAS, an afterschool Shakespeare program for Title I elementary schools. Over the course of six weeks, elementary students read, discuss, rehearse, and perform a shortened Shakespeare play under the guidance and coaching of undergraduates in my 300-level Shakespeare course. Student leaders—whom I recruit to return to the program as interns the spring after their initial semester in the course—take on directorial, design, and textual-editing responsibilities. Thus while the core of the service-learning project spans six to eight weeks of the spring semester, the planning and preparatory work that occurs with experienced undergraduate student leaders spans a calendar year, since much of the planning and preparation happens in the preceding fall semester. The project remains singular in a sense, but it now operates simultaneously at three school sites. I have recruited these partners deliberately, choosing Title I schools with the highest percentages of students qualifying for free and reduced lunch rates and the highest percentages of English language learners. This selection relates directly to the issues of cultural capital and social justice that I address in a 2011 article for *Pedagogy*, which I assign to my students for our discussion of the social-justice underpinnings of the project. But service learning is at its most effective when both aspects (service *and* learning) are given equal weight and consideration (Hansen, "'O Brave New World'"). Service is valuable in and of itself, but service learning demands meaningful connection to course content. The use of a service-learning project in my course has helped integrate performance as interpretation as a central concern, thus delivering on the course's learning objectives and in particular the teaching of literary analysis and interpretation.

While most Shakespeare instructors incorporate performance in teaching Shakespeare, my use of in-class performances coupled with a rehearsal-as-learning and production-focused project outside the classroom puts performance on equal footing with written literary analysis and interpretation. Using a performance-oriented service-learning project in which undergraduates see performances, perform, and teach Shakespeare through performance moves the learning dynamic beyond a standard two-constituency (student, teacher), two-role (student, teacher) learning structure and into a six-constituency (professor, undergraduate leader, undergraduate student, elementary school student, elementary school principal or teacher, elementary school parent) and three-role (student, student-teacher, teacher) structure. Elizabeth, a 2010 student who later became a leader and site director, observed that taking our college-level analysis of Shakespeare and passing along applicable reading and interpretive skills to elementary students allowed *The Tempest* (that year's production text) to "become more multifaceted and intriguing" than she felt it was on an initial reading. She observes, "This experience has challenged me to do the same type of rephrasing and re-communication with everything I read so that I can test my own understanding of a text." This same student, working closely with the elementary student playing Ariel, gained great insight from her elementary-age collaborator about the power dynamics between Ariel and Prospero. The elementary student, in discussion with Elizabeth, proffered the paradoxical insight that Ariel, possessing magic and doing the actual magical work, is more powerful than if submissive to Prospero. This thought led Elizabeth "to examine the text further and write my reading response on the support that I found that backed up [our Ariel's] initial interpretation" that "Ariel is the main source of power in the play." During in-class discussion about this particular moment, students took the observation further, connecting it to power relationships at work in the story of Aladdin and the genie, another manifestation of the magical servant who ultimately wields a power greater than his master but who must remain subservient to the master's wishes while yearning for freedom.

See One, Do One, Teach One

A performance-based approach to teaching Shakespeare runs through every aspect of the course. Students read the plays in whole (usually over a weekend) rather than in segments.[3] I organize optional, extra-credit group read-throughs of all the plays throughout the semester (see Hansen, "Learning"). Students are assigned to a performance troupe for the semester and work together in those teams, performing assigned scenes in class roughly every other week. After students perform, we discuss the performance as a class. We quickly come to understand the practicalities and implications of decisions related to blocking and movement, vocal intonation and facial expression. We discuss the merits and limits of those decisions and contemplate other choices either considered but not followed or choices previously unimagined. After each in-class performance, students submit a written self-evaluation of their performance, assessing their team's work overall, the insights gained from performing and discussing their performance, and their contribution to the performance.

We occasionally also view and discuss film clips of scenes and analyze the interpretive decisions underlying those performances. This process of seeing performances by their peers (and professionals on video), performing themselves, and eventually teaching younger students to perform introduces my students to the ways in which performance operates as interpretation, which involves their making concrete decisions to adapt the text but is not meant to be the only interpretation possible. As part of our postperformance in-class discussions, we explore how their learning through performance will be extended when they begin to teach in the SIUAS program, such as how we can help the elementary students block scenes to keep their faces visible to the audience and their voices audible. We also discuss how certain choices that are useful for performance in our college classroom might or might not translate successfully (or appropriately) to a performance by ten-, eleven-, and twelve-year-old performers. When performing scenes from *Titus Andronicus* early in the semester, for example, we discuss how that play's on- and off-stage violence (including the rape and mutilation of Lavinia) may or may not be appropriately managed. I hasten to add that *Titus Andronicus* is not likely ever to be a play I would select for SIUAS, but we have produced *Macbeth* and *Hamlet*. Discussing the violence in these plays with both undergraduates and elementary students takes thoughtful consideration but is not something that one should automatically reject or avoid. Elementary students are not immune to the constant presence of violent scenes on television and in movies and video games, and some of our refugee students know about violence and cruelty in unmediated ways. While we may be introducing terminology when we talk about Macbeth as a tyrant, we are not necessarily introducing new concepts.

Over the semester, the insights gained through in-class performance often find their way into my students' biweekly, written argumentative analyses. For Eva, a student in my spring 2012 class, playing Celia in act 4, scene 1, of *As You Like It* led to an extended exploration of what to do with the resistance in Celia's line "I cannot say the words" (4.1.121) and how to communicate the sister-like bond between Rosalind and Celia. Because I had situated *As You Like It* within a group of texts that explored sibling rivalries—and especially conflicts between brothers—Eva was able to meaningfully compare and contrast Shakespeare's positive portrayal of the relationship between Rosalind and Celia and the warring pairs of brothers in the play. Her insights ranged between practical considerations of performance informed by close reading and careful analysis to the applied work of performance as interpretation, first in performing the role of Celia herself and then in coaching an elementary student in an exploration of Celia's character and relationship with Rosalind.

In this way the dividing line between performance and written criticism grows increasingly blurry—fruitfully so—as students' mastery grows. As I explain to my students, we are adapting and adopting the approach used in medical education to teach procedures: see one (watch the procedure performed), do one (perform the procedure under supervision), teach one (teach someone else how to do the procedure).

Depth versus Coverage

Faculty members are understandably, even justifiably, wary of incorporating service learning into their teaching; they often feel that doing so will detract from course content (Strage 260). And because I incorporate service learning and make it the defining element of my 300-level Shakespeare course, my students study fewer plays than they would in my colleagues' sections of the course.[4] But I maintain that engaging in project-based learning that focuses on performance as interpretation and mode of learning is as valuable — if not more valuable — than covering more plays in less depth. Because we devote considerable in-class time to the play we then teach to elementary students and continue to study that play by teaching it while moving on to other plays for classroom discussion, undergraduates gain a deep and rich understanding of a specific play text. This understanding provides a strong foundation from which to make effective comparative analyses with other Shakespeare plays.

When we focused on *As You Like It* for the afterschool program in spring 2012, spending five weeks on in-class study of the play and eight weeks of afterschool programming meant we spent a total of twelve weeks (of a sixteen-week semester) engaging with *As You Like It*; during part of that time, students were helping produce *As You Like It* with elementary students while studying other plays.[5] The value of this deep understanding of *As You Like It* showed itself in students' writing and ability to think critically about the play and its relation to other versions of Shakespearean comedy we studied.

Not all my students agree. In anonymous course evaluations, one student remarked that he or she knew *As You Like It* "backward and forward but [had] trouble remembering anything from the other plays." In an addendum to his postservice reflection, a student noted that he was "concerned about how the [service learning] program has taken over the actual Shakespeare course. Class time was devoted to Shake It Up topics and if we had time we would discuss whatever play was scheduled on the syllabus." My current approach, accurately characterized by this student's comment, has also been a response to previous student concerns about imbalance on the other side: the regular course schedule of reading, discussion, and writing or performing assignments was too unrelenting in combination with the extraordinary demands of the service-learning project.[6]

Overall, the effort, in my estimation, is worth it. And as my students experience a meaningful way in which their interests in literature can lead to profound connections and shared learning with younger students of Shakespeare, I become only more convinced. Indeed, the preceding student comment about difficulty "remembering" other plays indirectly supports my point: my object in the course is not for students to recall

Shakespeare's plots. Since the comedies tend to be formulaic, some confusion is inevitable, a point that the fun and irreverent *The Complete Works of William Shakespeare (Abridged)* makes brilliantly (Long, Singer, and Winfield). Rather, I want students to understand how Shakespeare's plays work—to be able to analyze character, to imagine and articulate what the world of the play is like, to assess genre in relation to historical context and performance (as audience and as performer)—and to gain skills in parsing his language to determine if, how, and why Shakespeare is timeless.

Student reflections more often support my position and demonstrate that the work of the service-learning project opens up Shakespeare to them in ways that reading and discussion alone could not. Diana avers that her understanding of *As You Like It* "definitely expanded more than it would have if [she had] only read it in class." She discusses how rehearsing act 4, scene 3, with elementary students enabled her to see that in this scene Oliver and Celia meet and immediately fall in love. Together, Diana and the performers she was coaching realized that they had to convey this important aspect of the story. This insight then led to collaborative questions and experimentation: "How do you act when you see someone for the first time and have that love-at-first-sight moment?" Diana and the elementary student performers worked together to find an answer to this question, drawing on their own wealth of knowledge of such scenes as readers and as viewers of film and television.

Similarly, Tom gained deeper insight into the brotherly dynamics at work in Oliver and Orlando's relationship through rehearsal and directing. We had looked at relationships between brothers in our readings and discussed how the biblical precedents of Cain and Abel, Jacob and Esau, and the parable of the prodigal son informed aspects of the brother-versus-brother dynamics of *As You Like It* and other plays on the course reading list. But, as Tom writes, it wasn't until he saw a particular scene in rehearsal (act 5, scene 2) that he appreciated the "melancholy" Orlando must experience. When he saw and heard the actor playing Orlando speak the lines "as if in a mood of resentment because Oliver had found love and Orlando has yet to woo Rosalind," Tom "tweaked to melancholy." He concludes, "Orlando in this scene does not feel resentment, but feels joyous for his brother[;] at the same time [he] is in that state where you can't quite be happy for your friend, or brother in this instance, because you yourself are not happy." Sharing this insight with the actors he was coaching, he found they agreed, and together they were better able to understand for themselves and communicate to the audience the dynamics of the brothers' relationship.

Diane's and Tom's experiences are representative. In aggregate, student reflections demonstrate the power that performance and nuanced interpretation have in bringing Shakespeare's text to life and into far clearer understanding. Can similar effects be achieved simply through watching video performances or by carefully analyzing in-class student performances? Perhaps. However, student reflections and in-class discussions suggest that there is a unique value in teaching performance, because of the depth of understanding it requires.

In their preservice reflections, students frequently articulate a desire to become expert in the play chosen for the afterschool project to be fully prepared for the questions the elementary students may ask of them. Students often find that this expertise is actually achieved through the prolonged and overlapping engagement that occurs between our classroom study of the play and the demands of teaching and rehearsing with elementary school performers. Eva articulates the benefits of prolonged engagement with a single text directly:

> Spending so much time with the text and teaching it really helped to ingrain *As You Like It* in my brain. . . . In order to be intimate with the play enough that I could help these kids understand it, I had to make my own decisions about character behavior and mannerisms, and this forced me to look at *As You Like It* even harder. I feel like I developed a stronger connection with the characters and their nuances than I ever have with a Shakespeare play, because of this project.

Eva's observations demonstrate that it is the combination of prolonged focus on a single text and of the required mastery necessary to teach that material that facilitates deep learning here. In-class performances as I structure them open the text in important ways for my students, but the service-learning project, focused as it is on both performance and teaching, demands a still-higher level of understanding and analytic thinking. As Tanya, another student, concludes:

> [I]t is also a great opportunity to gain new ideas and insights that would be missed without the open discussion that this program facilitates. A great example was when we asked the kids what the play was about and a few of them answered, "girl power." At first it struck me as funny, but it

also has some truth to it and made me think about the play from an angle I hadn't previously considered.

The elementary students' response that *As You Like It* is fundamentally about girl power led Tanya to think more critically and, ultimately, insightfully about issues of gender and power in *As You Like It* and other Shakespearean comedies. In a response to *The Winter's Tale*, she judiciously compared Rosalind's power as it is achieved through disguise and the power exercised by Hermione, whom Tanya argued "acted with elegant gentleness despite the accusations of her husband." Similarly, Rachel argued from close textual analysis that "women held power and control through their voice" or powers of persuasion and linguistic mastery in *The Comedy of Errors*, *As You Like It*, and *The Winter's Tale*.

Undergraduate Student Learning: Literary Criticism and Performance as Interpretation

Because students developed a deep and nuanced understanding of *As You Like It* both as a literary text and as a text for performance, they were well able to compare and contrast that play with other Shakespearean comedies studied in the course. Student writing insightfully contrasted the lighthearted world and happy ending of *As You Like It* with the far darker and more complex ending of *Measure for Measure*, in which at least two individuals are punished by being forced to marry, thus effectively exploring the elasticity of a generic or modal label such as *comedy*. Amanda produced a reading response to *Measure for Measure* that offered "an in-depth look at Isabella, the Duke, and the ending of the play to analyze how these aspects differ" from the comic endings of *As You Like It* and *Much Ado about Nothing*. Erica likewise wrote insightfully about the ending of *Measure for Measure*, characterizing it as a "problematic element": "The Duke decrees that Angelo and Lucio must marry Mariana and Kate Keepdown, thus arguably ruining at least four lives. This is a far cry from Shakespeare's other comedies, such as *As You Like It*, which end with wanted marriages, happiness, and song."

Students likewise effectively explored the tonal differences between *As You Like It* and the tragicomic aspects of *The Winter's Tale*, again demonstrating increasingly sophisticated understandings of genre and mode. Diana examined the role of magic in the two plays—the seeming resurrection and transformation of the "statue" of Hermione in *The Winter's Tale* and the *deus ex machina* appearance of Hymen in *As You Like It*. In a reflection drawing on her peers' reading responses, Erica built on Diana's observations to argue that as fantastical as the conclusion of *The Winter's Tale* is, its lack of magic and inclusion of the death of Mamillius "makes the play more realistic, and therefore less like the idealized world of a comedy." When we produced two versions of *Hamlet* in 2011, one director, Elizabeth, saw the essence of the play in its own self-consciousness as theater, as play: "The play's the thing" (2.2.605–06). This insight led to a slight reconfiguring of the text in which the play's concluding scene was staged twice—as an opening tableau and as the concluding scene—to underscore the ways in which *Hamlet* is a story that is performed and re-performed. In her written reflection, Elizabeth connects this understanding to readings and theories about revenge, including recent scholarship on *Hamlet* and *Titus Andronicus*. Drawing specifically on Deborah Willis's work on *Titus Andronicus* and trauma theory, Elizabeth understood revenge as a "potentially endless cycle . . . of new traumas in need of containment by revenge" (Willis 33).

Relating this concept to *Hamlet* and her decision to modify the performance text in ways that caused a deliberate echoing effect, Elizabeth concludes:

> Thus, by immediately introducing the audience to a stage of death in *Hamlet*, they are constantly aware of the consequences of revenge. In addition, by opening and closing the show with the lines "Now cracks a noble heart. Good night, sweet prince, / And flights of angels sing thee to thy rest," there is a conflicting response within the viewer (5.2.341–42). There comes a sense of closure at hearing the lines spoken again, but also a foreboding at the repetition. There lurks the suggestion that the play will start again, that the revenge will again be enacted and the characters will once more lay motionless; a haunting ambiguity.

A reflection such as this demonstrates the richness of a prolonged engagement with the text as material for performance and material for teaching performers and audiences. Elizabeth's incorporation of relevant scholarship effectively demonstrates her growing sophistication as a literary critic. And although students can relatively easily cherry-pick choice quotations from a scholarly article without genuinely reflecting on it, the work of teaching a Shakespeare play by directing others in a performance of it can lead to the kind of integrative analysis we hope our 300-level students are beginning to achieve.

The particular approach to melding Shakespeare and service learning described here is, without doubt, not for everyone. Such an approach is demanding—in time, emotion, and energy—of both students and the instructor. In my experience, the rewards in student learning and community enrichment warrant the effort. The structure of SIUAS leads undergraduates and elementary students to focus in depth on a single play text through performance. While both groups of students, naturally, come to different levels of understanding, their shared engagement leads to teaching and learning that is multifaceted and multidirectional: we all learn and we all teach, together. As we coach the elementary students "off-book" and through dress rehearsals of their play, I frequently direct them to tell the story: while I would love for them to do that using Shakespeare's words, if they can't remember the precise words Shakespeare has given them, I would much rather hear their own paraphrase than silence. In one of our three 2012 productions of *As You Like It*, the elementary student in the role of Celia always altered Celia's exit line in act 1, scene 3, from "Now go we in content / To liberty and not to banishment" (135–36) to "Now go we forth not to banishment, but freedom." She understood the line and what it meant and arguably came up with a formulation that is more logical in its syntax than Shakespeare's in that it moves from the negative concept from which Rosalind and Celia are fleeing ("banishment") to the positive concept of liberty or freedom. The reformulation lacks Shakespeare's scene-ending couplet but makes at least as much sense. More important, it demonstrates the kind of ownership of Shakespeare that this program strives to make possible.

NOTES

1. For a rich alternative approach focused on male-positive literacy, see Gouws.

2. I am grateful to my students for their permission to quote their work. All student names used in this essay are pseudonyms.

3. All citations of Shakespeare's plays refer to Bevington's sixth edition of *The Complete Works of Shakespeare*. Several useful resources exist for those considering a performance-based approach to teaching Shakespeare; for superb

starting points, see Rocklin; Riggio. Practical suggestions for immediate application can also be found at the Folger Shakespeare Library's Web site, http://www.folger.edu.

4. Of the three of us who regularly teach the same 300-level Shakespeare course at Boise State University, one typically teaches seven plays, another six; I now typically teach five plays in a sixteen-week semester.

5. This was the outline for the 2012 course: week 1: introduction and overview; weeks 2–3: *The Comedy of Errors*; weeks 4–8: *As You Like It*; weeks 9–10: *Measure for Measure*; week 11: spring break; weeks 12–13: *The Winter's Tale*; weeks 14–15: *The Tempest*; week 16: semester review. The service-learning project began in week 7 and concluded at the end of week 15.

6. Typical service-learning courses at Boise State University require that students contribute fifteen hours of service over the semester. My course—which also offers an additional one-credit service-learning lab—requires forty hours. Many of my students end up serving far more than the minimum requirement.

Diana C. Archibald

Learning across "Different Zones": Bridging the Gap between "Two Nations" through Community Engagement

The Westford Street Landfill in Lowell, Massachusetts, is a sixty-acre facility featuring a capped and lined mountain of solid residential waste,
gathered from 1948 to 1992. With a two-hundred-ton-per-day permit, the
landfill eventually became a gigantic mound on the outskirts of what is
now the fifth largest city in Massachusetts. The imposing heap is dotted
with methane gas wells expected to become defunct in a few years since
the hill's cap keeps water from permeating and breaking down materials
inside. As Gunther Wellenstein, the coordinator of solid waste and recycling for the city of Lowell, remarked to a small group of Victorian literature students one day in the fall of 2011, if we opened up the entombed
landfill, we would find most items in the exact same condition as when
they were dumped there decades ago—even newspapers would be dry
and readable. A few years back a development company considered starting a landfill mining and reclamation project at the Westford Street site.
The students were surprised to learn that the mound contains many valuable materials such as aluminum, scrap metal, and rubber. It had never
occurred to them that garbage could be a desirable commodity. The deal
fell through, but Wellenstein dreams of turning this pile of refuse into a
recreational site, with a small ski lift and ice-skating pond in winter and a
picnicking spot in summer.

My four students and I admired the view from atop the heap after
driving the spiraling road to the summit. Meanwhile, three more groups
of my students were visiting other community partner sites: a homeless
shelter in a dilapidated part of the city, a career center on a busy downtown street, and an adult-literacy-program office in the local library.

One of the students at the landfill could have been speaking for all four groups when she remarked, "This wasn't what I expected!" In our case, the landfill was certainly not what one would imagine after encountering the "dust mounds" in Charles Dickens's *Our Mutual Friend*, a text we were studying in class, although echoes of the novel were ringing in our ears that afternoon as we traveled the "serpentining [road] up . . . the mounds, that gives you . . . a view of the neighbouring premises, not to be surpassed" (64). As Wellenstein regaled us with stories about our local landfill, we could almost hear Mr. Boffin discuss his "dust" mounds with his secretary: "Ay, ay, . . . I may sell THEM, though I should be sorry to see the neighbourhood deprived of 'em too. It'll look but a poor dead flat without the Mounds. Still I don't say that I'm going to keep 'em always there, for the sake of the beauty of the landscape" (186). The greedy Silas Wegg of Dickens's novel "kept watch with rapacious eyes" for possible hidden treasure while his employer's mounds were slowly carted away, but his miserly master had already "vigilantly sifted the dust . . . [and] coined every waif and stray into money, long before" (759).

Unlike Silas, we knew that we were perched atop a small fortune. Students wondered why these valuable materials were buried in a landfill in the first place and what that said about our society. They commented on the apparent superiority of the Victorians' adherence to the "reduce, reuse, recycle" motto. They asked how much this mound would fetch on the open market and wondered if its sale could help fill the city's budget gaps. Students argued about how the money should be spent: fixing potholes, paying for teacher aides, adding police? Could another investor be attracted to the project? Why had the first deal fallen through? Many scholars have discussed the importance of garbage in Dickens's last complete novel and examined the relation of "dust" to corporeality, social change, and sexuality, among other topics (see Brattin; Simon; Toker), and we had done so as well. But it was the site visit that piqued their interest in the complex and important issues surrounding waste in a way that class discussion of the novel had not done, and that engagement led back to a better understanding of the text and to a commitment to collaborative problem solving and community engagement.

Similarly, students working with the other community partners found that their service-learning experience not only helped them meet literary learning objectives of the course (analyze characters, themes, and styles of various works; argue a strong case for the interpretation of a text, on the basis of textual evidence and relevant sources; and explain how Victorian literature influenced Victorian society and how Victorian culture shaped Victorian literature) but also helped them recognize and analyze the connections between Victorian social issues and those we face today, thereby deepening understanding of the time periods and spurring them to action. The Victorian period is deeply significant to us, both as individuals and as a society, and service learning is an ideal tool for demonstrating this relevance. Service learning in a Victorian literature class can establish the pervasive connection of the period with our society, explode myths of past and present, and help students examine other problematic dichotomies such as art versus action, fostering lifelong learning and community engagement. Equally significant, the collaborative work completed also benefits the community.

The Disorientation of Crossing Zones: Critical Thinking and Service Learning

When I returned to campus, a colleague knitted his brow and queried, "What on earth does visiting a landfill have to do with the study of literature?" As Janet Eyler and Dwight E. Giles, Jr., note, "authentic situations generate questions" (86); my landfill group asked more and better questions outside the classroom than inside. Abstract information presented in the classroom may often seem fairly straightforward until students encounter a "complex situation" that upsets their vision of reality (86). The dissonance between what students expected or assumed and what they encountered or learned through their engagement in this project proved to be an excellent tool for deepening their understanding. It is the real work of service learning that often engenders a healthy disorientation, which sets the stage for critical thinking and perspective transformation, new understanding and problem solving (141–48).

In *Sybil; or, The Two Nations* (1845), Benjamin Disraeli, the young novelist and future prime minister of England, described his country as being "*[t]wo nations*; between whom there is no intercourse and no sympathy; who are ignorant of each other's habits, thoughts, and feelings, as if they were dwellers in *different zones*, or inhabitants of different planets . . . the rich and the poor" (66; emphasis added). The Victorians faced no greater challenge, perhaps, than dealing with the ever-widening gap between these "two nations," between the privileged and the disadvantaged. With recent debates about the growing chasm between the one percent and the ninety-nine percent, Disraeli's "two nations" ideas seem more pertinent to students today than to students even a decade ago. But students tend to see politics as something separate from good literature, and they have difficulty understanding the pervasiveness of the spirit of reform in the Victorian period. Rapid industrialization and urbanization of eighteenth- and nineteenth-century England led to a wide range of social problems that the Victorians worked tirelessly to try to address. Reform efforts in education, labor, environment, health, and politics led to significant changes in British society by the turn of the century, and novelists were an integral part of these movements, employing their craft to help their causes. Most undergraduate courses on the Victorian novel acknowledge the writer's additional role as investigative reporter, documentarian, polemicist, or advocate, but for many students, understanding this dual identity and the issues about which nineteenth-century novelists wrote can be difficult. They tend to compartmentalize writers and activists into different arenas, creating a false dichotomy. Service learning helps show how art and action can stimulate and enrich each other.

Further, students often assume that we hold little in common with the Victorians when, despite the significant changes in society, we share many of the same problems and attitudes. Students often believe that we have made great progress on social issues when sometimes the two nations continue to remain divided. Or students expect that scientific advances inevitably must have led to progress when, in fact, we are worse off in some ways. Through active engagement in service-learning activities related to carefully selected crossover issues such as waste, homelessness, unemployment, and literacy, students better understand Victorian social problems and their legacies, Victorian and modern community engagement practices, and the contribution that literature makes to our understanding of the human experience.

Service learning enables a deeper appreciation for the interconnectedness of our field to so-called real life. As Howard Gardner remarks, "Students must come to understand that the materials they encounter in a humanities . . . course are not drawn from a world apart" (237). Literature both reflects and affects society. Art and action can be and often are connected. Service learning enables students to cross multiple and overlapping zones to engage more directly with the world, thereby deepening their understanding of a complex web of connections.

The Course and Assignment Development

The University of Massachusetts, Lowell, is a comprehensive, urban university with fourteen thousand students, most of whom work half-time in addition to taking a full load of classes. The upper-division course Victorian Fiction satisfies a post-1800 distribution requirement for the literature major or an advanced literature requirement for creative writing or journalism and professional writing majors. Thus students in the course have very different career goals and literary analysis experience. The reading list provides students with a sampling of British fiction from the Victorian period, introducing them to a selection of different subgenres and focusing on these works as cultural productions or producers of a complex age. The service-learning project is worth twenty percent of the course grade, enough to signal that it is an important component of the course.

The assignment asked students to investigate several interrelated issues of concern both to the Victorians and to our own community and to complete a short-term service project helping meet the needs of a local organization. Students read five British novels during the semester, and the service-learning project was based on issues in the first two texts: Elizabeth Gaskell's *Mary Barton* (1848) and Charles Dickens's *Our Mutual Friend* (1864–65). Topics included waste, homelessness, unemployment, and illiteracy—all notable for their importance then and now, all present in many literary representations, and all likely to surprise students when investigating connections to current conditions. The course was informed by new historicist theories of the referentiality and subjectivity of history. We examined how Gaskell and Dickens attempted to bridge the gap between two nations through their writing and through their personal involvement in reform efforts, noting how these authors were both products and producers of history and culture. We investigated our own time- and place-bound biases and modern assumptions about literature, history, and social concerns through classroom discussions, reading, research, and active engagement in the community as students crossed many zones: historical, socioeconomic, geographic, and political, among others.

Working with community partners in a meaningful and respectful way takes time and careful communication. I sought organizations that were connected to the issues we were exploring and that were able to work collaboratively with students. Before the semester began, I approached several potential community partners whom I thought would be ideal coteachers for the assignment, deciding on four sites: the Lowell Transitional Living Center, a 120-bed shelter and soup kitchen; Literacy Volunteers, an adult-literacy program at the local library; the city's career center; and the recycling office at the Department of Public Works. All our partners were enthusiastic about working with students to meet some of their organization's needs. I asked each of the on-site supervisors to provide a brief contextual reading for the students about their contemporary issue, to come to class to meet with their group, to lead a site visit and work collaboratively with students to design a project to meet one of their organization's needs, and to provide students with feedback on their work.

Assignment steps included a mix of reading, doing, and reflecting activities: study the contextual material about the issue and write a two-page response paper; meet with the supervisor in class and visit the site; write a mid-project reflection; work collaboratively with peers and partner to develop a suitable end product to meet an identified need; submit a draft to the instructor, revise, submit to community partner, revise, and submit final draft; and write a final reflection essay or speak at a public service-learning showcase. Since about half the students were writing majors, many of them had previous experience with professional writing. Others drew on the knowledge they had gained from classes in other disciplines. Still other students learned directly from the community partner how to create the end product. With a scaffolded assignment and plenty of support, students were able to develop projects that built on their strengths and to produce acceptable work.

Assignment Outcomes

Problematize Notions of Historical Progress and the Stability of History

Belief in the forward march of history runs rampant in today's student population. We have all heard students assert that women receive equal pay for equal work, that racial prejudice is an anomaly, and that Americans enjoy a better standard of living than anyone else in the world. The idea of unequivocal progress is as attractive and pervasive as it is misleading and dangerous. While surely some advances can be touted, history is a moving target, and historical meaning is difficult to construct. When students relegate the Victorians to a time far inferior to ours, they not only lack understanding of the subject matter but also lose a stellar opportunity to use understanding of the past to inform engagement in the present.

All the student groups to a certain extent were surprised at the persistence of social problems from Victorian novels in today's world. In the case of the landfill group, we see the most extreme example of how this service-learning project problematized notions of historical progress and stability and thus enhanced students' understanding of the material. Students became much more attuned to themes of waste and reuse in the novel, showing a deeper understanding of the thematic and social significance of Mr. Boffin's dust mounds and Mr. Venus's taxidermy shop than my previous students, who had not engaged in service learning.

Although the Victorians as a group were appalling polluters, they were remarkably good recyclers, reusing almost everything down to ashes and bits of bone. In many of Dickens's novels, characters work within the system of waste management. During the early Industrial Revolution, such frugality and careful reuse of every scrap was a matter of survival for the poor. Although recycling rates today are going up relative to waste produced,[1] our levels of waste are much higher than the Victorians'. The students researched such Victorian and contemporary waste and recycling issues as a part of their service-learning assignment, but their site visit enabled them to feel the stark contrast between past and present. Standing on top of a modern-day mound filled with inaccessible but reusable materials, they felt their notions of contemporary superiority shatter.

The collaborative service project that emerged from their experience that day met a real need: assisting in the city's efforts to increase recycling rates. During these tough economic times, the students argued, we should be following the Victorians' lead by making better use of our resources. The group worked under Wellenstein's supervision to create an informative flyer for residents of the city, showing that a five percent increase in recycling citywide would translate into $100,000 in savings for the city. The students researched the city budget to determine what that amount of money would mean in concrete terms: enough to pay the salaries of two firefighters or four teacher's assistants. The students' flyer was sent to over twenty thousand homes in Lowell on the back of a mailer from the city. The same document has also been uploaded to the city's Web site, and Wellenstein is planning to create a *YouTube* video based on the students' Victorian-inspired ideas about how to promote the city's recycling campaign.

Learn to Critique Notions of Charity and Speaking or Acting for the Other

In class we discussed Dickens's involvement with Urania Cottage, a home for "fallen" women that sought to redeem prostitutes by helping them change their sinful ways and live a clean new life in the colonies. Well-meaning but highly problematic paternalism was often at the core of Victorian reform efforts. Students cringed when reading Dickens's open letter to streetwalkers and approved of Gaskell's more tempered approach to serving the poor in her native Manchester, England. Once the four groups began their service-learning projects, however, students had to make the difficult leap to understand how our own efforts might become equally problematic. We discussed the differences between charity and collaboration, between acting for and working with. The idea of working with the community, listening to their needs, and engaging more fully was both exciting and a little scary to the students.

The group working with the career center was able to complete a project designed to give clients a voice. The career center's supervisor asked these students to phone people who had only attended one employment-assistance session and never returned. The goal was to discover how the center might better meet the needs of their clients. Students found that language barriers accounted for most of the dropouts, and the rest were due to learning disabilities or homelessness.

The students saw the ways in which factors outside an individual's control could influence employability and how many social problems are entangled with one another. Having discussed the use of unemployment as a recurring theme in *Mary Barton*, where random events led to characters' unemployment, the students were able to connect the past and the present through their work. While students noted that there was no place like Lowell's career center in the novel, we also discussed the ways in which middle-class Victorian charitable institutions tried to assist the poor. The career center gained valuable feedback that they would not have been able to gather themselves, since five employees at the center had recently been laid off because of city budget cuts.

Expose Stereotypes and Question Assumptions about Past and Present

The group of students who visited a local homeless shelter experienced great personal transformation, as is clear from their end products—public impact statements used by the shelter to combat negative stereotypes and bolster the shelter's image. Each student wrote that her visit to the shelter had challenged her ideas about homelessness and given her a different perspective on her own life. Their work at the Lowell Transitional Living Center was powerful because the students were working directly with this population—homelessness now had a face. Their impact stories reveal significant shifts in their thinking. Jennifer, for example, wrote of how her service-learning experience made her "think about how selfish people can be when they complain about insignificant things like not having the newest shoes, the latest cell phone, or the nicest hair color." As in the other groups, the students working with the shelter noticed the interrelatedness of the issues we were examining. As Lowell has begun to become more gentrified, pressures on the downtown shelter have grown. Students' impact statements are useful commendations of the good work the center is doing for the city and morale boosters for staff members who have become discouraged by the monumental task of providing a safe and pleasant temporary home for some of the city's most vulnerable people.

Examine the Connection between Literacy and Social Justice

From my critical perspective, all texts are valid and valuable for what they reveal and conceal. Our service-learning work enabled us to examine and problematize the privileging of the literary text while also grappling with the social-justice issues connected to literacy. A rich conversation emerged about the ways meaning is conveyed and why certain modes of communication are favored. My students working with the Literacy Volunteers program, like my other students, were also moved by their experience and saw many connections to the course material. They noted that illiteracy was a much bigger problem these days than they thought and carried a greater stigma now than it had in Victorian times. We discussed how illiteracy was and remains tied to socioeconomic factors and discussed how Lizzie Hexam's illiteracy in *Our Mutual Friend* was linked to her status as a poor woman. Indeed, Lizzie's goodness, like many illiterate Victorian characters, seems to stem at least in part from her separation from text-based knowledge.

My students discovered that many of the clients of Literacy Volunteers are ashamed of their inability to read and have tried to hide the deficit for years. With the help of the community partner, students learned that, because of the particularly sensitive nature of illiteracy, the tutor-client relationship must be one of great trust. Thus recruiting new volunteer tutors is essential, and the group's work creating a brochure to help with that task felt important. Since the organization had no printed materials to recruit volunteers, the students' basic but effective brochure proved acceptable to use. The community partner brought a stack of color-printed brochures to the service-learning showcase at the end of the semester, and I have seen them around town as well.

See and Value the Power of Art and Action Combined

It was relatively easy by the end of the course for students to be able to discuss how the Victorians viewed the artist as working for the common good, how writers like Dickens and Gaskell took on a dual identity as creator of fictional worlds and influencer of real life. But did the students see themselves in this way? Did they combine art and action? The deeper their reflection about their experience, the more likely students were to recognize the power of their art to transform their world. As a baseline, all students in the course seemed to have understood that their work was valuable and valued. Three students' ongoing work in the community, sparked through the service learning in my class, offers evidence of further success in this outcome.

One student, Megan, began volunteering with Girls Inc., a local after-school program for girls from low-income families. She helped launch a literacy program celebrating the two hundredth birthday of Dickens in 2012. The curriculum was so successful that the organization decided to continue the program with Edgar Allan Poe in 2013 and others in the future, and they credit Megan with being instrumental in their initial success. She used her talents to help the girls embrace literature and create their own Girls Inc. version of *A Christmas Carol*. At our service-learning showcase, in her presentation, entitled "Our Mutual Dickens: Bringing Dickens Back to Life for Girls, Inc.," Megan discussed the particular challenge of making "the past relevant to the present," explaining how important it was to empower the girls to make the text their own. She concluded that her service-learning engagement offered her "a more comprehensive and diverse opportunity to expand [her] education on literature of the

Victorian period through detailed research in a deeper way" than through a traditional essay. "Most importantly," she adds, "I was able to share my enrichment and share my work with . . . someone else."

A second student, Brad, set up a project for a youth organization that offers a job-training program in media for high school dropouts. Brad created a script of Dickens's travel narrative, *American Notes*, for a virtual walking tour of Dickens's 1842 visit to Lowell. Working with archival materials and the published book, and with the help of a local historian and the media center at our university, Brad created the backbone of an ongoing digital humanities project that will not only provide job training for the youth involved in video production but also offer an effective public relations tool to promote Lowell as a famous destination.

A third student from the course engaged in direct art action in a subsequent semester. Stephanie volunteered with the Nigerian Association of the Merrimack Valley as the costume and poster designer for their original play *Asking for More: Dickens in Nigeria*. This play was devised and performed by an ensemble of Nigerian immigrants from Lowell. A primary school class in the 1970s reads *Oliver Twist* and imagines the famed protagonist as a young boy in Lagos, Nigeria. *Asking for More* explores the power of literature in reimagining identity and fueling purpose. Stephanie attended rehearsals, researched Nigerian fabric designs, and talked with the actors about their lives as immigrants and their mutual love of Dickens.[2]

At the end of the term, students in Victorian Fiction completed a final reflection for their project: either a three-page essay describing how the project contributed to their understanding of Victorian literature and culture as well as how the experience affected them personally or a public presentation for a department service-learning showcase. The goal was for students to create an end product that would help them see and communicate the value of their experience. From these final reflections and from anonymous course evaluations, it was clear that students saw service learning as a valuable learning tool. In their literary research papers and other course work, the students demonstrated a complex understanding of the Victorian period. That they also came away from the course knowing they had helped meet real needs in our community and seeking additional ways to learn and serve was undoubtedly a positive outcome as well. They bridged the gap across the different zones of community and campus and reached out to the disadvantaged in a meaningful way. As many of the students remarked to me in class, they gained as much as they gave.

NOTES

1. According to the Environmental Protection Agency in a document that our community partner provided, in 2010 Americans generated 4.43 pounds of waste a day, with a 34.1% recycling and composting rate. That is a marked improvement over the 1975 recycling rate of 9.3%, but then again, waste tonnage has doubled since that time to a whopping 249.9 million tons in 2010 ("Municipal Solid Waste").

2. This play and the walking tour Brad helped with can be viewed online at http://library.uml.edu/dickens.

Lisa Rabin and Jennifer Leeman

Critical Service Learning and Literary Study in Spanish

In this essay, we describe several service-learning programs that grew from our efforts to integrate the critical analysis of language and language ideologies into Latin American literature courses. These efforts are rooted in critical pedagogy (Freire, *Education*), critical approaches to the teaching of Spanish (Leeman, "Engaging"; Martínez), and critical approaches to service learning (Marullo; Ochoa and Ochoa; Calderón; Rabin, "Literacy Narratives" and "Culmore Bilingual ESL"). As we demonstrate, combining a study of language ideologies in literary texts with hands-on work in community language activism provided structured opportunities for students to combat language-related inequities while also enhancing their understanding of some of the major theoretical claims of twentieth-century literary studies. In particular, the programs augmented the study of Mikhail Bakhtin's notion of literature's accommodation of heterogeneous discourses; Benedict Anderson's, Doris Sommer's, and John Guillory's theories on literature's role in the reification of written discourse and social hierarchies; and Raymond Williams's claim for literature's access to the "structure of feeling" of a society—or the hegemonic, emergent, and resistant forms of culture to which creative writers give voice (132, 134). Further, in an age in which market forces have come to dominate language education (and schooling in general), critical service learning provided students with opportunities to engage in community language activism and democratic leadership by addressing educational inequities and working to make the public sphere more inclusive of multilingualism, hybridity, and linguistic difference.

From Classroom Study of Language Ideologies
to Hands-On Language Activism

At George Mason University,[1] we have integrated the study of "language ideologies"—the "cultural systems of ideas about social and linguistic relationships, together with their loading of moral and political interests" (Irvine 255)—throughout the Spanish curriculum. The first step of this curricular reform was in the courses Spanish for Heritage Speakers and Spanish in the United States, in which students engage in the critical examination of the role of language in constructing knowledge and power, as well as the relation of language varieties and practices to various social discourses. Students interrogate the historical erasure of non-English languages in the United States, the monolingual ideologies that denigrate code switching and language mixing, the assignation of greater moral and intellectual value to "standard" and "national" language varieties, and the role of educational institutions in enforcing language hierarchies (see Leeman, "Engaging").

Next, we incorporated the study of language ideologies into Latin American literature classes, as we have described elsewhere (Leeman and Rabin). In these courses, literature students discuss the subordination of indigenous languages, the reification of written texts over oral culture, and the role of language in performing identity. The examination of language issues in the literature classroom complements the course material in Spanish sociolinguistics courses while also offering new insights on the literary texts.

The goals of the revised Spanish curriculum include promoting students' critical understanding of social inequities linked to language and fostering student agency regarding how ideologies might be actively resisted and transformed. Critical perspectives on language in both linguistics and literature classes have great valence for our students, in part because many of them have personal experience with multilingualism, both in their own families and in their local communities. Many students have intimate, though frequently unexamined, knowledge of the public stigma of speaking a minority language, the overwhelming school pressure to abandon home languages, and the vilification of "nonstandard" language varieties and practices in "foreign" language classrooms, as well as personal experience and recognition of the expressive, social, and creative possibilities of bilingualism.

Early on in our incorporation of the study of language ideologies in the Latin American literature classroom, we noticed that students' personal and intellectual engagement with these issues was accompanied by the desire to resist or transform dominant public discourses on bilingualism in their local communities. In one particularly animated discussion on the lack of school board support for bilingual education and the underfunding of adult courses in English as a second language (ESL), a student expressed hesitancy about how to engage in social action, asking her classmates, "What can we do?" Observing students' enthusiasm for participating in social change, we began to think about how linguistic activism in the local community could become part of their education in Spanish. Since our courses include critical analysis of language ideologies and their political, social, and material consequences, it seemed that critical community-service learning opportunities oriented toward language education and activism would have the most coherence with our academic program. Such opportunities would allow students to use their new knowledge in the way that Paolo Freire proposed: toward social change, in the very communities where they resided (*Education* 37–78). Following a classroom discussion of support for bilingual children's development of biliteracy, several heritage speakers of Spanish proposed starting a Spanish-language book club at a local elementary school. That proposal became the impetus of the Spanish literacy afterschool class for young heritage learners that we describe below.

Critical service-learning proponents stress that to avoid a "charity model" of service, community-based programs must lead students to understand the structural underpinnings of the social problems they seek to address (Marullo; Ochoa and Ochoa; Calderón; Mitchell). As Tania Mitchell points out, faculty members' and students' direct collaboration with community partners toward the democratic solution of problems is paramount (50). Thus, we established partnerships with local schools and a workers' rights organization and sought input from staff members, parents, children, and community residents in the development of three collaborative programs in language activism: an afterschool Spanish class for heritage speakers at a local elementary school, a bilingual book club at a local middle school, and a Spanish literacy and ESL class for day laborers at a workers' rights organization. Our students were primarily responsible for the teaching of these programs, although parents at the elementary school sometimes gave presentations on the cultures of their home countries and labor organizers from the workers' rights organization occasionally spoke on labor issues at the ESL classes.

One challenge that arises when service learning is a course requirement is that some students may not have the interest or availability to engage fully with the project, a limitation that can harm the program as well
as the community participants. For this reason, we offered service learning as an optional credit-bearing internship rather than as a requirement
of the literature course, and students who participated in service learning
shared their experiences with other students both inside and outside the
literature classroom. The internship required forty hours a semester of on-
site teaching or lesson planning in accordance with national standards
for internships. In addition, students were assigned readings on theoretical and practical issues related to the specific site where they were teaching: bilingual education and heritage language for the elementary school
class, literacy and social justice for the book club, and popular education
and bilingual ESL for the day laborers' class.

Faculty members met regularly with interns on campus and at the
project sites. We used blogs and wikis to direct discussion of the readings,
lesson plans, community activities, and connections to course work, and
we encouraged interns to share teaching and classroom management
strategies online.[2] The remainder of this chapter describes the reciprocal
relation of students' critical interrogation of language in literature courses
and their language activism. In each section, we describe a unit of a survey
course on Latin American literature from the colonial to the contemporary periods, underlining how critical perspectives on language were first
integrated as discrete themes in students' analysis of literary texts—such
as multilingualism in the colonial period, language variation in the independence and modern periods, and language hybridity in the contemporary one—and then reinforced by critical service learning in the community. We wish to stress here that these themes were exclusive neither to
discrete periods of literary study nor to discrete activist programs; indeed,
they were woven continually throughout the survey class and the service-
learning projects. What follows is merely an attempt to show some ways
that these three modules of literary study, the study of language ideologies, and critical service learning can be successfully integrated.

Multilingualism and Diglossia in Texts and Community

The first unit of the Latin American literature course focuses on the colonial era. Produced within the Spanish historical conquest and colonization that displaced, destroyed, and discriminated against indigenous and

African populations in the New World, colonial texts frequently contain multiple, competing discourses of different ethnic communities. Examining the diverse languages, language varieties, and belief systems in colonial texts offers students a rich opportunity to grasp the Bakhtinian notion of literature's possibilities for the representation of heterogeneous discourses. Students' community-based work with speakers of indigenous languages reinforces this facet of their literary study.

Central to this unit is a historical chronicle written by an indigenous noble from Peru in the seventeenth century, Felipe Guaman Poma de Ayala's *El primer nueva corónica y buen gobierno* (1615; "The First New Chronicle and Good Government"), a protestation to King Philip III of Spain on the horrific treatment of the Andean peoples under Spanish colonization and a defense of their right to self-rule. Guaman Poma's manuscript, written in a combination of Spanish, Quechua, and Latin, provides a context for students to explore literature's potential for containing heterogeneous and competing discourses as well as to reflect on multilingualism in local Latin American immigrant communities.[3] The participation of some students in the critical service-learning programs enhanced the classroom discussions for everyone; interns in the heritage speakers' afterschool class, for example, shared with their classmates that several children from Bolivia spoke Quechua, and interns in the day laborers' ESL class spoke about the array of Guatemalan indigenous languages spoken on the day laborers' corner, with Spanish used as a lingua franca. The bi-, tri-, and even quadrilingualism of many Central American immigrants underscored the ideological basis of both the widespread trope of immigrants unable or unwilling to learn new languages and the triumphalist myth of Spanish as universal language that rapidly replaced indigenous languages during the colonial period (see Kamen).

Guaman Poma's text came to bear on the multilingual environment in which interns worked. From their readings and online discussions, the interns in the heritage learners' afterschool class had learned that the incorporation of children's home experiences into the classroom is linked with academic success (Moll), and they recognized the political as well as social implications of their work with young children. In an afterschool session dedicated to minority languages in Latin America, the intern leading the lesson asked if any of the children spoke languages other than Spanish and English. When a little girl from Cochabamba, Bolivia, volunteered that she spoke Quechua, the intern encouraged her to teach the class several words in that language. Remarking on the girl's delight and pride at sharing her heritage with the class, another intern suggested that the recognition and promotion of the child's home language might lead to a more positive engagement with school. Another student commented on the class blog how surprised she was by the little girl's knowledge of Quechua. Interns' service-learning experience helped all students (whether they taught in the program or heard about it from their classmates) recognize and destabilize the erasure of indigenous languages from the Spanish curriculum as well as from broader representations of Latin America.

Interns' personal experience with multilingual speakers in various community projects also enlivened their discussions of Guaman Poma. Grace, for example, who taught in the day laborers' ESL class, drew a parallel between language ideologies and educational policies in the United States and Latin America, pointing out that the ESL class, which was taught in Spanish, did not address the historical subordination of indigenous languages. She explained how the devaluing of indigenous languages in Central America had contributed to low educational attainment and Spanish literacy among the day laborers, which, in turn, made learning English even more challenging for them.[4] Ethan added that these challenges inhibited day laborers' educational opportunities and sense of agency. He spoke eloquently of the need for ESL curricula to be sensitive to the multilingualism and low literacy rates of Latin American immigrants.

Language, Literacy, and Nation Building

The second unit of the Latin American literature course focuses on the period of Latin American independence and nation building from 1812 to 1930 and includes critical theoretical work on writing and nation building such as Anderson's classic analysis of the relation of print culture to the national imaginary in *Imagined Communities*, Sommer's treatment of "foundational fictions," and Guillory's scrutiny of literacy ideologies underlying the study of literature in *Cultural Capital*. Two "foundational fictions" anchor this unit: *Facundo: Civilización y barbarie* (1845), by the Argentinian Domingo Faustino Sarmiento, and *Doña Bárbara* (1929), by Rómulo Gallegos of Venezuela. Literature students reflect on Sarmiento's and Gallegos's employment of the artifacts and practices of written culture, such as education, literacy, and the legal code, as central motifs in these nation-building texts, and they examine the construction of rural varieties of Spanish.

Interns in the bilingual book club drew parallels with how minority language speakers are disempowered in schools in the United States and expressed their desire to address these inequities by valuing the young learners' language varieties and practices. Interns encouraged the children to voice their opinions on literary readings, as well as to create texts like hip-hop songs, graffiti murals, and short stories, without focusing on "correct" usage. One intern, Madeleine, verbalized the relation of linguistic acceptance, educational achievement, and social justice on the class blog: "If every educator would discuss the use of English and the power of the way we express language and put aside the importance of meeting a standard, then . . . every child—wealthy or poor, male or female, black or white (or Hispanic or Asian)—would meet a standard, or rather a goal to reach their maximum potential." One highlight of the book club was the children's creation of a school Web page with original stories that heritage learners based in part on legends they had heard in their families' home countries; this project provided a means for the children to value their families' cultures within literacy lessons. Claire, another intern, pointed out that this and other book club activities elevated the children's unique cultural knowledge and improved their feelings of self-worth—an increasingly rare phenomenon in our age of standardized testing.

Through critical service learning in the middle school book club, interns gained deeper understanding of how educational institutions and policies—such as those buttressed by the "foundational fictions" they read in class—serve to construct various types of literacy as forms of social sorting (Guillory 3–82). Interns then sought to transform these ideologies with literacy modules consistent with children's interests and needs, in which the children were not only able to become critics of literature but also to create literature through their own voices, language varieties, and cultural perspectives. In this way the book club provided all participants, interns and middle school students alike, with a renewed appreciation of the significance of literature and of what Williams has named as literature's capacity to make an active intervention in the social world (309). As the children discovered that they could produce verbal constructions that were valued in the school—songs that could be shared in the hallways, graffiti murals to be shown in the classroom, stories to be published on a school Web site—they came to see how they could develop a public voice even as they continued to maintain their sense of cultural and personal identity. Madeleine encapsulated the club's social accomplishments in the following commentary:

> Through the past twelve weeks of the [book club], I have noticed that the youth have become much more confident in their abilities as well as in their overall personal identity. . . . As we [interns] have provided them with visual, written, and oral texts that they can relate to, they have progressed [at] a very impressive rate in their abilities to think for themselves and to have a constructive debate.

Language and Identity: From Nationalism to Hybridity

In the final unit of the course, which concerns the modern and contemporary periods, students expand on the examination of reified notions of national identity and the one-to-one relation of nation and language. They consider how these ideologies have evolved in the 1960s and 1970s Boom literature of Carlos Fuentes, Gabriel García Márquez, and Mario Vargas Llosa (see Levinson) and then read twenty-first-century transnational and bilingual novels like Roberto Bolaños's *2666*, Sandra Cisneros's *Caramelo*, and Junot Díaz's *The Brief Wondrous Life of Oscar Wao*.

Heritage speakers of Spanish contributed significantly to discussions on hybridity, identifying with Cisneros's descriptions of feeling "in-between" anglophone and Spanish-speaking cultures in the United States and Mexico. One student, Natalia, spoke of attending schools in the United States where her bilingualism had positioned her as a "deficient" speaker of English, an identity she understood as not "sufficiently American." Another student, Gabriela, an immigrant from Venezuela, said that on summer visits to her home country, family members made fun of her Spanish, which they deemed not suitably "authentic." When they worked in the community projects, heritage speakers increasingly saw hybrid linguistic practices and identities as something positive that could enrich their daily lives as well as their interactions with family, community members, and other multilingual groups. Santiago, a heritage speaker who taught ESL to day laborers, wrote in a class journal that his community work had allowed him for the first time to see the value of his bilingualism for connecting with the local immigrant population. Another student, Luz, a bilingual mother of two children, wrote in a final assessment that the program had cemented her commitment to speaking in Spanish to her children so that they could be bilingual and had inspired her to become a bilingual education teacher. Their literary study of hybrid identities and their community work helped these students gain the means to visualize a wider and more inclusive community, where bonds were forged across different generations, countries of origin, ethnicities, and genders. This view served as a counterpoint to contemporary discourses that frame Spanish language maintenance and learning as a commodified skill to be deployed on the job market or for the national interest (Leeman, "Value"; Leeman and Martínez; Pomerantz); it also enriched the curriculum.

Literature's role as a purveyor of multiple discourses, as a representation of language ideologies, and as a stimulator of students' affective connections with critical analysis of language is central in our Latin American literature courses. Critical understanding of language ideologies strengthened in literary study can be brought into play in students' work as language activists in local contexts—work that contributes to the greater public good in its democratic and collaborative nature, cultural inclusiveness, and commitment to social justice.

One indication of the impact of the critical service-learning programs on interns' consciousness is the striking number who have gone on to pursue further work in social justice and language education after graduation. Of the fifty-two interns, at least eight have become public school teachers in bilingual education or Spanish, one has worked with AmeriCorps, another is an assistant director of a local day laborers' organization, another is pursuing international work in urban planning and social justice, and another, Noah, now works in the favelas of Río de Janeiro and is planning a career in grassroots or not-for-profit organizations. Noah, who taught in the day laborers' ESL class, came back to Mason recently and gave a guest lecture in a Spanish class on his experience in Brazil. He said that his work teaching day laborers had radically changed the way that he viewed himself as a speaker of Spanish; previously he had felt his language abilities were limited to the classroom, but the activist project showed him how his Spanish could have an immediate and significant effect on breaching class and ethnic boundaries with the day laborers, several of whom were close to his age, in turn giving them new perspectives on their social world. This experience had made him feel like a social actor in the world, an identity he now fully embraced in his career.

Student activists bring their community work back to the literature classroom to illuminate and enliven the literary texts, where older stories of men and women in history like the multilingual Guaman Poma, the rural characters speaking local language variations in *Facundo* and *Doña Bárbara,* and the code-switching protagonists in *Caramelo* and *The Brief Wondrous Life of Oscar Wao* resonate with those of real-life men, women, and children that they have come to know. In this way, literary texts can have some bearing on the work of social change.

Although the projects described here were created for students of Spanish and arose out of the Latin American literature class, the language ideologies that students engaged with—attitudes toward regional language varieties and notions of literacy as cultural capital and nation building—are broadly representative of the kinds of themes that literature professors who wish to incorporate critical perspectives on language or implement critical service learning can look for in other national or global literatures.

NOTES

1. George Mason is a large, ethnically, racially, and linguistically diverse public university in Fairfax, Virginia, in the suburbs of Washington, DC. Twelve percent of students in the university's College of Humanities and Social Sciences self-identify as Hispanic ("Official Student Enrollment").

2. See Leeman, Rabin, and Román-Mendoza, "Critical Pedagogy," for a full discussion of the theoretical framework and logistics of the community-based activities; Leeman, Rabin, and Román-Mendoza, "La Web 2.0," provides details on the use of online technologies.

3. See Leeman and Rabin for an examination of the language ideologies in this text and suggestions for classroom activities.

4. Higher levels of first-language literacy have been shown to be advantageous to adult learners in the acquisition of English (Bigelow, Delmas, Hansen, and Tarone). Many immigrants to the United States (including those from Latin America) since the 1990s have been determined to have low literacy rates in their native language (Fix, Passel, and Sucher; Wrigley and Powrie).

Part III

Service Learning in Creative Nonfiction and Memoir

Kristina Lucenko

Generation(s) of Narratives:
Life Writing and Digital Storytelling

In her essay "Memory and Imagination," Patricia Hampl argues that the work of the memoirist is to conjure resonant images from a personal past and transform them into stories that explore "profound matters" such as "life and death, . . . love, despair, loss, and innocence" (788). These enduring human concerns are what connect us, and we talk with one another about them by sharing our personal life stories. But just as the memoirist must humbly acknowledge the limits of point of view, the reader must recognize the complexity of truth in autobiographical narrative. A life story can be both factual and conditional, both recalled and fashioned. Further, in Hampl's view, autobiography is an affective, ethical, and social act, not a self-absorbed pastime:

> [It is] a personal confirmation of selfhood, and therefore the first step toward ethical development. To write one's life is to live it twice, and the second living is both spiritual and historical, for a memoir reaches deep within the personality as it seeks its narrative form and it also grasps the life-of-the-times as no political analysis can. (791)

In this interpretation, memoir is a critical, creative, and collective exercise in truth seeking.

Hampl's essay acutely illustrates key concepts in autobiography theory, such as memory, authority, experience, subjectivity, history, and self-representation, as well as the ethical value of literature and literary studies. Life Writing and Storytelling is a 200-level seminar in the Honors College at Stony Brook University, on Long Island, that introduces students to theoretical approaches to autobiographical practice, innovative forms of life narrative, and the ethical and social aspects of autobiographical acts. In this course, I ask students to consider these concepts both in the classroom and through a community-based learning partnership with Stony Brook's chapter of the Osher Lifelong Learning Institute (OLLI), an enrichment program for retired community members. This four-week, collaborative, intergenerational life writing workshop reveals for students the real-world applications of critical concepts we analyze in course readings. We explore, for example, how autobiographical subjects interpret and reinterpret their experiential histories or how autobiographical writing is a communicative representation shaped in part by memory and narrative choices and thus does not hold one stable truth. The workshop culminates in a digital storytelling project that students and OLLI members create together.

A learning objective of the course is to complicate the notion that autobiography is simple and transparent—a straightforward recollection of facts of a life. Students become aware that self-reflexive narrative is a complex, multipart act in which a subject's memory and experience are transformed into art and then interpreted and assessed by an audience. Through the literary texts we examine, students see that autobiography is at once provisional and unstable and that it articulates enduring themes that underscore our common humanity. As readers, students develop interpretive skills and a deeper understanding of autobiography's cognitive, emotional, aesthetic, and moral value. I want students to consider how autobiography as a genre particularly relies on a reciprocal relationship between writer and reader: the writer's authority influences the reader's assessment of the story, and the reader's historical position affects the way the story is interpreted.

Linking service learning to autobiography studies foregrounds this important and ever-shifting relationship between readers and narrators. In an intergenerational writing workshop, the classroom becomes, both literally and figuratively, an intersubjective discursive space where readers and writers come together to make meaning. This collective meaning-making enterprise highlights relationships and binds together communities and echoes the benefits of service learning, especially its reciprocity. Thus the course's multimodal, multigenerational, experiential project is the creative materialization of that shared dialogic space, a reflective and critical exercise, an artistic and ethical practice, and a community-building activity.

Life Writing and Storytelling is an interdisciplinary seminar that is part of Stony Brook's Honors College core liberal arts curriculum. Students do a good deal of reading, analysis, and critical writing, and the seminar format emphasizes discussion and participation. The students in this course are mostly premed or science majors and are motivated and high-achieving. To draw on students' disciplinary strengths and interests and to explore the interconnections of literature and medicine, I assign literary and cultural texts on health, illness, disabilities, and healing. We read personal narratives of patients, doctors, and family members and also listen to several podcasts of the National Public Radio program *Radiolab*, hosted by Jad Abumrad and Robert Krulwich. These different modes highlight key elements of narrative (plot, time, space, character, vocalization) used to shape life experiences into stories, both written and spoken, and offer students a multiplicity of human experiences, perceptions, and beliefs about health.

Sidonie Smith and Julia Watson's *Reading Autobiography* serves as a critical introduction to the course, and assigned memoirs include Jean-Dominique Bauby's *The Diving Bell and the Butterfly*, Alison Bechdel's *Fun Home*, Edwidge Danticat's *Brother, I'm Dying*, Barbara Ehrenreich's "Welcome to Cancerland," Brian Fies's *Mom's Cancer*, and Lucy Grealy's *Autobiography of a Face*. Marshall Gregory's *Shaped by Stories: The Ethical Power of Narratives* provides a critical framework for OLLI sessions. In the context of reading or hearing a range of literary forms — from digital stories to memoir to graphic narratives — students analyze a rich cross-section of life narratives and consider what these texts can teach them in their own writing practices. Course work includes extensive journal writing, two analysis essays of 1,500–2,000 words each, the OLLI collaborative project, and a final project or presentation. The OLLI workshop happens around week 10 of our fifteen-week semester. By the time students begin the experiential portion of the course, they are well steeped in the critical language and concepts of life narrative.

The role of students in our four-week workshop with OLLI is twofold: they participate by writing their own brief autobiographical texts in response to a series of in-class writing prompts and by responding to the work of others, and they facilitate the creation of the digital narrative for the OLLI members by managing data collection, storyboarding, audio recording their partner, and producing the digital project. Two instructional sessions (a library session on general resources and a media lab session on audio recording) provide students with guidance about the technology used to create digital narratives. Digital stories can be simply defined as narration with digital technologies (i.e., a combination of spoken word, music or sound effects, and images to narrate a story in a short video). Bryan Alexander sees digital storytelling as a tool for understanding, curating, and presenting complex information, and subjects can range from personal stories to historical events to scientific ideas (215). The educational uses of digital storytelling have grown over time, from digital storytelling assignments to entire courses to community-outreach initiatives to bachelor's and master's programs in digital storytelling. Some notable examples of pedagogical and practical resources for digital storytelling include Alexander's *The New Digital Storytelling: Creating Narratives with New Media*, Georgetown University's *Digital Storytelling Multimedia Archive* (Oppermann and Coventry), University of Houston's *The Educational Uses of Digital Storytelling* (Robin), and Stony Brook University Libraries' *Digital Storytelling: Research and Subject Guide* (Chase).

The first two weeks of the semester begin with broad definitions, distinctions, and traditions. Using Smith and Watson's useful critical introduction, we outline the relation of self-referential writings such as memoir, biography, and history to the truth status of autobiography. During these early weeks we also read Anne Hunsaker Hawkins on pathography as a subgenre or form of autobiography that focuses on personal illness and treatment and again consider the role of the truth in self-narration. Hawkins argues that in stories about illness, feelings are especially heightened, memories imperfect, and meanings given in reflection that are only latent in the moment. And, finally, to get students thinking about the everyday uses and role of self-referential narrative, we read Jerome Bruner's brief yet influential 1987 essay "Life as Narrative," which explores the relation of lived experience and narrative, between how we each "live time" and how we recount or self-report the events of our lives. These various theoretical texts provide students with an interpretive lens and a vocabulary they can use to engage critically with the literary texts that will make up the bulk of the semester's work and with the memoirs of the OLLI members.

Closer to our OLLI session we read Danticat's *Brother, I'm Dying*, which provides students with an opportunity to examine mutuality, history, and memory in life narrative, concepts that are particularly relevant to the OLLI collaboration. The memoir traces the intertwined stories of Danticat, her father, and her uncle and takes place in both Haiti and New York. In class we observed places in the text where Danticat's authorial voice foregrounds her role as family storyteller and discussed the ethical and artistic responsibilities of telling another person's story. At the end of the first chapter, for example, Danticat writes, "This is an attempt at cohesiveness, and at re-creating a few wondrous and terrible months when their lives and mine intersected in startling ways, forcing me to look forward and back at the same time" (26). Students can see that life writing is an interpretative and provisional practice in which subjects employ memories and experiences, often in an attempt to assert agency. In an essay analyzing the text, one student, Hannah, identified Danticat's text as a constructed assemblage, noting specifically her use of transcripts from Krome Service Processing Center, where her uncle was detained and subsequently died. This student observed that the memoir was a "merging of various truths, a recorded truth and a personal truth as [Danticat] questions the immigration policies of the United States." Hannah then noted that Danticat's strategic use of historical documents "ensures the reader of the validity of her story as much as possible while refusing to relinquish her beliefs of what must have been true," despite her lack of firsthand evidence. We discussed Danticat's interpretive agency and tactical use of evidence and considered what was at stake for Danticat and for the reader in accepting her narrative as "truth," both as a personal memoir and as a historical document of Haiti's repressive government and United States immigration policy.

Danticat's political critique illustrated for students memoir's ethical dimensions and the importance of trust and goodwill between readers and writers. As students began to anticipate the partnerships they would form with OLLI members, the stories that they might hear, and the critical and ethical analyses that they would exercise in the workshop, they wondered if they were up to the challenge. One student, Jeremy, wrote in his journal, "I'm just scared that what I make will be a poor, poor substitute for what could have been and what [my OLLI partner] was expecting. . . . I only hope I can do the story justice." Jeremy is recognizing the difference between what happened (the experience and the memory of an event) and "what I make," which is the art and craft of personal narrative. Part of this recognition is the contingency of storytelling, which means asking the questions, What do I include? What do I leave out? Is it ethical? Am I being true to the story? Collaborating on an autobiographical project with a person from another generation allows students to see the complexity of autobiographical truth—that it is real and fashioned, transformed but not transparent.

In preparation for the first OLLI session, I ask students to post a series of writing prompts for our workshop to our university's course management system. In future workshops, I will also invite OLLI members to post writing prompts to emphasize from the start our work together as participatory and shared. Students generate prompts about important memories and formative experiences. Some ask writers to describe a memorable place, a conflict they had with a parent, or the worst advice ever received (we learned that bad advice is ever present). The initial meeting between students and OLLI members consists of a round of introduction, writing prompts, and a round of sharing favorite in-class writings. Like their undergraduate counterparts, OLLI members are highly motivated, and they are very strong readers and writers. Unlike the undergraduates, however, who to some extent see the writing classroom as compulsory, OLLI members participate in the workshop because they enjoy writing and want to work with and learn from students. This self-directed ethos shows students that learning is not just something that we do for a degree and then stop; it shows students that writing is a sustained, lifelong practice that hones our interpretive imaginations, is a form of introspection, and allows us to connect to others. In their journal entries, several students wrote about coming to a new understanding of learning as "life-wide." Students noted that "it is easy to forget that life extends beyond college and that college is just one stage of my life" and that the experience is an inspiration to "keep learning."

While students are working with their OLLI partners, we return to the idea of autobiographical truth as a negotiation between the writer and reader. Students often commented on the narrative and editorial choices they made as they gathered a range of artifacts—photos, textual documents, artwork—to tell their partner's digital story. Fatimah, for instance, noted how narrative choices can shape the "truth" of the story:

> The first thing I noticed . . . was that [my partner] . . . had two copies of the same story but told differently because she focused on a different angle for each one—one told the story of how she met her husband in a way that put it in context with the rest of her life while the other version focused more directly on how she met her husband. . . . The fact that she had two versions shows how different narrative can be depending on the way you remember the past and your present situation.

Students referred back to texts we read earlier in the semester, such as *Brother, I'm Dying*. They saw, for example, that Danticat's metacommentary on her writing process paralleled their own understanding of their partners' narrative process and was similar to the editorial choices they made in the collaboration. In bringing together literary analysis and service learning, students recognize the complexity of autobiographical truth and subjectivity and the polyvocality of narrating subjects.

OLLI's National Resource Center at the University of Southern Maine collaborates with the university's Life Story Commons, a resource for intergenerational storytelling programming. A shared goal of OLLI and Life Story Commons is to encourage "dialogue that examines the benefits of storytelling and personal narratives while also exploring questions of growth and change across the life cycle, the passage of tradition across generations, and the making of meaning across time" ("About the Life Story Commons"). Coincidentally and fortuitously, these goals converge with both the curricular goals of the course and the State University of New York's strategic plan to promote a "seamless education pipeline" in New York State ("Power of SUNY"). An underlying principle of an education pipeline is the link between generations—most notably, the ongoing flow of learning and the importance of intergenerational mentoring. In composing and sharing life narratives in the university classroom, young and old participants can experience the manifestation of the word *generation* as age group(s) and as a productive site of writing and renewal. In a postworkshop evaluation, one OLLI member, a retired high school English teacher, wrote:

> I loved being with the young people; that they were intelligent, articulate, and receptive to our sessions with them was just an added bonus. The writing prompts were fun—I am pursuing my general interest in writing and this gave me practice. For so many years I edited and corrected student work, now it is time to write for myself!

At the same time, the OLLI members served as important mentors, sharing valuable lessons with students. In a journal entry, Jia wrote about her partner, who returned to college to pursue a bachelor's degree as a single mother of two young children:

> She felt like giving up so many times because it was so difficult to manage a family, a house, a budget, and college at the same time. Yet it was her teenage son who gave her the motivation to keep going. . . . He told her that she got them this far, and she would get them the rest of the way, because he believed in her.

Reflecting on her partner's story, Jia wrote, "She is such a strong, independent woman who . . . gives me the motivation to do something with my own life that I can look back on, like she does, with wonder, happiness, and fulfillment." The reciprocal benefits of mentorship are clear.

At the same time that students are introduced to learning as a holistic, lifelong process, both young and old learn about new media as a mode and context for autobiographical narratives. We discuss in some detail the two tracks of meaning in this project—the auditory and the visual; doing so allows the group not only to understand composition methods in a new way but also to reconsider the meaning and use of a range of communicative forms, from text to photographs to video to sound, in telling stories about themselves and others. One OLLI member, an addiction psychiatrist, created a digital story about being honored with the Knight's Cross of the Order of the Icelandic Falcon. She wrote this about the workshop:

> Before I joined this class, a memoir was always a written essay. . . . I can now appreciate the value of using audiovisual techniques. [My student partner] motivated me to dig for photos and souvenirs of my experiences in Iceland. . . . [My partner also] decided to make use of my drawings and a couple of paintings as part of the memoir. The resulting video was enriched by that decision. It was quite an enlightening process for me, and an enjoyable one.

Through this creative collaboration, OLLI members explore a new art form for their life stories. At the same time, the ethical responsibilities of collaboration become real concerns for students. This OLLI member's student partner, Beth, expressed some anxiety about her role as editor-producer:

> Every bit of [the digital story] was important to her and was carefully constructed by her. Who was I to ask her to edit out sentences, phrases, and images? It is difficult having to edit something so personal; it feels like telling a person that a certain aspect is not important, when just the opposite is true.

Playing several roles in the project—editor, collaborator, and reader—gives students an intimate view of the complicated ethical issues involved in assembling and organizing life narratives.

The OLLI members' stories were quite remarkable and illustrated for students the idea that we are each historical: one member recounted her experience as a woman in the United States Air Force in the 1950s;

another told about learning as an adult that his mother had died giving birth to him, right before the family emigrated to Israel to escape Hitler's regime, and that the woman who he believed was his mother was actually his stepmother; another, a retired teacher, described the room she recently created in her home, a space where she now has the freedom to write. These deeply personal narratives taught students the importance of memory, of not only describing what happened but also explaining why it matters. As Hampl states, "in the act of remembering, the personal environment expands, resonates beyond itself, beyond its 'subject,' into the endless and tragic recollection that is history" (790).

In a postworkshop assessment, one student, Oona, noted that she now understood "the importance of storytelling not only to share with others but always for oneself, to understand that we can either let our memories shape us or shape our memories as we develop new insights." Oona wrote, "Since many of [the OLLI] stories were from a while ago the writers also incorporated a lot of reflection and had a positive outlook on things that were hardships during the time." Another student, LJ, remarked, "I realized that we all have unique life experiences, but in order to transform them into fluid autobiographies we must find an underlying theme or message that links them all together. Readers must be able to relate to this message and/or be inspired by it." Students recognize the twofold mission of autobiography: to vividly narrate an experience as it was lived while also analyzing the experience's meaning. And as students develop these analytic skills, they can see the ongoing value of literary interpretation as they continue to find meaning in their own lives and in the community in which they live.

Although many of these digital projects were outstanding, it is important to recognize the challenges of assigning a digital storytelling project. Students must devote significant time both to learning numerous software applications and to creating, assembling, and editing multimedia files. Teachers must have clear assessment criteria in place. Furthermore, course work must cover copyright and compliance, fair use, and Creative Commons licenses within complex and rapidly changing digital media environments (see Seiter and Seiter).

My experience with service-learning writing workshops at Stony Brook University has shown me that students are eager for ways to enrich their educational experience and connect with people off the traditional pathways of their studies. A digital storytelling service-learning project that explores personal narratives of students and community members who make up the education pipeline in New York State—learners at all life stages—can offer another perspective on the idiosyncrasy and expansiveness of learning and literacy, of modern information ecosystems, and of the creation of literary narratives from real-life experiences. In addition to illustrating critical definitions and concepts through interpersonal interactions, intergenerational programs in higher education strengthen learning communities, as students begin to see education—and autobiographical narrative—as a meaningful lifelong practice.

Kathleen Béres Rogers

"The Boldness of Imagination": Illness Narratives outside the Classroom

As we pushed the screen door open, [my partner] glanced back at me with an unsure face. We gazed upon the sight of Mr. P, lying on his bed with his shirt rolled up, exposing an enormously bloated stomach completely unproportional to his twig size legs and arms. A tube was attached to his stomach that was used to give him medicine while he stayed in the hospital. [My partner, the hospice worker, and] I all grabbed a seat around Mr. P lying in his bed and asked how he was feeling. I felt uneasy. . . . I remember at first truly having to hold back tears. I am not one to cry easily, so I feel as though being in such a new experience, overwhelming and not what I expected, caught me in the moment. Although it may sound like the situation could be sketchy, I would never want to trade my situation. Talking to Mr. P has made me realize so much of something I had never really thought about. The way our world works, treating the less fortunate with the least efficiency of healthcare.

This journal entry, written by one of the students in our First-Year Experience learning community Healing Narratives: Understanding Illness through Storytelling, attests to one of the ways in which narrative, whether oral or written, can be used by students to imaginatively enter into another's real-life experience.[1] Rita Charon, the founder of what has now arguably become a narrative medicine movement, writes that "telling stories, listening to them, being moved by them, are recognized to be at the heart of many of our efforts to find, make, and honor meaning in our lives and the lives of others" (11). In her 2006 *Narrative Medicine: Honoring the Stories of Illness*, Charon argues that medicine practiced with "narrative competency" allows practitioners to understand how patients conceive of their stories and how these stories, in turn, allow patients to make sense of their experiences (107). Charon stresses the notion of personhood, what she calls "singularity" (46). Simply put, every story is singular and unique, and generic conventions simply help us code it as a story.

Whereas these stories are individual, Arthur W. Frank's equally influential *The Wounded Storyteller* argues that they can be broken down into three types. The first type, the one advocated by pharmaceutical advertisements and hospital pamphlets, is the "restitution narrative." The plot of the restitution has this basic storyline: "Yesterday I was healthy, today I'm sick, but tomorrow I'll be healthy again" (77). In conjunction with the restitution narrative is the "quest story," in which illness teaches the protagonist something integral to her or his life quest (115). The most problematic type of illness narrative, according to Frank, is the "chaos narrative," in which life is chaotic and illness is never resolved. Understandably, in our Western culture, "chaos stories are as anxiety provoking as restitution stories are preferred" (97).

Yet it is the chaos narrative, the most "anxiety provoking" form, that, I argue, prompts us to consider illness narratives not in terms of their form but in terms of their function: as a means of social action. This approach, recently considered in narrative theory, allows us to reconcile tensions between Frank's formalism and Charon's emphasis on singularity. Read in this way, genre becomes a form of social action, connecting the individual concerns of the writer with his or her reading pubic. Carolyn Miller famously argued that "a genre [connects] . . . the private with the public, the singular with the recurrent" (163). A chaos narrative, for instance, would connect the private, here a narrator's sense of discomfort and depression, with the public, embodied in the idea of this chaotic series of emotions being labeled as an illness narrative. By viewing their stories as not only individualistic but also recurrent, people begin to feel that illness, an often uncontrollable event, can be both cathartic and active.

Often, the individualism of these stories forces their readers to engage differently with their communities. As Charon writes, "The boldness of imagination is the courage to relinquish one's own coherent experience of the world for another's unexplored, unplumbed, potentially volatile viewpoint" (112). These volatile viewpoints are what lend a voice to social critique and often form the impetus for change.

In the journal entry quoted at the beginning of this essay, my student, Laura, struggles with an "unexplored" viewpoint: one that is culturally and politically other and, therefore, volatile.[2] Mr. P.'s narrative is affected by, in Laura's words, "what he had been through": unable to afford a liver transplant, this man waits for death, losing trust in close friends as well as the American health-care system, what Laura refers to as the "least efficiency of healthcare." Embedded in this small scenario are discourses of race (Mr. P. is African American), socioeconomic class, space (the "sketchy" area of town in which Mr. P. has to live), and social justice (the imbalance in the American health-care system that puts the poor at a disadvantage). Laura is overwhelmed and uncomfortable as she deals with a different perception of the world, one outside her previous realm of experience.

This example illustrates how stories from the surrounding communities push students to question their internalized expectations of illness and the narratives that portray it. Through their socialization, students have been subject to an "unconscious modeling of . . . specific narratives upon master narratives in the culture" (Rimmon-Kenan 15). Most of these "master narratives" are restitution or quest narratives, so what would happen if we allowed students to hear authentic, often chaotic stories?

To answer this question, students in my Healing Narratives class, in pairs, listened to and documented such community stories, producing the narratives that they individually analyzed in the context of the literature we read. Our elders also took an active part in the storytelling process by acting as editors. Just as Charon, among others, thinks it crucial for the patient to contribute to his or her own "parallel chart" (157), students found it powerful to have elders or caretakers read over their narratives. This not only enabled the elders to have a voice in their stories but also allowed for grammatical and linguistic critique, ceding some of the power in the relationship from the academy to the community. For instance, in her journal entry, Jennifer writes that her resident, who continues to write poetry and submits writing to the local newspaper, "really is looking forward to editing my paper, and giving me tips to improve my writing."

In this class combining civic engagement and memoir, the service-learning component both helped students draw connections between real life and the stories they read and allowed them to grapple with the realities and social issues of residents' chaotic narratives, lending credence to the notion of genre as social action. Over and over again, students referred to the memoirs we read as they wrote journal entries about their service-learning experiences and participated in class discussions. Conversely, they discussed their community members' experiences as they attempted to make sense of the published memoirs we read in class. Specifically, students used the elements of literary analysis—in particular, an understanding of genre and point of view—to become more nuanced readers of both published memoir and community illness narrative; gained insights about diversity, including issues of gender, class, race, socioeconomic status, physical disability, and, of course, age; and became active agents in their new communities, deepening their understanding of the politics of social justice. They evidenced their learning through journal entries, a final paper, and a presentation that considered their elders' stories within the prescribed genre of illness narrative, asking questions of that genre and its social work.

When I initially designed this course, I sought medical patients who would tell their stories. Because of HIPAA laws and because time spent by patients in a hospital is limited, I ended up working with two hospice organizations that served predominantly low-income elders in their own homes but sometimes worked in more socioeconomically advantaged nursing home settings. In each subsequent offering of the course—begun in fall 2009—we became more intentional about the diversity of our service partners. To the two hospice organizations, we added a modified-rent elderly residential community with residents representing many races and cultures and an extremely wealthy, almost exclusively white, senior community. Our two constants were age and chronic illness, with most of the patients or residents being at least seventy-five years old.[3]

As patients and elders put their experiences into words, they became stories. If the self is a collection of stories, then this activity enabled elders, as well as the family members and organizations reading the stories, to narrate and form a coherent idea of subjectivity. At the course's conclusion, students gave copies of this narrative to family members and to our community organizations. According to Dana Madanski, the manager of volunteer services at Odyssey Hospice, Charleston, "It appears that hospice patients feel empowered to share their stories with the younger generation. Patients are often identified by their general illness, not their personal health story, and through the use of healing narratives, a patient becomes a person."

Acting and Inventing Genre

To work with the elders' stories, students needed to understand the illness narrative, a new and increasingly ambiguous genre, and to analyze how people's words, space, and bodies tell their stories.

With this in mind, I provided students with models of illness narratives to read, analyze, and juxtapose with their residents' stories. One of the most frequently mentioned early texts, Frances Burney's 1811 letter to her sister, Esther, describes the process of a mastectomy without anesthesia in a graphic manner. This is, in many ways, a straightforward restitution narrative: Burney is diagnosed, undergoes an incredibly painful surgery, and lives to write about it. When conceived of under the rubric of genre as social action, however, the tale is not as straightforward; she expresses that even nine months after the incident, "I have a headache from going on with the account! & this miserable account, which I began 3 Months ago, at least, I dare not revise, nor read, the recollection is still so painful." Burney's psychological trauma, occasioned by the abruptness of the surgery and the seeming callousness of the surgeon, works to perform a social action—to critique the eighteenth-century medical establishment (see L. Clark; Epstein; Lang-Peralta; and Simons).

Lauren Kessler also writes for a rhetorical purpose: to change our understanding of Alzheimer's disease. Unlike Burney, however, Kessler writes from a modern caretaker's perspective. Kessler's 2008 *Finding Life in the Land of Alzheimer's* is her quest narrative about her time as a volunteer at an Alzheimer's facility. The experience not only teaches her that these patients are vibrant individuals but also enables her to complete her quest: to come to terms with her mother's death from the illness. Again, by considering the rhetorical function of this quest narrative, we can see that Kessler hopes to effect social change by enlightening her audience about the individuality and vivacity of Alzheimer's patients. Sally Brampton's 2008 *Shoot the Damn Dog* is a relatively straightforward restitution narrative that narrates her journey through debilitating, incurable depression. It also functions rhetorically as social critique: Brampton undergoes trauma due to her disease as well as to society's misunderstandings of depression. This part of her narrative is left for us, the readers, to resolve and act on.

Kessler and Brampton's books are what Anis Bawarshi would call "imitative" ("Genres" 84), in that they imitate the more socially condoned genre conventions by fitting into the genres of the restitution narrative (Brampton) or the quest narrative (Kessler) with which readers are more comfortable. In this sense, the two texts fit the generic conventions of American autobiographies, which "have comic (in the cosmic sense) masterplots that validate the movements that enabled them to speak— testaments to endurance, survival, triumphs over adversity" (Bloom 153). Burney, for instance, miraculously recovers from her surgery; Kessler learns to understand her mother's Alzheimer's and resolves her feelings toward her; and Brampton conquers her depression and returns to living a productive life.

The chaos narrative is more difficult both to write and read, but it is represented well in our class readings by Lucy Grealy's 2003 *Autobiography of a Face*. While this memoir does describe an illness, detailing Grealy's struggles with jaw cancer and the resultant facial reconstruction surgeries that forever define her sense of beauty and self, there is no climax, no denouement, and no positive ending (see Brown; Couser; Garden; Mintz; and Todd). When we read Grealy's chaotic *Autobiography*, therefore, students were perplexed by an ending that was not particularly "poetic" and did not testify to "endurance, survival" or any sort of "triumphs over adversity" (Bloom 153). As opposed to Burney's, Brampton's, and Kessler's, Grealy's narrative does not allow for much healing; the author continually undergoes facial reconstructions, deals with depression, and, as we learn in the afterword, dies prematurely at the age of thirty-nine.

While Frank would view Grealy's story as a formalized narrative type— the chaos narrative—one can also perceive it as a process of "invention," which, as Bawarshi writes, "takes place within genres and can be a site of conformity and/or resistance" (*Genre* 46). Although Grealy uses the illness narrative to communicate her critique of our appearance-centered society to her audience, she nonetheless resists the generic conventions of the restitution and quest narratives in her ending, leaving readers as bewildered, confused, and depressed as she undoubtedly felt. By doing so, she knowingly resists audience's optimistic expectations in order to interrogate them. Again, her narrative functions rhetorically to allow readers to critique and intervene in socially accepted norms.

These types of social critiques were replicated in service experiences as students and elders worked together on narratives. While the narratives could be read through Frank's genre categories or Charon's emphasis on singularity, they all shared in common the desire to tell a story, affect readers, and effect some form of social awareness. Formally, they were mostly chaotic: hospice patients would most likely not recover, and elder-care residents ended up with new medical issues to replace the old. These narratives were difficult for students to grasp. In class, we discussed the culturally acceptable notion of narrative and tried to map out how a real-life narrative, with its circles and curves, might look. Here, form, by alerting us to the complex realities of illness, already began to serve a social function. It allowed students to see that neither the individual nor the social aspects of illness are linear or comfortable. Yet because students had to produce printed products, most of which followed a more linear structure, they remain confused about how a nonlinear narrative might look. What would hold these chaotic, often atemporal, narratives together? In asking this question, we experimented with form; students ended up writing journal entries, jumping back and forth in time, or even writing stories from different perspectives.

That these spoken narratives were given the same weight as printed, canonized ones meant that students paid more attention to the social issues inherent in what might otherwise be categorized as elderly ramblings. We discussed the fact that literary and oral texts share remarkable similarities in terms of metaphor, imagery, and figurative language. Instead of setting up literature and oral expression as binaries, students learned to see the literary in everyday language (Hall 32). They saw authors as well as their elders using extended metaphors of battle, precipices, falling, and more to describe what Elaine Scarry has argued are indescribable feelings of pain (43). In addition, my students experienced the ways in which oral stories tend to take on a narrative form; they learned to recognize both spoken and written language as texts.

One of the unifying textual elements students consistently witnessed was a social critique or action of the way(s) in which the ill are objectified. Burney, in her letter, depicts herself as a lone woman covered by a "veil," unacknowledged and dehumanized. Even though the cultural context is very different from modern-day Charleston, students quickly drew parallels between Burney and their assigned residents or patients. Often, people who have undergone an illness will talk about being "abandoned by their doctors, dismissed in their suffering, disbelieved when they describe their symptoms, or objectified by impersonal care" (Charon 21). Whether in 1811 or today, they tell their stories graphically, using a recognizable form to convey their social needs.

Again and again, community members and published authors alike worked with narrative to show how they become identified through their illnesses. As Rosemarie Garland-Thomson puts it, people with illness or disabilities often function "only as visual difference that signals meaning . . . stripped of normalizing contexts and engulfed by a single stigmatic trait" (11). This became clear in our reading of *Finding Life in the Land of Alzheimer's*. As Kessler gets to know the people with whom she works, she begins to experience a "paradigm shift . . . away from disease, disability, and dementia, and toward personhood" (120). Students and I discussed the illness narrative as a way to make this "personhood" clear, to progress toward the individuation on which Charon and other theorists focus.

To achieve this goal, students needed to balance their desire to work within a dominant narrative form with their desire to maintain each person's singularity. In her first journal entry, Mary was worried about getting the story down, about making it a socially condoned restitution or quest narrative: "Every time I felt like I was coming closer on a topic I could write a paper on, the subject was changed. I was more worried about thinking of a paper topic than I was about creating a good relationship with our patient." Worried about completing an assignment and uncomfortable in a nursing home setting, Mary was deeply influenced by a character in *Finding Life in the Land of Alzheimer's*, the irreverent, always funny Alzheimer's patient named Hayes. Therefore, she decided to focus on the iconoclastic use of humor in coping with illness:

> I think my patient uses humor as a way to cope with serious issues or hurtful events that have happened. After a few of these comments, a light bulb went off in my head. I had a flashback to Hayes, a character in Kessler's *Finding Life in the Land of Alzheimer's*. Hayes was one of my favorite characters in this book, and I realized then that I wanted to relate my patient back to Hayes in my paper.

Mary, who entered the class wanting to write the narrative she most often reads or hears, was redirected by Kessler, whose Hayes doesn't have a linear life story; every time we see him in the book, it is through little vignettes and jokes. Mary's final presentation featured many of her patient's jokes and commented on humor as a coping mechanism for illness. By focusing on the patient's unique way of narrating his story through jokes, both the patient and student work here at using the element of humor to make coherent and singular an otherwise jumbled chaos narrative.

Natalie, assigned to the wealthy nursing home, was initially terrified at the thought of talking about illness:

Most people do not scare me, especially elderly people who are in a comfortable, stable environment. Diseases, on the other hand, scare the hell out of me. There are so many different types of illnesses and diseases that can not only be extremely physically destructive, but also emotionally and mentally destructive.

Natalie initially thought of disease as the only element of an illness narrative. Yet in Grealy's book, very few of her pages feature her jaw cancer, and more space is allotted to her human need to appear pretty. Thus her narrative combats restitution and quest narratives by redirecting the focus away from the illness. In her final paper, taking a cue from Grealy, Natalie focused on the elder's need to be perfectly put-together all the time: "She showed us year books from the Citadel and Clemson, neither of which she attended, in which she was in the section titled 'Beauties.' And man, was she beautiful." This resident is now in a wheelchair, but the focus on beauty implicitly critiques our social tendency to define her according to her disability.

At our end-of-semester presentations, students talked about the fact that, like the beauty in the wheelchair, the person they interviewed was ultimately defined not by illness, class, race, gender, or disability but by what Kessler calls "personhood" or by Charon's singularity, which allows us to see beyond form and realize the social action accomplished through the simple communication that patients are individuals. Mr. P., for instance, loves Western movies; another resident enjoys singing, especially "You Are My Sunshine"; yet another writes poetry and stories. In her final paper, Darla wrote:

[My elder] is a person. He is not the guy who has cirrhosis of the liver or the man that has a feeding tube poking out of his stomach, but a real human being. A man that I am honored to have met and a man I respect.

Students learned that an illness narrative is the narrative of life lived in the midst of illness, not necessarily of the illness itself.

Imagining Social Action

Like Kara Mollis, who taught a service-learning course based on multicultural literature, I feel strongly that connecting literature and community service allows students to see larger or even previously unconsidered social patterns and to draw conclusions from them (51). For Laura, the student who worked with Mr. P., "the experience of Healing Narratives has allowed us to create such meaning out of some one's life that embodies such a diverse array of events." While students were quick to comment on the relationships built with the residents, they had also started to see patterns, ranging from race and class to the use of humor in the face of illness. We talked about the ways in which gender affects responses to physical disability, especially mastectomies; the socially constructed idea that people with Alzheimer's are, as Pat Robertson put it, effectively "dead" (qtd. in Breen); the ways in which race and culture affect people's responses to illness; and the ways in which these discussions intersect with our current health-care inequities. We discussed alternative medicine and its role in healing, and we talked about cultural attitudes toward caretaking. All this emerged from both the literature we read and the elders' texts, creating a rich fabric of social meaning.

So what does narrative as social action look like? It might look like Laura realizing that "[p]eople will die, not because they have a terminal illness or a disease that has no cure, but because they cannot afford treatment." By hearing and internalizing Mr. P.'s story, she can take a political generalization and grant it a very human face. Or it might be as simple as a person's story presented to and heard by hospice workers who normally don't have time to hear it. Madanski, from Odyssey Hospice, writes:

> Partnering with the Healing Narratives course at the College of Charleston reignites our employees' passion for caring for those in this critical time of life. We may lose sight of the personal stories and personalities of the people we interact with on a daily basis. This partnership helps us not only see a patient and an illness, but a person and a journey.

It might result in a level of comfort with community and with diversity, leading to increased volunteerism. According to Julia,

> Just by talking to this family, I have gained more confidence in myself, more empathy for others, and I gained a wonderful friendship and bond with them. Also, I am thinking about volunteering for another hospice or health care group.

By combining service learning and memoir, students move toward a true understanding of others' stories and of narrative not as beginning, middle, and end but as a verb, as something that acts to influence social action, one story at a time. With this understanding, students learn to develop a bold imagination, an imagination that accounts for diverse, individualized stories, both literary and oral. As Ben wrote, "I think it [the service learning] opened my eyes to experiencing new things and not judging people. It's made me more well-rounded and eager to try new things." This is how students can begin to make imagination matter: to take oral, personal stories and transfer them onto a broader social canvas.

NOTES

1. This course was a team-taught course in English and psychology in the fall 2011 semester. While I focus here on the English literature component, I am thankful for all of the help and support (not to mention the journal entries) provided by Dr. Silvia Youssef Hanna.

2. I have used pseudonyms for all student names to protect anonymity.

3. In 2010, Charleston reported a population of 120,083; 12.2% of these residents were sixty-five or older. Over a quarter of residents identified as black or African American; few other minority groups reported. Although the median household income is $49,448, 16.4% of residents reported living below the poverty level from 2006 to 2010 ("Charleston").

Joan Wagner

Care, Compassion, and the Examined Life: Combining Creative Nonfiction and Community Engagement in a First-Year Seminar

"A name and a story dignify a life."

—*Amy Goodman*, "Democracy Now"

Plumbing the depths of the self is a lifelong task—not the least because we continuously undergo changes within and outside ourselves, both perceptible and imperceptible. The territory of self is vast and ever expanding. To journey inside can be at once terrifying and exhilarating, yet ultimately illuminating. No one else can take this journey for us; however, paying careful attention to how others navigate their inner terrain can productively assist us in gaining the confidence, if not a purpose, to explore our own interior space. This chapter considers how the study of creative nonfiction and the application of community-engaged learning pedagogy combine to challenge students in examining the ways in which personal experience influences their identities, assumptions, values, motivations, behaviors, and worldviews.[1] Using this approach, students gain not only a deeper appreciation for the value of various nonfiction literary texts but also first-hand experience in constructing such texts. In addition, they learn that when we see ourselves in others and they in us, our common humanity is revealed, our capacity for compassion is enhanced, and our sense of belonging and responsibility within a connected community is realized.

Overview of the Course

My focus is a first-year, writing-intensive seminar entitled The Examined Life: The Art, Craft, and Impact of Memoir. The seminar originates from a tradition of theme-based courses designed to guide entering college students in developing foundational skills in critical thinking, reading, writing, and dialogue. At least one goal of the seminar is to move students away from an overreliance on one-dimensional writing approaches and toward an expanded notion of the skilled writer's ability to draw from a range of strategies in making intentional and effective authorial choices. Creative nonfiction, as the animating theme in this course, embraces an array of forms, from letters, diaries, and journals to diatribes, reportage, prose poems, analytic meditations, autobiography, memoir, and personal essays (Gerard; Lopate; Roorbach). Because of its partiality toward the use of crossed genres and amalgamated rhetorical stratagems, creative nonfiction is both an elegant and a versatile vehicle for facilitating the transition to college writing for incoming students who, as Keith Hjortshoj points out, often arrive in the college classroom having been fed a steady high school diet of the five-paragraph essay or other such formulaic arrangements (36–40).

In The Examined Life, we looked to a variety of texts representing a broad spectrum of voices to consider how others interpret their life and place in the world. Using Lynn Z. Bloom and Edward M. White's anthology *Inquiry: Questioning, Reading, Writing*; Jay Allison and Dan Gediman's collection *This I Believe: The Personal Philosophies of Remarkable Men and Women*; and James McBride's full-length memoir, *The Color of Water: A Black Man's Tribute to His White Mother*, we entered the interior worlds of both ordinary and well-known individuals, novice and professional writers. Here we witnessed individuals exploring how their identities and values and beliefs were shaped by their educational experiences, relation to language and literacy, gender, social positions, cultural traditions, historical moment, family, and occupations.

The first year of college—recognized as a crucial time for cultivating the "intellectual habits of inquiry" that drive student behavior and success throughout their college career and beyond—is also a critical time for developing the habits of civic engagement (Mehaffy 6). Thus important parallels can be drawn between the classroom as a setting for students to develop into a community of peer learners and off-campus environments as places for students to exercise their roles as active participants in a multigenerational and diverse world. The Examined Life rests on the belief that an outward-looking gaze is an important, if not essential, part of the study of one's self; therefore, a community-engaged learning component complemented our textbook readings by bringing students in contact with living texts: throughout the semester, students met regularly with members of the senior community at the Program of All-Inclusive Care for the Elderly in Vermont (PACE VT) to gain the perspective of individuals outside their typical social and generational sphere. Using their developing skills as writers, students assisted their senior partners in writing a series of creative nonfiction works based on their partners' lives. Course themes were largely based on the thematic structure of Bloom and White's text, which explored in turn issues of identity, diversity, ethical behavior, values, family heritage, and interpretations of the past (xv–xix). The activities with PACE intentionally prompted students to consider how such themes played out in another person's life as they simultaneously turned an introspective lens on themselves.

As a writing-intensive course driven by inquiry and process pedagogies, assignments consisted of both informal and formal writing throughout the semester. Students drew from their weekly informal writing to shape more carefully constructed formal essays requiring them to blend together evidence from the text with illustrative material from their own or their senior partner's experience in considering course themes. In addition to the community writing project, each student had the task of crafting a short memoir based on a specific aspect of his or her own life.

The educator Parker Palmer suggests that "the most practical thing we can achieve in any kind of work is insight into what is happening inside us as we do it. The more familiar we are with our inner terrain, the more surefooted our . . . living becomes" (6). Therefore, each of the two major writing projects culminated with critical self-reflection essays in which students tracked their growth in writing and assessed how various elements—the literary texts they read, the people they encountered in the community, the peer and instructor feedback they received—contributed to the writing process and assisted them in examining their lives more deeply. Ultimately, students tried their hand at journal writing, poetry, formal academic essays, personal essays, biographical vignettes, and reflective compositions. The course design was intentionally multilayered and multidimensional, offering a rich variety of intellectual, artistic, and practical tasks to complete as well as resources for helping students make sense of the texts, their experiences with the elderly, and the various approaches to writing creative nonfiction.

Writing with and for the PACE Community

Thomas Deans differentiates between three service-learning paradigms regarding community writing: writing for, about, or with the community (17). In this case, the community was PACE, a not-for-profit health-care program committed to helping older adults remain independent in their own homes by providing direct medical and social support at the program's center during the day.[2] PACE's goal is to keep individuals out of hospitals and nursing homes whenever possible so they can enjoy personal freedom and the positive effects of being in familiar surroundings yet also receive the daily social, psychological, and medical support they require. Our class was invited to work with the seniors at PACE because members of the staff perceived what little knowledge they possessed about the personal lives of their participants beyond their formal medical profiles. The purpose of the creative nonfiction writing project, then, was for students to assist the caregivers in gaining a holistic perspective of the PACE participants they interact with daily. Students were also expected to provide one-on-one companionship for the participants and to contribute intellectually stimulating activities to PACE's programming, thus embracing PACE's mission of preserving the dignity of the elderly in the community by joining in a valuable part of their client-centered approach to care. In The Examined Life, students alternated between Dean's "with" and "for" paradigms by writing in collaboration with their elderly partners to benefit the community of families, caretakers, and peers that surrounded the PACE participants. This approach not only empowered the seniors to voice their stories but also empowered the students to serve as valued listeners and writers, thus aligning the mission of the PACE organization with the objectives of the course. Such alignment is noted to be a vital component to a successful community partnership (Clayton, Bringle, Senor, Huq, and Morrison).[3]

Students began meeting with their partners during the third week of classes. Thereafter, they met two hours each week throughout the semester for a total of ten visits. A service lab was built into the course schedule to ensure we had regular and substantial blocks of time dedicated to community engagement as a group, thus fulfilling a desire on my part to shape this endeavor into a consistent, unified, and mutually agreeable effort as opposed to adopting a logistically challenging and potentially fragmented "placement" approach (Morton), where students visit as it fits into their schedule.[4] Service-learning literature suggests that the commitment demonstrated by the former strategy is desirable for both community partners and the integrity of the endeavor (Sandy and Holland; Stoecker and Tryon, *Unheard Voices*).

The collection of works produced for the community writing project consisted of three components. The first involved creating a "Where I'm From" poem that names items—both ordinary and unique—from a person's past and present experience. What begins as a sort of inventory of recalled smells, favorite foods, time-worn family sayings, cherished values, books read, and places visited is shaped into a poem with the common refrain "I am from. . . ." The inspiration and structure for this poetic form originates from the Kentucky writer and teacher George Ella Lyon, who believes that "writing comes from abundance. We all have a wealth of feelings and experiences to write from and we all have a voice we can trust in putting words on paper." As students helped their partners assemble their poem, the conversation uncovered future topics to explore, for behind every remembered artifact or value or aphorism, there lived an extended story.

The second writing project for the PACE collection involved composing an essay modeled after *This I Believe*, a National Public Radio series and a published collection wherein thousands of individuals over the years have sought to identify one principle they believed in and publicly expressed it in a brief essay about a personal life experience (Allison and Gediman). Lastly, students composed a set of biographical statements about their partners to complete the collection, thus providing PACE staff members with a variety of products to know the persons in their care.

As the weeks unfolded and together we made our weekly afternoon visits to PACE, each student-senior relationship proceeded on its own trajectory. Some senior participants, hungry for one-to-one connection and eager to present self-described portraits of themselves, were ready to disclose intimate details about their lives within minutes of meeting their student partners, whereas others proceeded with more reserve during the initial encounters. Although I did not prescribe the use of direct interviewing techniques, suggesting instead a conversational approach based on relationship building—what Philip Gerard refers to as the "human factor" involving "many hours of close companionship" as one prepares to write about a subject (67–68)—many students' first attempts at dialogue took a journalistic approach. Students later noted in their reflection essays a shift over time from somewhat forced and awkward question-answer sessions to conversations that developed organically. The more relaxed approach proved to be the ingredient that produced the most meaningful interactions and the better avenue for getting to know their partners. Students learned to become comfortable with silences, pauses, and, at times, nondirection in the effort to let their senior partners reveal themselves in their own time.

What makes a story interesting is that the characters and the world they inhabit are not painted too simply; that is, "for the story to come alive, the people in it must come alive" (Gerard 117). The first creative nonfiction pieces students and their partners completed were the "Where I'm From" poems. The poems were then used to reorient both students and senior participants from the focus on the self to focus on the other or on "us." Each student and participant read aloud his or her poem in small groups. In this way, students had the chance to hear about an array of personally poignant life moments, significant relationships, and what mattered to others. Likewise, the senior participants were intrigued to learn new things about their peers and the students that sparked new conversations and connections. As trusting bonds formed, we began our work on the *This I Believe* essay and the biographical sketches. Here, a keener sense of their partners' complex characters began to emerge.

Phillip Lopate reminds us that "[p]ersonal essayists from Montaigne on have been fascinated with the changeableness and plasticity of the materials of human personality. Starting with self-description, they have realized they can never render all at once the entire complexity of a personality" (xxviii). Therefore, in class, we spent a good deal of time exploring the concepts of identity and character. Do we view or characterize those we know as one-dimensional beings, or do we see them as complex individuals with multiple and frequently contradictory personae? How do we choose to see others, and what do we gain by moving beyond initial impressions to know others on a deeper level? The characters students encountered in our texts and those they met in person demonstrated the need for recognizing the depth of people, both in literature and in their own lives.

In "On Being a Cripple," a reflective essay on the physical self, Nancy Mairs considers the tensions between the personal construct she built of herself and the social construct others have projected on her as an individual living with multiple sclerosis. Her struggle with a progressively debilitating condition prompts a continual reexamination of her identity that resonated with students as they faced an elderly cadre similarly grappling with who-I-was-then and who-I-am-now identity quandaries. In class, we discussed the ability of Mairs's essay and other aesthetic models like it to challenge preconceived notions based solely on external cues, to redefine (or refine) personal identities, and to shift readers' perspectives. With each new text we read, students confronted their assumptions and labeling habits by getting to know people from the inside out. A parallel process occurred at PACE. Students who presupposed that the population we'd be working with would be sleepy, quiet, disinterested, cranky, or out-of-step came to appreciate the spiritedness and depth of character displayed by their partners. James admitted that his "ideas on the elderly were very narrow" entering the course: "I did not expect such outspoken or social people."[5] Martina found that she had "never met anyone whose drives were as powerful as [her partner's], at least in terms of self-discovery and inner reflection. [Her] story is the story of a woman who struggled constantly throughout her life; it is the story of endurance, of self-discovery, of little rewards, and inspirational meditation. It is the story of *being*." Students consistently articulated similar revelations about their partners throughout the semester, testifying to the impact that the PACE participants had on students' perceptions of the elderly. Each participant would remain, in Callie's words, "a vivid character in my life."

Around the seminar table, students discussed various authors' depictions of the complex characters inhabiting their lives and began to see how challenging a decision it can be to determine which features of a person's character to reveal. Scott Russell Sanders epitomizes Lopate's "multiple personae in action" (xxix) in two works: "Under the Influence: Paying the Price of My Father's Booze" and "The Inheritance of Tools." The essays present two very different, even opposing, portrayals of the author's father and the relationship they had. I assigned these two essays without drawing attention to the fact that they were written by the same author. It was only after a full discussion about the qualities of each essay, the themes raised, and the techniques used that I asked if anyone noticed that the essays were written by the same person about the same father. This revelation sent students back to the text for a closer look. Was it really possible that this could be the same father and son? Is an author who presents only a partial view of a character trustworthy? What are a writer's responsibilities to the characters and the veracity of a story? The joint consideration of these essays revealed new strategies for students to consider in their writing and underscored the conscious decisions writers make in presenting a particular story.

As students worked on their own memoirs and completed the collaborative pieces with their senior partners, we concurrently read McBride's memoir. A fitting parallel existed between McBride's and my students' writing experience, for in his memoir McBride formulates the story of his boyhood coupled with the telling of his mother's life story. He reveals that it took fourteen years and many interviews to accumulate the bits and pieces necessary to tell just a portion of her story and unveil the many facets of her character. Students' challenges with accurately capturing their partners' characters provoked an appreciation for the effort and attention required of McBride to provide a faithful rendering of his mother's story using her voice and her perspective. Students used a variety of methods to make new discoveries about their partners. On one visit, students read aloud a selection of the essays published in *This I Believe*, prompting their senior participants to speak about the influence of faith, struggle, compassion, ambition, acceptance, harmony, courage, and self-respect in their lives. They recalled cherished relationships, pleasurable pastimes, stunning transitions in nature, and kindnesses others had done for them. Further, students and their partners exchanged opinions on spiritual matters, political views, what gave them strength, and the path to joy.

At the end of the semester, selected readings from our project served as the central part of a fourth-anniversary event for our PACE site. Students and their senior partners read from these works to a rapt audience made up of staff members, board members, senior participants, their family members, and community supporters. It was not only a moment of literary pleasure but also a celebration of each senior participant's unique human experience. Our inclusion in the program further solidified the project's alignment with PACE's approach to elder care. Dolly Fleming, the executive director, later shared that "the project brought vibrancy to the day center and modeled an activity that reflected person-centered care. It is easier to keep the care in caregiving when we actually see the person for who he/she is." Each participant received a keepsake portfolio of his or her works. To the organization, we presented the full collection to be made available for current and prospective participants, staff members, and family members.

Fleming explained the benefits for the elderly participants and PACE's expectations for the project this way: "The lives of the participants were genuinely enriched. Their unique stories and memories were acknowledged and affirmed and celebrated. Any intentional effort that brings out the person behind their presenting disabilities or frailties helps shine light [on] and reveal the genuine person." She noted that as a result of the project "staff and caregivers had a better and more genuine sense of who the participants actually were. This knowledge deepened their interest and strengthened their relationships and interactions [with participants]."

The Role of Care and Compassion in Student Development

Just as writing-process pedagogy should provide students with "an ever-expanding repertoire of strategies for enhancing their own way of producing text" (Kirby, Kirby, and Liner 15), community-engaged learning pedagogy should provide students with an enlarged understanding of how disciplinary knowledge coupled with care and compassion can be applied to strengthen the communities in which they live, work, and play. In writing courses, we talk about the process being just as important, if not more important, than the product. In a similar way, the community-engaged learning venture is about the experience itself, the process of patiently and purposefully getting to know another person. This process was critical to developing the perceptiveness necessary to capture each partner's essence on the page and for students to learn something about themselves. The following excerpts from student essays demonstrate changed perspectives as a result of their community project:

> I would never have considered myself a patient person, until now. Working with [my partner] has made me realize that sometimes it is alright to slow things down. I thought to enjoy a person's company, you need[ed] constant conversation. After sitting with [my partner], I came to the conclusion I was wrong. . . . This project made me realize that there is more to life than just the "me" aspect. (Kylie)

> This [experience] really took my narrow . . . view of life and opened it up. I have become much more self-aware. It makes me look at all aspects of my life and wonder what else I might be able to improve. (Sam)

> With her belief of reaching out to others, [my partner] made me reflect on my own way of extending my love for those around me. She has made it clear what distinctly matters in life. (Callie)

The approach to The Examined Life was significantly informed by Katherine Kirby, a veteran practitioner of community-engaged learning. She calls on the ethical framework of the French philosopher Emmanuel Lévinas to argue that "[c]ourses in ethical or moral education should not only teach students how to conceive of moral codes or laws or virtues. They should also help students to acknowledge the urgency of ethical action and foster a certain kind of concern and care on the part of students as ethical agents" (154). Such a philosophy aligns with Nel Noddings's conviction that the development of a caring sensibility is the necessary foundation for leading a full life, which includes "neighborliness, aesthetic appreciation, moral sensitivity, environmental wisdom, religious or spiritual intelligence" (14). Thus the course cultivated in students an ethic of care and compassion as a foundational element of engaged citizenship by prompting students to extend concern for the well-being of others and to play a meaningful role in enhancing that well-being.

If care and compassion rest on a better understanding of the other and if this understanding is arrived at through the recognition of the individuality, dignity, and depth of others, then our foray into creative nonfiction helped take us there. Students powerfully demonstrated these abilities when they used creative nonfiction as a tool for examining their lives and as a way to meaningfully engage with the community. In the process, students learned there is much to be discovered about how individuals communicate their paths to personal knowledge. Literary texts, especially personal narratives, by their design offer an intimate look into the inner landscape of another person's mind. In their quest to delight or sway or awaken readers through the written word, writers of creative nonfiction simultaneously satisfy their own curiosity about the self and the world while inevitably expanding someone else's concept of the world.

NOTES

1. I choose to use the term *community-engaged learning* to emphasize reciprocal, socially just, college-community relationships.

2. In 2011, eighty-two PACE programs were operational in twenty-nine states.

3. For an excellent discussion of transactional versus transformational partnerships, see Jacoby and associates, *Building Partnerships*. To assess a community partnership, see Clayton, Bringle, Senor, Huq, and Morrison.

4. In a first attempt at service learning, I established four brief placement options that students were expected to pursue independently. I learned that my lack of involvement and an absence of structure in the community project produced inconsistent student commitment and results. In the 2011 course discussed in this essay, the service project was fully integrated into the course, and all students were engaged in the same, sustained experience. The selection of just one community partner and the addition of a "lab" contributed to an improved level of communication among the students, me, and the community partner. Setting up the service project as a shared and consistent experience allowed for more meaningful integration of the community work into class.

5. Pseudonyms are used for all students' names.

Part IV

Service Learning
in Literature-Based Writing

Elizabeth Parfitt

Teaching Literature to Raise a Voice in the First-Year Writing Course

The City and Service Learning

Labor Day in Boston marks the arrival of thousands of college students who call the city their campus. They'll return fresh from internships, summer jobs, and suburban high schools, where they drive instead of walk to the 7-Eleven. The sidewalks will teem with urban hipsters near Boston Common and backpacks on every corner in Cambridge. Coffee sales will increase—along with alcohol sales—and the trains will swell with chatty groups of new best friends, direct from first-year student orientation. To the students' credit, the city would not be the vibrant place it is if not for the energy and enthusiasm of their influx. The result is an exchange of intellect, space, energy, and power that enhances the culture of the city. With each new semester, the city gains a wealth of knowledge and innovation that allows it to flourish as a center for creative capital. Students remind citizens that the youth generation is a powerful agent both in Boston's economy and in its identity as a destination for research, travel, and leisure. Yet, as a composition lecturer who frequently discusses civic engagement with her first-year writing classes, I am aware that most first-year students never seem to question their right or privilege to live in the community. They enter into the collegiate world as independent citizens but rarely stop to consider the impact the community might have on their scholarship at Emerson College. In addition, there is little sense of what it means to be an engaged citizen in an urban environment or of how their campus community borders a much larger social scene. They are at once insiders and outsiders, earning the right to call the institution their home yet often knowing little about the community that lies just beyond the academic gates.

This intersection of community and campus, citizen and student, creates an ideal moment for exploration and research in a service-learning class. Likewise, the first-year student—traditionally just beginning to comprehend his or her place in both the institutional social climate of the university and the freedom of the world outside the familiar—is an ideal candidate for entering into the urban exchange that the city can provide. In particular, the simple act of leaving one home for another signifies a transitional period during which intellectual inquiry and reflection might provide a path to comfort. Moreover, staking a claim in the community structure can be a challenging process and one that might be aided by collaborative learning both on and off campus.

For the last few years, I've taught a first-year writing course that intends to create this service-learning experience for students by using the cityscape as one of our literary texts. In Writing for Civic Engagement—Case Study: Boston we use writing, literature, and service learning as forces that link knowledge of the city and culture around us to narratives of social activism and community empowerment. Students serve over ninety hours at a combination of organizations; community partners share space, knowledge, experience, and a sense of belonging with students—most of whom have not yet fully realized a community identity. At the end of the course, students use this new knowledge and understanding to create an online magazine, titled by the students *The Sky Is Wicked Huge*, that echoes the aims of activist literature: it initiates a conversation that raises consciousness and, ideally, inspires a community of readers to act.

Course Structure and Goals

Case Study: Boston is a first-year Research Writing course that begins by asking students to consider their roles and responsibilities to the surrounding community.[1] In a letter the students receive the first day, I explain our common goals:

> Welcome to WR121: Writing for Civic Engagement—Case Study: Boston. For the next 14 weeks, you will be investigating, exploring, and studying the city of Boston and recording your findings through a variety of writing projects. This semester, I encourage you to walk the city, get lost in the city, and talk to people in the city. In fact, I require that you do it. Your mission, should you choose to accept it, is to research the question, What

does it mean to be civically engaged in Boston? Through a series of writing and research projects, you will be working individually and in groups to break down the barriers between student and city.

Case Study: Boston pairs literary texts—related to Boston and to the issue of civic engagement—with community-based service-learning projects that ask students to engage with diverse populations and new physical, mental, emotional, and geographic experiences. Students in the course partner with Boston Cares, an organization that manages service projects for hundreds of citywide not-for-profit organizations with volunteer needs. An affiliate of the HandsOn Network,[2] Boston Cares works with three hundred not-for-profit organizations in Boston with varied missions and impact areas—including the environment, youth education, senior services, arts and culture, and hunger and homelessness. Each student is required to complete three community service projects of roughly two to four hours each at a host of local agencies of their choosing, for a combined total for the class of over ninety service hours.

Boston Cares provides students with the freedom to choose service projects that relate to their career paths or individual interests. Students commit to projects on an independent schedule and have the opportunity to repeat projects with well-matched organizations or move on to new projects for different perspectives on the meaning of service. Among others, these projects include serving dinner at the New England Center for Homeless Veterans, choosing books for inmates with the Prison Book Program, cleaning up one of Boston's many parks with the Charles River Conservancy, and assisting in treatment and recovery centers through the Pine Street Inn. As part of the exchange, Boston Cares enters our classroom, provides a service orientation, and mobilizes students to track projects through an online portal. Boston Cares serves as a project-management tool for hundreds of organizations, and so students are responsible for all communication with the partner organizations.

The four key components of the course are research, writing, literature, and service projects. To illustrate, during one week of the term, a student might be assigned to explore South Boston and record observations on the neighborhood's structure, while at home she is reading excerpts from Michael Patrick MacDonald's memoir *All Souls*—an account of growing up in the South Boston housing projects. That same student might volunteer to work at the Boston Food Bank, sorting and providing food to clients in the South End on Saturday morning. When she returns to class on Monday, she'll recount this experience with a written reflection shared in class conversation. Then we turn toward that week's writing project: a memoir about a place that has affected the student since arriving in the city. Research comes from service reflections, literature, and short written pieces that are later honed and crafted into formal writing projects.

These coordinated activities prepare students for the capstone project in which they design, write, and edit a collection of original work for a public audience. Students choose representative pieces from their portfolio and combine them into a cohesive publication that contributes to Boston Cares's mission to put the service experience at the forefront of community action. For the spring 2010 section I discuss in this chapter, students chose to use the magazine as a platform for exploring and defining civic engagement. Upon completion, the magazine was published online, shared with Boston Cares, and launched at the Emerson College First-Year Writing Program Showcase of Student Work.

In addition, for students in a first-year writing course, the culminating magazine pedagogically signifies that the community work is not over but has just begun. Much like the literature we read throughout the course, the writing in the magazine can be viewed as part of an ongoing conversation about civic participation. For these students, situated in the center of downtown Boston, simply entering unfamiliar neighborhoods and exploring those sidewalks through various organizations creates an opportunity to encourage civic involvement and establish an investment in community impact during the first year on campus. As Ellen Cushman writes in "The Rhetorician as an Agent of Social Change":

> Activism begins with a commitment to breaking down the sociological barriers between universities and communities. And if we see ourselves as both civic participants and as preparing students for greater civic participation, then activism becomes a means to [a] well defined end for approaching the community. (12)

Once students have found that entry point, the work leads toward an exchange that must be assessed at the end of a fourteen-week term.

For Case Study: Boston, the first course of its kind at my institution, strong efforts were made to track hours served. By the numbers, the requirements for the course were as follows: fourteen semester weeks, seven formal writing projects, three service projects per student, and three written reflections per student. In total, the students served at roughly thirty agencies in the following impact areas: adult and youth education (over thirty-nine hours served), arts and culture (over ten hours), the environment (over ten hours), health and wellness (over ten hours), and other miscellaneous areas (over fifteen hours).

Although these projects are all one-time student experiences, Boston Cares introduces students to community service, and many organizations use Boston Cares as a recruitment tool for gaining long-term or repeat volunteers. Considering students often choose their service projects with personal and career interests in mind, the partner organizations are able to obtain some volunteers who will make a continuing contribution to the organizations throughout their college career in Boston.

Our class provided additional benefits as well by exposing students not only to Boston Cares as a potential organization for future involvement but also to hundreds of smaller not-for-profit organizations that might better fit their interests and passions. Of the impact areas, education, both adult and youth, received the most service hours. The most popular organization overall was the Learning Ally, formerly known as Recording for the Blind and Dyslexic, which hosted four students who trained and then recorded books for more than fifteen hours. Other popular education organizations included Jumpstart, an organization promoting early childhood education in low-income neighborhoods, and the Jewish Vocational Service, which aids in career development for diverse populations. Both organizations worked with two students each for over ten hours. In addition, the Central Square Theater and the Commonwealth Shakespeare Company hosted two students, each for over ten hours of service helping as ushers and with the administrative side of auditions. Students' majors played a large role in the projects chosen. Students majoring in theater tended to choose the arts and culture projects, whereas one writing major chose projects that might add to his skill set, such as working in the after-school creative writing program at 826 Boston.

Although it is difficult to quantify precise benefit to community and student,[3] many studies indicate that civic leadership skills in particular are recognized by alumni in postcollege surveys, and these skills are, in part, attributed to service-learning course work (Astin and Vogelgesang). Therefore community impact from this service-learning experience may provide long-term benefits that will not surface until years later, when students become more involved with professional work in the community.

Service also benefits the students' experience with literature in the classroom. Ultimately, when literary study is combined with service-learning research and writing that asks students to confront and explore their interactions with the local community, students begin to see that literature can be an agent of change. When published, student work becomes community literature with a public audience.

Experiential Research that Connects Service with Literature

The writing projects in Case Study: Boston elicit specific inquiries in literature that focus on our guiding research question, What does it mean to be civically engaged? Readings include poetry, fiction, and nonfiction, and writing assignments push students to examine current social problems, research unfamiliar neighborhoods, or observe social trends in the campus community. To illustrate, when reading Robert Frost's poem "Mending Wall," students examine their personal experience with boundaries in their relationships with neighbors, roommates, and other people and with nature. They discuss, visualize, and draw what Frost's "wall" might have looked like, and they write about experiences they've had with human-made barriers. Further, we analyze the poem, working through the language, coming to terms with the metaphors and imagery that Frost imbues in his reader. Structure plays a key role as we deconstruct the rhetoric to better understand the stance the author has crafted and how he develops and builds a relationship with the audience. But beyond that, we discuss boundaries in the city of Boston and the invisible lines created between various neighborhoods. We look at census data to see where race, ethnicity, gender, and family makeup statistics create separations and define groups throughout the city. These divisions signify important distinctions at an institution that reported 76.8% of the 2011 incoming class was white ("Creating").

Finally, adding in the service-learning component, students discuss where they've found physical walls in their service and experiential research—as well as where they've uncovered metaphoric and symbolic fences. In his final commentary project, one student, Chris, writes:

> I know I was personally impacted by this poem as it inspired me to choose volunteer work where I would get to speak to and interact with people. . . .
> It makes you question what you may be losing by keeping people at a dis-

tance. It is this very idea that inspired me to choose to participate in a game night at a senior citizens' assisted living facility.   (Peck)

As shown in Chris's comments, we examine why these fences exist and how we might negotiate them in our urban lives. Writing, research, and service act as the vehicle by which students tackle these inquiries.

In addition, the course emphasizes reflection as a research model for recording experiences. To illustrate this process, I look to Justin, who, like many students, used his service reflections to track his roles as student and citizen. Whereas many students chose projects within walking distance to campus, Justin consistently chose service opportunities that put him on the train or the bus and sent him to unfamiliar neighborhoods. In his second project, Justin helped renovate the warehouse of Boston ReStore, an organization in Dorchester's Four Corners neighborhood that works to rebuild neighborhoods by distributing donated office furniture and supplies to schools, not-for-profit organizations, and lower-income populations. He observes that "[w]hat I found most interesting about the project was the assortment of people that showed up to work[:] . . . the man who was fulfilling hours to become an AA advisor[,] . . . the brothers from Providence [who] were giving up a Saturday of the spring break." He wonders "why any of these individuals would give up their Saturday mornings to help a two-man organization re-do a used furniture warehouse in the middle of one of Boston's more dangerous areas" (J. Chun, "Boston ReStore"). These required yet ungraded reflections served as a space for Justin to work through his ideas about civic engagement. A trend in his reflections relates his conversations and interactions with other volunteers in local communities that he visited. By the end of this particular reflection he argues, "I think this was the most influential project for me as it showed me that no matter where you are in life, a sense of civic service can unite you with anyone from anywhere who has a similar set of moral values." Here, his persona moves beyond that of student writer to become part of a greater community of citizens. The connections Justin cultivated through his service represent the beginnings of a dialogue between diverse groups of people—something the student magazine aims to establish.

Justin's experience is only one example of the ways in which students demonstrated knowledge of the exchange involved in service, and his point echoes one from Cushman, who explains, "Once we locate an access route into the community, we can begin the long process of self-disclosure and listening from which we can begin to identify with each other" ("Rhetorician" 18). For some first-year students, this act of self-disclosure and identification might begin with other volunteer activities and then move toward greater commitment to community work and more intellectualized service. This small success is an important step, especially at a predominantly white institution where a 2009 diversity climate study indicates the following:

> While all three constituent groups [students, faculty, and staff] felt respected by their peers and were likely to indicate that they fit in socially, constituents also perceived the racial/ethnic diversity at Emerson to be lacking. Additionally, all groups were unlikely to indicate that their experiences at Emerson had improved their ability to interact with people from different backgrounds.   ("Climate Survey Summaries")

This finding seems to be the opposite of what Justin argues in his final commentary, in which he illustrates how he moved beyond himself and his comfort zone through the service projects by drawing connections between the public work and the course literature:

> In ["Mending Wall"] the line "good fences make good neighbors" is repeated several times and hints at the central theme of the poem which is about the walls people put up to separate themselves from others. . . . There are few requirements that you have to meet to be a Boston Cares volunteer, but you do, however, have to have at least several common "walls" taken down. To be a good volunteer . . . you can't enter a project with the attitude that you are being forced to be there or that you're only there because a project needs you. In a way the project doesn't even need you, there are plenty of volunteers that they can find, but . . . [i]f you have the courage and initiative to take down a few walls . . . you might be surprised at what you learn. In the end it doesn't matter where you are in life or why you are being civically engaged, but doing so can teach you "facts of life" that you can't learn in a history or science textbook.
>
>   (J. Chun, "Commentary")

Here, Justin shows how service and literature help make sense of civic engagement on practical and philosophical levels. His point that the project "doesn't need you" shows huge growth from his perspective at the beginning of the course, when he admitted to "wondering how I could switch into the research writing class about video games or pop culture and avoid the dreaded 4 community service projects." These small steps toward breaking down the walls of the classroom may not be new, but in a writing class examining literature, Justin's work shows a strong emphasis on the importance of providing a space for this type of critical confrontation of community and self to occur.

Literature as Civic Inquiry and Writing as Community Work

In part, the writing projects, civic reflections, and service components in the course are designed to challenge student perceptions of their communities and the multilayered roles they play as citizens and scholars in our society. In Case Study: Boston, students are only just beginning on this journey toward engaged citizenship, and Boston Cares provides the entry point. Anne DiPardo explains:

> Few would dispute that the best thinking and writing is at once personal and public, both infused with private meaning and focused upon the world beyond the self. The goal of writing teachers is of course to help students learn to negotiate between the two, to locate those dynamic points of connection where experience gives rise to inquiry. (2)

Through the service work, students gain access to a world beyond the university gates—one that is often intimidating in size and diversity, as well as in intellect. But through writing and literature, students uncover ways in which they can ask questions of society and use their voices to reflect. Though students are studying the ways in which the community engages in the local scene, volunteerism is only one dimension of the work. Literature connects the community work with the writing projects and shows students that there is more than one way to act and respond to each rhetorical situation.

Thus the course serves as a response to critics of composition service-learning discourse who believe that many service-learning courses focus primarily on student learning and not community benefit. To remedy this imbalance, these critics suggest reframing discussions about service learning in terms of engaged citizen work. Kevin Ball and Amy Goodburn argue that it is necessary to "reframe the positionalities of students, community members and teachers involved in such work" (91). This project replicates just such a reframing by creating a project focused heavily on community activism, student involvement, and questions of civic engagement. Our class becomes a narrative of interrelated stories linked together through common objectives and experiences: the Boston community and its social triumphs, challenges, and hurdles as seen through student eyes. This insight is exemplified through the editorial letters that introduce each of the four sections of the student magazine: "Explore," "Move," "Reflect," and "Imagine." Designed by the students as representations of the research strategies used and the themes present in the course literature, these sections signified four ways the service intersected with the reading and writing process. The "Imagine" team, for example, asks its audience, "Consider this: 7681 Boston men, women and children didn't go home after filling out their 2007 census, because they had no home to go to. And the homeless rate in our city is rising. Ignoring our homeless won't help them. What can each of us do about it?" (Acosta, Drutman, Hiestand, Nunez, and Williams). *The Sky Is Wicked Huge* sends a message from the students (and the university) back into the community: we value your work, and we value our community.

As students documented their experiences living in Boston, they were also documenting the stories of the community partners through the service reflections and testimonials to be included in the magazine. The digital record not only preserves the stories in a unique and easily disseminated mode but also allows students to experiment with innovative methods of documentation related to narrative structure, genre, and rhetorical stance, since they knew that the stories would be read online by a public audience. Furthermore, the digital platform allowed us to present the material to our primary community partner in a way that permitted them to use the project for further communication, fund-raising, grant support, and community awareness. Providing this material to Boston Cares is part of the reciprocity involved in effective service-learning partnerships. The online magazine also created a digital narrative of the student work. With the guidance and editorial supervision of a senior student who was majoring in writing, literature, and publishing, class discussions covered the rhetoric of digital media and design, specifically highlighting the importance of audience and writing for the public.[4]

The publication of our magazine signifies the first step toward taking that civic awareness and positioning student writing as community work. In their editorial letter, the "Reflect" team writes, "We are not asking you to go out and change the world single-handedly. But we as the writers are convinced that by reflecting on the work that we do, we can create a more effective, civically engaged community" (James, Maietta, Peck, and Sinkiewicz 25). Perhaps inspired by poems that examine the citizen role, like Frost's "Mending Wall" or W. H. Auden's "The Unknown Citizen," the students align themselves with the audience to promote a cause. Bruce Herzberg argues that "the effort to reach into the composition class with a curriculum aimed at democracy and social justice is an attempt to make schools function . . . as radically democratic institutions, with the goal not only of making individual students more successful, but also of making better citizens" (317). Case Study: Boston aims to extend Herzberg's notions about citizenship by emphasizing that a composition class is also an ideal place to bridge the gap between the academic community and the intellectual citizen by providing a space for students to explore public narratives, literature, and service experiences in a meaningful, scholarly, and creative way. After the students have come to terms with the narratives in the classroom, empowering them with a voice to send a message back to the public is the next step in joining the conversation.

Moving toward Change

The staff at Boston Cares praised the student involvement and requested permission to share *The Sky Is Wicked Huge* within its organization and beyond. This initial success has encouraged us to think about how this type of project might be better served by working with only one organization—creating a partnership in which students were crafting narratives with the partner—or perhaps by setting it up as a group project among a few organizations. Although it is unclear how far the magazine has reached into the community, we do know that as of August 2013 it has been viewed over four hundred times since it was posted online and distributed electronically throughout the Emerson community.[5]

Community partnerships create a bridge for student narratives to the public world, but they also serve to promote organizations like Boston Cares, advancing their missions, developing and funding programming, and establishing connections between students and the greater community. The interaction signals an exchange of skills, personnel, and knowledge that enhances the academic experience with a practical backdrop to the course's literary landscape. Throughout our partnership, Boston Cares symbolized the greater community audience who might read and take part in the change that the students were advocating through their writing and work for the class magazine.

While one goal of our magazine is to bring student voices to the community, another is to give back to the partner in a way that signals how much the college values its contribution to the classroom. This kind of validation from academic institutions can help establish the partner as a leader and innovator in community relations, notably when seeking out foundation, governmental, and corporate grants that might require these types of university affiliations.

Fostering partnerships like the one described here requires great amounts of time and resources by dedicated educators and community leaders. In the early stages, these partnerships can be difficult to assess, which makes a magazine like ours an integral part of the growth process. A shareable publication, along with a record of hours of service, creates a body of work that can be used to drive bigger projects down the line. While Emerson students are only beginning to define activism and their roles in the local community, what I hope the partner organizations and community gain from the student narrative includes a difficult-to-obtain but necessary documented record of the ways in which service participants are affected and inspired by their service work.

In a general education service-learning course, small achievements are often the biggest rewards for the instructor, the community partner, and the student. At the end of my opening letter to students I tell them, "The goal of this case study is not to come to any singular consensus, to learn all there is to learn about the city, or to become experts in urban research. Rather, my aim is that you will determine what role you want to play as a citizen and scholar in the greater Boston community." If I can show them how to work as scholars and citizens using literature and writing as a guiding force, the students might someday become rhetorical and literary activists in their own right, giving back to the community in new ways. In his commentary project, Chris writes, "The thoughts derived from the examination of art can be the very catalyst that drives the doers of the world, who make the civic contributions for all to relish in. In this respect, artists are a vital component in enacting the perpetual cycle of change across all mediums" (Peck). For Chris and many others in the course, literature creates the connections necessary to bridge practical community work with theoretical interpretations of civic study and rhetorical awareness.

A service-learning course does not have the ability to change the world, but it might move student scholarship forward by asking questions about what it takes to raise a voice.

NOTES

1. Generically titled Research Writing, this course is the second in a required two-semester sequence in first-year writing. The course takes a genre-based approach to writing and research, using various rhetorical situations that call on writers to do research. In spring 2010, when I piloted this course, I had eighteen students in one section. I chose to incorporate service learning in my personal course theme, Case Study: Boston.

2. The HandsOn Network consists of two hundred fifty centers in sixteen countries worldwide and aims to mobilize volunteers toward community action. It is the largest network of volunteers in the nation, and it works with corporations, faith groups, and not-for-profit organizations to craft innovative solutions to community challenges. In terms of impact, the network delivers over 25 million hours of volunteer service, valued at $579 million ("Our Network").

3. This problem of assessing impact in service-learning institutions is reinforced by the results of the Campus Compact 2011 annual membership survey, which reports that few institutions have established mechanisms to track and assess this kind of data, a missing step that leads to a failure to "highlight not only the value [of] their own work, but also the role of higher education as an agent of positive change" (*Deepening*).

4. A seed grant from the Emerson College Office of Service Learning and Community Action funded the final course project, which included hiring a senior student to serve as publication editor for the course magazine.

5. Students were encouraged to distribute the magazine through their local communities and social networks as well.

Claudia Monpere McIsaac

"Beneath Thatched Shelters, We Paint Wide-Brimmed Straw Hats": Creative Writing and Social Justice

On a warm April evening, six women write poems, far away from husbands who have hit them, belittled them, filled them with fear. Here in this room, my students display a picture of a shimmering ocean and wildflower-covered bluff. In the picture's corner is a small fence. My eye is drawn to the water and flowers. The women write of the fence. It is, a student reflects, for them both protection and barrier.

For one academic quarter at this transition residence for single-parent families, my students and the mothers read and write poetry together in Spanish and English, laugh and cry. It's an ideal placement, with challenges certainly, but one that leaves both students and community members deeply satisfied. Other students face greater challenges at a residential treatment center for previously homeless people with diagnosed mental illnesses. Earlier placements were successful, but there's been staff turnover and miscommunication. Before, residents gathered to read and write poetry, some eager and some skeptical, but all engaged once things got going. Now students search for participants who are watching television or smoking outside. "Our presence," writes a student, "is like that of an uninvited guest crashing a party."

In 2009 I designed the course Creative Writing and Social Justice, with support from the Jesuit institution Santa Clara University (SCU), where I teach, and with valuable assistance from our campus program, Arrupe Partnerships for Community-Based Learning. In their placements, students work in small groups reading and writing poetry with community members. Each group works in one of these settings: transition housing for women and children who were victims of domestic violence; a residential treatment program for adolescent girls, ages twelve to sixteen, who have been in and out of foster care, many of them victims of abuse, neglect, or sexual violence and some in treatment for substance abuse; an afterschool program at a youth community center in an area of San José with high gang activity, where children and adolescents come for homework assistance and enrichment activities, such as gardening, outdoor play, and art; transition housing and short-term shelter for recently homeless adults with a diagnosed mental illness.

My students are primarily juniors and seniors majoring in a mix of subjects, some experienced in service learning, and others not. SCU recently developed a core requirement, Experiential Learning for Social Justice, which my course fulfills. Among outcomes for students is the ability to "interact appropriately, sensitively, and self-critically with people in the communities in which they work and appreciate the formal and informal knowledge, wisdom, and skills that individuals in these communities possess" (ELSJ Course Design). In addition, beyond empathy for community members, my course fosters an understanding of the complexity of social problems, a commitment to social change through community partnerships, and an awareness of poetry as a catalyst for human growth and social change.

Most of my students and most of the community members have little exposure to poetry. What they recall from school often intimidates them. So a critical outcome for both groups is the ability to enjoy reading and writing poetry. For community members, the service learning aims to empower them through their poetic voices. For students, literary course outcomes include the ability to analyze poetry through a combination of formalist and multicultural lenses and to write poetry that is aesthetically pleasing and that addresses justice issues.

Creative Writing and Social Justice

The service-learning placements are challenging at first, particularly for the students working with community members with a mental illness diagnosis, since most students have little experience with this population. Although the recent experience at this particular placement frustrated students, they said they learned how to listen, withhold judgment, and, in one student's words, "be comfortable around homeless people." In the six times I've taught this course, most students found their experiences deeply rewarding and educational. The service learning and literature speak to each other compellingly, echoing not only common themes but also the complexity of social issues. Laurie Grobman notes that "literary texts and community service can work reciprocally to heighten (and in some cases to introduce) awareness of the complexities of race, gender, and class as they intersect in people's lives" ("Is There" 133), to which I would add complexities of disabilities, such as mental illness. Stigmas toward people with mental illness are widespread; they're often characterized as "dangerous, violent, unintelligent, isolative, and impersonal" (Barney, Corser, and White 66). Through the combination of service learning and literature, my course identifies the needs of this extremely marginalized group and introduces to my students empathy and understanding.

Regardless of the population with whom students work, some critics worry that courses linking literature and service learning foster a narrow perspective, encouraging students to read literature solely as sociology and ignore its aesthetic elements or to respond too personally and ignore systemic roots of injustice. My experiences have demonstrated that including nonfiction along with literature helps students see these systemic roots. Further, having students write creatively helps prevent sociology from subsuming the aesthetic in literature. It also brings an intensity and depth to students' thinking about service learning.

At the course's beginning, I want students to grasp key facts about the systemic roots of inequality, so I have them read David Elliot Cohen's *What Matters: The World's Preeminent Photojournalists and Thinkers Depict Essential Issues of Our Time* and Nicholas D. Kristof and Sheryl WuDunn's *Half the Sky: Turning Oppression into Opportunity for Women Worldwide*. These nonfiction texts also illustrate the importance of identifying community needs in partnership, whether the community is a Kenyan village or an American neighborhood. Early in the course we are visited by residents from the transitional housing and short-term shelter program where some of my students have their placements. All three visitors have been recently homeless, and all have a mental illness diagnosis. One year, for example, the visitors were a woman with an MBA who has schizophrenia, a former Navy SEAL with PTSD, and a man raised in eight foster homes. They tell their stories, touching on ethical issues about language ("I've been diagnosed with a mental illness" not "I am mentally ill"), about responding to people on the street asking for money ("You can smile or say hi. You don't have to give money. When people ignored me, I felt like an

insect."). Students say these stories are critical in helping dispel stereotypes, such as that homeless people are "lazy" or "dirty and dangerous."
"I was awestruck at their courage," a student writes, explaining how hard
it must be to confront and try to solve such serious problems. Many students comment that although they've served meals to homeless people,
they've never taken time to hear their stories.

The literature we read—primarily poetry and a little fiction—explores
issues of poverty, homelessness, mental illness, race, and gender and includes canonical works by writers like Adrienne Rich, Rita Dove, Jimmy
Santiago Baca, and Edwidge Danticat and poems by teachers at San Francisco WritersCorps, social workers, therapists, and homeless people. My
course differs from most creative writing courses in not only including service learning but also incorporating poems written by underrepresented
voices, such as those of homeless people. Including these noncanonical
writers allows the traditionally voiceless to be heard in an academic setting and delivers an important message: poetry is not a bastion for the
elite; every poetic voice has value.

Working in groups at their service-learning placements, students initially do whatever is needed: tutoring, serving meals, playing with children. Later, they read and write poetry with community members. During
several class sessions, we develop curriculum students can use in their community classes, aided by a poet who works in nontraditional settings.

My students' writing primarily consists of poetry about justice issues,
community placements, and their lives, which often enter the curriculum:
a home foreclosure, a schizophrenic brother, an alcoholic parent. Early in
the course students write reflections about community placements and
some of our texts. As they become more comfortable with poetry, they
increasingly write in that genre, experimenting with style and structure.
Students tend to form tight bonds, and the course concludes with a public
campus reading of their poetry.

Discussions moving between literature and the students' experiences
with community members create an environment of deep reflection, cognitive dissonance, and empathy that can lead to transformation. Hearing
about community members who lost families, jobs, and homes because of
mental illness, students certainly witness suffering, but the course reading
draws out the enormous complexity of community members' struggles.
One student at the shelter, for example, watches a community member
sort her medication: for high blood pressure, sleep, anxiety, depression.

"How can she keep track of it?" my student asks. "How effective is it?" we ask, while considering a stanza from Jane Kenyon's "Having It Out with Melancholy" that is a litany of failed medications (lines 21–27). "What are the side effects?" we ask as we look at Eileen Malone's lines in "The Visit Secured" about her schizophrenic son. Malone's gripping poems highlight deficits in our health system, in one of which a young man is dropped off in a town where he knows no one by a hospital psychiatric technician, given $172 and "instructions to memorize corners / [and] the phone number for Vocational Rehab" ("Outdoor Sky," lines 9–10).

Malone's poems highlight another theme that students encounter in their service learning: the need for human connection. Our class discusses Malone's poems as well as an incident at the shelter in which community members mocked a man who spoke in a confusing, passionate way about religion and money. Unsure how to respond when others in the treatment program laughed and called him crazy, my students were silent at first, nodding, trying to maintain eye contact with the man. One student writes, "I certainly didn't want to laugh, but I did not want to offend the other residents who were . . . expecting me to laugh." We discussed the situation in class, acknowledging its difficulty, brainstorming responses, and validating the students for remaining respectful.

Poetry's Power for Community Members

I help students develop curriculum with a basic format: a brief introduction to poetry, a reading of several short poems students think community members will enjoy, discussion of the poems, and then poetry writing. Community members are encouraged to read their poems aloud or have someone else read them, if they prefer. The books by the WritersCorps training coordinator Judith Tannenbaum are instrumental in developing curriculum (see, e.g., Tannenbaum, *Disguised as a Poem* and *Teeth*; WritersCorps, Tannenbaum, and Bush). Among poems that work with all age groups are odes, lyrics about nature or animals—often accompanied by calendar images or, with children, their drawings—narrative poems, and poems structured as anaphora and haiku. I encourage students to use a range of subjects and never to require poems about personal subjects. Students and community members write alongside one another.

My students have had success and challenges bringing poetry to varied age groups, although most adapt well to challenges. With restless children, students incorporated physical activity and drawing. At a community center for teens, students found that providing pizza heightened the teens' willingness to engage. Sometimes students are unnerved by a youth's seemingly casual attitude toward violence or saddened by poems about abuse or neglect. We discuss ways to deal with these feelings; I remind students that while the groups they're working with are getting some treatment and support, many are not. But as the community members read and write poems, students become aware of poetry's power to communicate and connect, with one's self, with the environment, and with other people. In dazzling shorthand, poetry speaks about being human: the sorrows and joys of our lives, the beauty, chaos, and injustice of the world.

Research on the use of poetry in community settings shows clear benefits to community members. Stressed family caregivers caring for elders with dementia report that weekly poetry writing resulted in "a catharsis of negative emotions and validation of positive emotions such as increased confidence, pride, and greater empathy for their loved ones" (Kidd, Zauszniewski, and Morris 601). Seriously ill community members found an eight-week poetry-writing program more useful than an illness support group, saying that writing gave them some control and "an outlet to try to untangle some of the confusion within" (qtd. in Rickett, Greive, and Gordon 267). WritersCorps brings poetry to youth in detention facilities, inner-city schools, and community centers. Some medical schools, such as those at the University of California, San Francisco, and Duke University, incorporate poetry into electives and sponsor poetry workshops and conferences.

Writing poetry seems to provide some agency to people who have been marginalized or traumatized; many community members with whom my students work refer to the freedom and empowerment that writing poetry gives them, an idea voiced by Trevor Clark, a man with schizoaffective disorder, who writes that poetry writing strengthens him during recovery and that it is "a non-invasive way of expressing my emotions" (S105). Larry Brewster's study of California's prison arts program, which incorporated poetry along with other arts, shows impressive results; current and former inmates say it gave them "a sense of purpose, . . . self-esteem, and self-discovery" (9). WritersCorps teachers who work with youth in detention facilities and other community settings speak of poetry as a catalyst for hope, community, personal growth, and social change. Uchechi Kalu adds that for her students "poetry was a subject in which they could shine because it allowed for minimal language with maximal impact" (155).

One student in my class comments that poetry can help heal the soul; another who had been skeptical that poetry had anything to do with social justice now sees it as giving people a voice. These poetic voices help shatter stereotypes. Hearing them, students at the shelter, for example, learn to see people with schizophrenia or bipolar disorder not as their disabilities but as multidimensional men and women. Students express surprise at how "creative, witty, and wise" many of the poems are and at the passion and intelligence shown in discussions with community members.

Students have varying degrees of success introducing poetry to community members. Students who worked with youth in transitional housing found that while the children welcomed poetry writing, the two teens resented shifting to poetry after weeks of discussing popular culture, asking my students about everything from sex and alcohol to college classes. "I felt they were almost mad at us for forcing them to read and write poetry," writes a student. "B. even crumpled up her poem and threw it in the garbage." My students shifted next to spoken word, which worked well with B., but not for the other teen, who stopped coming. Ultimately, the outcomes were positive with the children and less so with the teens. But in the residential treatment program for female adolescents, poetry sessions were very successful, partly because of careful listening and flexibility. One student promised herself she would "learn from these girls by keeping my mouth closed and listening[;] . . . it helped them trust us with their writing which included some pretty heavy subjects." Although I'd cautioned my students not to focus on personal subjects, they quickly adapted to the girls' desire to write about those issues. Worried the girls "wouldn't like poetry because it was like more schoolwork," one student is surprised by the positive response. Describing one teen's poem, she says, "It was beautiful. It was written as if addressing her abusive dad and drug-abusing mother, asking for memories of her childhood, of happiness, but there were none. After we read it and complimented her, another girl gave some constructive criticism which she took really well."

The service-learning experience inspires intense feelings among students; occasionally these feelings result in personal blame: anger at parents for neglecting children or frustration with youth who dismiss homework assistance. Here the nonfiction and literary texts work together, helping students see such behavior in a broad economic and social context, such as parents struggling to get by with multiple low-wage jobs, food-insecure households, and underresourced schools. Kristof and Wu-Dunn write about well-meaning aid groups who raid overseas brothels, bringing young women back to their communities—only to have some return because they feel stigmatized or because of drug dependencies they developed while being held captive (35). Helping others, students see, is complicated.

Students' Poetry—Aesthetic and Justice-Oriented

Where is literature as literature in all this? Grobman asks how "we balance the . . . tension between the literary text as a work of art and the literary text as a source of cultural or social truth" ("Is There" 136). I believe that when students write imaginatively and thus try to replicate specific literary techniques in their writing, they read literary works not solely as cultural documents but also as works of art. Repeatedly, students say writing poems brings an intensity and depth to their thinking about service learning. One student comments, "I can convey a multitude of emotions not possible in a reflection" and "I reflected outside the box, which helped me engage in a different kind of thinking . . . and in deeper issues." Student poems often reflect deep empathy, such as this one by Claude Donnelly:

> The cards are ashtray black,
> Torn, tattered.
> Crushed between two tattooed fists
> Each card shutters,
> Gasps, wheezes. . . .
> "Like everybody here I've been diagnosed.
> I gotta see my child soon, man.
> I'm not taking my meds anymore.
> Can't write, can't think when I'm on those things."

Blackened by cigarette ashes, the playing cards are daily sustenance to Tim, who desperately misses his child. This poem conjures his pain powerfully, acknowledging the issue of medication, which some argue should be forcibly given. By including Tim's voice, the student's poem complicates that view.

Another student, Alex Hierl, in his poem "The Chicken or the Egg," critiques a common characterization of homeless people:

They say mental illness is the third
Leading cause of homelessness.
Which came first?
How cool and calm and collected could you stay
If you had nowhere to stay?

Alex's lines illustrate the pitfalls of a diagnosis that neglects the context of homelessness.

Some student poems explore an intense connection with community members, such as Raquel Roque's poem written about a child:

As we played
That tiny finger
Reached for mine
And your not so tiny heart
Pulsated love
And spread through me
A jolt so fierce
I knocked over the Legos

This poem illustrates students' frequent observation that writing poetry creates emotional depth. One student says it lets her "bring detail to a whole other level . . . a deep emotional level." Why is this? Poetry, more than other genres, requires an intense focus on language: every word matters. Most effective poetry relies on details more than abstractions—and in a short, compressed space. Poetry also rarely incorporates transitions, instead inviting associative leaps, unusual juxtapositions. Perhaps it's not surprising that students see it as deepening their feelings and thoughts about service learning.

Aiming for authenticity in poetry, one student notes the importance of resisting "the temptation to exaggerate and dramatize . . . suffering." Writing about another's suffering raises issues of representation and risks of stereotyping. Early student poems occasionally include gratuitous details illustrating poverty or homelessness, such as one describing a man's dirty skin and clothes and his hair containing bugs. I ask my students, "When does depicting someone's life become stereotyping?" I encourage them to consider the fullness of every life, an idea they support, perhaps because they see themselves as multidimensional. This student poem by Alison Rogel humanizes Harry, a homeless man:

> Harry recalled laboring on hot afternoons
> Thirst quenched by his wife's lemonade
> And his daughter's sticky cake breath kisses
> Across his prickly whiskers.

We see Harry not as a faceless man without a home but as a man with fond memories of a loving wife and daughter.

A poem, because of its compressed form, sometimes reveals assumptions more clearly than a prose work. Some student poems long for simple solutions. "All he really needs is a friend," one student repeats in several stanzas. Another writes:

> We are striving to help you
> your biggest fans.
> Do it.
> It is in you.
> Push, push.

While compassionate, these lines imply that individual initiative, aided by the speaker's short-term help, can solve big problems. The service-learning theorists Lisa Langstraat and Melody Bowdon note that "compassion can easily mask unequal power relations" and warn that personal responses "may influence students' perception that social problems such as homelessness are chiefly or only personal, rather than systemic" (7, 8). I try to address this complexity by examining with students both gender violence and craft choices (i.e., language and style choices) in Frances Driscoll's powerful book *The Rape Poems*. Incorporating elements of formalism, I explain the importance of Driscoll's language and style, and students practice these techniques in their own poems. We examine Driscoll's fragments, which heighten her struggle to understand who this rapist is and stress his insatiable hunger; even unborn, he is a terrifying mouth of want. Driscoll's images, both literal and figurative, are masterful, such as these lines from "Difficult Word" describing the rape:

> I run. I run very very fast, Kate. But really Kate,
> > I am not
> running. And really I am not even crawling. Really

I am trying
to slither myself along the way you sometimes in TV
movies see soldiers under fire move. And really Kate,
it is only inches that I do move. Like used
    dishwater,
there is nothing left of me now. I am going to die,
      Katie.   (lines 25–30)

Seeing the power of imagery here and elsewhere in Driscoll's poems to evoke horror, despair, chaos, and isolation, students turn to their own poems eagerly. In revision, they add and refine images. Alexandra Cook, for example, working to convey the happiness in some children's artwork, incorporates this effective image: "smiles that spring up like daisies." Her poem then describes the bleak drawings by another child, J.:

Mother had purple on her cheeks
Dad's arms were raised
A white man in uniform
gun raised, aimed.

Later in the poem, other children complete their drawings and play outside, but "J. continues to paint trails of darkness."

The Rape Poems not only helps students write stronger poems but also speaks directly to service learning. Some of the community members my students work with have been molested by relatives; some were raped when homeless. The nonfiction texts in my course provide an intellectual, cultural framework for this trauma; the literature presents emotional urgency. Used in training programs for police, rape counselors, and the military, *The Rape Poems* is literature that effects change. It is also literature that challenges the tendency to interpret community members and their problems simplistically. The poems depict the aftermath of rape as long-term trauma, not something that can be fixed by kind friends or a little therapy. In "Page 134," Driscoll screams, terrified to read in a novel the same last name as the rapist: "This is over 2,000 days later" (line 4). In "That She May," a poem about suicidal thoughts, students learn "one in five attempt" (line 17). They learn, too, about culturally imposed guilt:

Maybe
no
isn't really
the right answer.   (78–81)

Driscoll hears frequently from readers; she's shared some of her e-mails with me, and I in turn have shared them with students. This one refers to her reading at a rape support group: "After I read 'Island of the Raped Women,' this beautiful young woman who had dropped out of school at grade 8 following rape said, 'I understand that poem. I've spent time in jail. I love jail. It's the only place I've ever felt safe.'" Students are stunned by this—its implication that our society is inherently unsafe for females. Yet in class discussions, some women agree. Male students tend to stay quiet. I gently acknowledge the difficulty of our discussion, complicating it by reading in class another e-mail from Driscoll, one about a male student confused by the poem "Island of the Raped Women" (from which the quotation in the title of this essay is drawn). Driscoll writes, "He said 'I get all that rape stuff, but the baking cakes and painting hats. . . . I don't get it.'" After I read the e-mail—silence. Finally, several women speak about compartmentalizing feelings, focusing on a small manageable task, creating something pretty to keep one's sanity. The language is coded, the class a mix of men and women. "Island of the Raped Women" concludes:

> At breakfast, we make a song, chanting our litany
> of so much collected blue. We do not talk of going
> back to the world. We talk of something else
> sweet to try with the oranges: sponge custard.
> Served with thick cream or perhaps with raspberry sauce.
> We paint hats. We paint hats.   (27–32)

Some readers see a happy ending here; Driscoll does not intend this. We've had fascinating class discussions about human beings' desire for hope and tidy endings and discomfort with complexity.

Our work challenges us to make room for both hope and the reality that social change is difficult and complex and that problems such as violence against women, racism, and poverty have deep, systemic roots. Class discussions, readings, assignments, service-learning placements—all can hold both hope and the realities of injustice. Our nonfiction texts explore devastating problems alongside case studies of success and Web sites that offer students a way to take action. One student writes that empathy alone "does nothing to help. It is in action that we make change." Another student, Andy Dalton, writes a poem that holds both injustice and possibility about a boy at his service-learning placement with a speech impediment. The boy is mocked by his peers as he responds to their request that he pronounce Mississippi: "The words sounded fine in his head / but came out as spit-filled, monosyllabic grunts." But the poem closes with this same boy in imaginative play with others:

> He was flying. He held a jump rope.
> I mean a steel cable
> that connected him to the mother ship.
> We were orbiting the Earth. It was beautiful.

Part V

Service Learning
in Cross-Disciplinary Studies

Carol Tyx and Mary Vermillion

Literature Goes to Prison:
A Reciprocal Service-Learning Project

I feel a deeper connection to the texts we've studied and to my community.
　　　　　　—*Ali*, a Mount Mercy University Book Club participant

Book Club . . . allows me to feel and stay connected to society.
　　　　　　—*Michael*, an Anamosa State Penitentiary Book Club participant

Since fall 2008, we, two English professors from Mount Mercy University, have taken literature and our students to prison through a service-learning project informally called Book Club. Small student groups plan and facilitate discussions of literary texts with small inmate groups at the Anamosa State Penitentiary, a maximum-security prison for men in Iowa. Research shows that higher education reduces recidivism, yet the Anamosa State Penitentiary, like most prisons in the United States, has no funds for such offerings.[1] When Anamosa's associate warden learned about a liberal arts prison program created by another Iowa college,[2] he asked a Mount Mercy criminal justice professor about collaborating with our university. She, in turn, conferred with us. We recognized that the warden's request fit with Mount Mercy's mission: "service for the well-being of all humanity and action in the cause of justice in the world" ("Our Mission"). From this intersection of mission and request, the idea of Book Club emerged.

　　The impetus continues to fuel the project over forty Book Club sessions later. We value Book Club because it bends "the arc of the moral universe . . . toward justice" as it promotes the intellectual and moral development of both inmates and students (King). We have used Book Club in general education classes and in courses for English majors ranging from Shakespeare seminars to American literature surveys. A flexible and effective pedagogical tool, Book Club requires only a small time commitment but produces big results for both prison and university participants. For the Anamosa participants, Book Club provides the opportunity to read more widely and to connect with people outside the prison. For the Mount Mercy students, Book Club dispels prison stereotypes and demonstrates the relevance of literature outside the classroom. Both groups develop an appreciation for two important capacities of literature: enriching readers' ethical frameworks and connecting readers from differing backgrounds. All participants build confidence in their abilities to communicate and negotiate difference. While both inmates and students enhance their understanding of the interpretive process, their focus differs. Anamosa participants expand their awareness of possible interpretations and the range of topics that can be discussed — irony, narrative structure, point of view; Mount Mercy students experience firsthand that interpretation is shaped by social positioning. Besides these immediate benefits, a project like Book Club enhances our understanding of why literature matters beyond the academy. Our service-learning project reveals literature's capacity to foster self-reflection, ethical thinking, empathy, and a more inclusive community.

An essential part of Book Club has been establishing a shared vision with our community partner, the Anamosa State Penitentiary. The prison staff members see the project as an opportunity to broaden inmates' reading and to open "their minds to places they may have never ventured" (Feeney-Wilfer). We likewise see Book Club as an opportunity for our students to broaden their perspectives as they discuss literature with a diverse community of readers. These goals require contributions from both partners. Our university provides the books, which then remain in the prison library, and our students provide a discussion guide for each Book Club and facilitate the discussions. The prison provides an orientation and tour for our students, and the prison's education coordinator, Mary Feeney-Wilfer, helps schedule Book Club, ensures that the literary texts are on the prison's approved list, selects inmate participants, distributes books and discussion guides to inmates, answers questions from inmates as they read outside sessions, and participates in each Book Club.

To prepare ourselves and our students to work effectively with the inmates, we scoured materials about prison culture and literacy. Repeatedly, we read about prisoners who found sustenance in literature. The prison educator and poet Judith Tannenbaum recalls prisoners who responded to poems "as though they'd received bread, actual matter with the power to nourish" (*Disguised as a Poem* 21). Wilbert Rideau, who spent most of his forty-four incarcerated years in Angola, describes his own hunger: "The biggest pain in prison . . . is the way you are assaulted psychologically and emotionally, the way in which you are robbed of any dignity as a human being and told in countless ways that you don't matter" (338). Reading and talking about literature helped Rideau counter that loss, bolstering his sense of identity. Obtaining books from the black market and later through a prison library, he discovered that reading helped him "feel empathy" and emerge from his "cocoon of self-centeredness and appreciate the humanness of others—to see that they, too, have dreams, aspirations, frustrations, and pain" (45–46). Rideau's experience exemplifies the philosopher Martha Nussbaum's belief that literature can foster social justice by increasing readers' capacities for empathy (see, e.g., *Poetic Justice*). Rideau eventually became an award-winning editor of the prison magazine the *Angolite*, and he played a key role in improving conditions for Angola inmates, not only by doing investigative journalism at the prison but also by learning to see the humanness of prison staff and cultivating relationships with trusted administrators (140–43).[3] Rideau attributes the maturity needed to accomplish these goals to the literary education he gleaned through reading (45–46).

A similar faith in the transformative power of reading fuels the alternative sentencing project Changing Lives through Literature. Because the founders so strongly believe that reading and discussing literature can literally change lives, offenders take part in a literature class in lieu of being incarcerated. Jean Trounstine and Robert Waxler, English professors and founders of the project, describe the benefits of discussing literature:

> As we hear others talk about their experience with the text, and as we talk about the characters with those who may see the world far differently than we do, we experience a paradox: We begin to see perspectives other than our own and, at the same time, we realize that our lives have brought us unique insights. A good story not only calls on us to exercise our minds, it asks us to reach deep into our hearts and evoke compassion for the characters, for each other, and for ourselves.   (8–9)[4]

Similarly, Nussbaum argues, "I defend the literary imagination precisely because it seems to me an essential ingredient of an ethical stance that asks us to concern ourselves with the good of other people whose lives are distant from our own" (*Poetic Justice* xvi). Here, scholars who ponder the ethical implications of reading literature get at the social justice aspects of reader-response theory: as we read about characters that live in circumstances unlike our own, we are moved to imaginatively inhabit and value those lives. Talking about that reading with people who live in circumstances unlike our own adds another potential layer where insight and compassion can be cultivated. Bolstered by these insights, we developed our ideas about what Book Club might teach both inmates and college students about the purposes of literature.

To prepare our students, we introduce Book Club on the first day of the semester. We include Book Club as an option on our syllabus, and we provide all students with a one-page handout that lists the basic requirements of the project: attending the prison orientation and tour, reading some brief sources about prison culture and literacy, planning and facilitating at least one Book Club, and writing a reflective essay about the experience.[5] Later in the semester, we provide students with a packet of more detailed materials, including the short required readings and tips for facilitating effective discussions.[6] Following Janet Eyler's lead, we attempt to weave reflection throughout our project, creating reflection activities that students can do alone and with classmates before, during, and after their service (36–42). For instance, before the orientation and tour, we provide students with questions to prompt individual and group reflection. Some of the group reflection occurs during our drive to and from the prison.

The orientation lasts about an hour and details the stark differences between academic and prison cultures. During the tour, we see the cafeteria, the yard, the library, the classroom where we hold Book Club, a housing unit, and a cell. The tour increases our students' knowledge about prison life and thus builds their confidence as they prepare to lead Book Club. Students also feel confident because they have already discussed the literary text in their Mount Mercy class.

Yet first-time Book Club participants often fear that the discussion will fall flat, that no one will talk. Fortunately, that's not what happens during the hour-and-a-half session. Participants argue about whether Captain Vere was right to execute Billy Budd; they draw pictures of Caliban and speculate on what he represents; they engage in a CSI simulation while examining Susan Glaspell's *Trifles*.[7] Inmate participants have often read the text more than once; they bring questions, perspectives, and an eagerness to debate. College students sometimes take literature and the opportunity to discuss it for granted, but the inmates are excited about joining a community of readers. The fervor of Book Club discussions often stuns our students: literature *matters* to the Anamosa readers.

It is when our students witness the inmates' passion for reading that Book Club becomes reciprocal. Our students enter the prison believing that they will teach the inmates. And they do: our students help the inmates make sense of Sherman Alexie's irony, Shakespeare's subplots, or Herman Melville's winding sentences. Yet once the Mount Mercy students recognize the inmates' high level of engagement, they also realize that the inmates have much to teach them about why literature matters.

Such learning can, of course, occur in traditional classrooms, but it is heightened in Book Club because the project brings together two radically different groups of readers. In Book Club, nearly all the Anamosa participants are men of color from urban areas;[8] most Mount Mercy participants, like the rest of the Mount Mercy student body, come from small, primarily white rural towns. Educational backgrounds also differ: most Anamosa participants complete their high school education through a prison GED program. They have limited experience with literature; none of the inmates in our first Book Club (*Othello*) had ever read a play. All these differences in social identity intertwine with the most obvious difference: after Book Club, Mount Mercy participants leave the prison and Anamosa participants return to their cells. Often, the biggest interpretive differences in Book Club seem to stem from the demographic and cultural differences between the two groups. These differences, in fact, strongly contribute to the project's learning outcomes.[9]

For our students, these outcomes are best demonstrated in the three-part reflective essay they write about Book Club. In the essay's first section, students describe and reflect on the ways in which Book Club reinforced, challenged, complicated, or enriched their interpretation of the literary text. In the second section, they discuss their learning about the purposes of literature and about the interpretive process. Instructions for the second section vary according to course objectives. Students in a course that introduces literary theory, for example, consider where Book Club participants primarily seem to look for meaning: the text itself, the author, or the reader. In the essay's third section, we ask students to reflect on ways Book Club affected them, suggesting topics such as emotional, spiritual, or social growth; the development of transferable skills; or the achievement of Mount Mercy's mission and goals.

Excerpts from our students' essays and inmates' written feedback reveal the ways in which Book Club strengthens their understanding of how and why literature matters. They discover for themselves the ideas put forth by the long line of thinkers who extol literature's potential for building community and for helping readers lead fuller, richer, more examined, or more ethical lives. Consider, for instance, the comments of one Mount Mercy student, Katie, about a discussion in which Book Club participants grappled with the question of whether Dr. Jekyll was responsible for Mr. Hyde's crimes. Robert Louis Stevenson's novel, she observes,

> allowed us to engage . . . in a conversation about right and wrong . . . without feeling vulnerable or self-conscious. Sitting in a room of criminals discussing innocence and responsibility would have been significantly more stressful had we not been able to do so through a story. This allowed them to . . . discuss freely their feelings on these issues without feeling hypocritical or judged.

Although Katie has not yet moved past an us/them conception of the interpretive community, she nevertheless echoes a key idea behind Changing Lives through Literature: "We are able to consider even the most awful of human actions through a character and come to grips with the most dreadful of our own experiences through someone else's story" (Trounstine and Waxler 9).

Key to this ethical thinking is the way in which literature expands our capacity for empathy. For Michael, an Anamosa participant, Book Club reading is "a door to the world of interacting. It creates a hunger to understand . . . not only your views but that of your fellow neighbors." This hunger to understand is often evident in our students' essays. Writing about a Book Club that featured *A Streetcar Named Desire*, Cody, a Mount Mercy student, describes a moment in which a young African American inmate ruefully reflected that he was a lot like Blanche. Just as Blanche resorted to prostitution in an attempt to achieve her dreams, the inmate resorted to selling drugs. Both of them, he believed, had trapped themselves in a vicious cycle. The inmate's empathy for Blanche in turn sparked Cody's, and the student began "to consider Blanche's dilemma from a larger social perspective." Cody writes:

> It's easy to look at how condescending and immoral Blanche is with disdain, to hate how manipulative she appears to be in kissing the paper boy and always trying to stay out of the light. What's difficult to look at is the

bigger picture, to see her as a person like anyone else, with hopes and aspirations that tragically fall apart after the death of her parents and suicide of her husband.

Here we have a double-layered imaginative act. Cody glimpses the life of the inmate, so different from his own, who had imagined the life of Blanche, so different from his own: a powerful domino effect of empathy.

Like Cody, many students write about the inmates' identifications with characters—especially identifications that surprise them or differ from their own. It is this topic that often triggers students' richest writing about the interpretive process. The strongest essays speculate on the reasons for interpretive differences. Students attempt to understand the ways in which reading is influenced by social positioning—both that of the inmates and their own. Writing about a Book Club focused on *Othello*, for instance, Josh reveals that he expected the inmates, who were all African American, to identify with the title character. Like the rest of the Mount Mercy group, Josh was surprised when most of the inmates were more interested in and sympathetic with Iago. As Josh processes his surprise, he explains, "We focused on the corruption of Othello through the trickery of Iago." Josh continues:

> [But] the prisoners seemed to focus on the idea of . . . self-reliance. . . . It seems that our experience led us to focus more heavily on the theme of corruption, of how far and quickly a man can fall—one of the more obvious themes of *Othello*. However, the prisoners, dependent as they [are] on the authority figures of the prison, valued the discussion of self-reliance the play elicited: How much should we trust one another? How much should we depend on one another to help us and guide us responsibly and morally? In a prison, when one is sequestered with other men, some guilty of serious crimes, these are real questions bearing real consequences.

Josh realizes that social positioning is more complex than he once thought—not only a matter of race and class but also, in this case, a literal position or location. He implies that the Mount Mercy students' interpretations were shaped by a university setting and the privilege it confers, whereas the inmates' interpretations were shaped by a prison setting and the volatile power relations within it. Josh imaginatively constructs an example of how different readers make meaning and how different environments "make" readers.

As students examine spaces of dissonance, they deepen their understanding of how identity shapes interpretation. In a session on F. Scott Fitzgerald's short story "Babylon Revisited," the major interpretive crux involved whether Charlie, a high-living, roaring twenties tycoon, has reformed enough to be granted the custody of his daughter. Inmates overwhelmingly believed Charlie had reformed and was wrongfully being denied his right to his daughter. Mount Mercy students were skeptical, citing instances where Fitzgerald hints at Charlie's lack of transformation. The inmates refused to be swayed. On the ride home in the van, students suggested that the inmates needed to believe that a person could change and that this need limited their ability to acknowledge the story's ambiguity. Students became aware of the blinders our social positioning can put on us, constricting our vision and distorting our interpretive lenses.

When Mount Mercy students reflect on their own distorted lenses, they often focus on their attitudes toward "criminals." Nearly all our students become wary of the media's negative or overdramatized depictions of prisons and prisoners and more wary of stereotypes in general. Joseph, an Anamosa participant, describes one reason for this shift: "Seeing that some inmates do use their time constructively . . . they can relate to us in ways they may not have thought prior to their visits here at the prison." Once students have grappled with moral complexities among a group of articulate, thoughtful, witty inmates, insiders and outsiders are no longer so sharply delineated.

As students detail the ways that Book Club has helped them grow, they describe several additional benefits of service learning that Janet Eyler and Dwight E. Giles highlight in *Where's the Learning in Service Learning?* (see esp. chs. 2 and 6). Our students note that they have developed skills in collaborating, planning, and facilitating discussions; greater agility in thinking and speaking on their feet; and greater ease in negotiating difference. They also describe attitudinal changes such as increased self-confidence and the ability to take meaningful risks. The Anamosa participant Joseph also notes some of these changes: "During my early teenage years I was a shy and reserved person. . . . I gained the ability to express my views and thoughts with unfamiliar people and in group settings."[10]

The ripple of effects extends beyond individual iterations of Book Club. Many students develop a long-term commitment to the project and participate in more than one Book Club throughout their tenure as English majors, becoming increasingly skilled facilitators.[11] Students, including alumni, volunteer to staff Book Club in the summer. After seeing the meager offerings in the prison library, the English Club organized a book drive. Recently, Carol Tyx and a veteran Book Club participant collaborated on a series of poetry-writing workshops at another local prison.

Beyond its immediate benefits, what implications might projects such as Book Club have for the field of literary studies today? The reading environment of such a project emphasizes the richness of reader responses, including how texts interrogate our ethical frameworks and cultivate our empathy. In *Uses of Literature*, Rita Felski suggests that "to engage seriously with ordinary motives for reading" may be a helpful move at this moment in literary studies (13–14). In *The Word on the Street: Linking the Academy and the Common Reader*, Harvey Teres likewise advocates a renewal of academic literary studies by bringing what literature can offer into the community (2). Such ventures can enrich the conversation about why literature matters and to whom it might speak.

Book Club takes literature outside the academy and into the world. As we examine the ways in which our social positioning shapes our reading, we can connect deeply with other readers. Kim, a Mount Mercy student, describes this reader-to-reader link: "Literature can be a leveler, a key that unlocks a group of thinkers from very different backgrounds and experience to discover common ground, new ways to look at a piece of literature, and respect for each other's impressions and opinions." As an Anamosa participant puts it, "We might have very different backgrounds, but through . . . reading, we are all the same. Seekers of justice, of happiness, love, friendship and equality for all." Perhaps this is what the future university might resemble: collaborations of shared knowledge between those inside the walls of the academy and those on the outside. Through shared reading ventures, insiders and outsiders build a communal belief in the power of literature to connect us.

NOTES

1. A key reason for this lack of funding was the 1994 revocation of Pell Grants to prisoners. For other reasons and for the correlation between higher education and inmate rehabilitation, see McCarty 87–89.

2. For a brief description of Grinnell College's Liberal Arts in Prison Program, see "Liberal Arts in Prison."

3. In his memoir, *In the Place of Justice*, Rideau focuses several chapters on his role as editor of the *Angolite*, a magazine written by inmates at the Louisiana

State Penitentiary. Under Rideau's leadership, the *Angolite* shifted from reporting activities to investigative journalism, winning numerous awards for articles that exposed injustices in the prison system. The *Angolite* Web site no longer exists, but, for more information on the *Angolite*, see "Doing Time."

4. For further information on the history and philosophy of the project, see *Changing Lives*.

5. Usually at least two-thirds of the students in a course choose to participate in Book Club. We create alternative assignments for nonparticipants.

6. For sample course materials, see "Prison Book Club." Our short required readings include two sources from the Web site *The Sentencing Project* that provide context for the fact that nearly all inmate Book Club participants are African American ("Facts"; Mauer and King 1–5). The other two sources emphasize the transformative power of literacy and literature in prison settings (Jackson; McLaughlin, Trounstine, and Waxler 5–9, 18–21, 29–32).

7. Because most of our courses are canonically based, many Book Club texts are classics such as Shakespeare's *Macbeth*, Williams's *A Streetcar Named Desire*, Shelley's *Frankenstein*, Hurston's "The Gilded Six-Bits," and Olsen's "I Stand Here Ironing." The most effective Book Club texts feature thematic plenitude, complex characters, and protagonists that make life-changing decisions or fight back against society.

8. African Americans are incarcerated at nearly six times the rate of white people. Iowa has the highest ratio of black to white incarceration: nearly fourteen African Americans for every one white person (Mauer and King 3).

9. The book club format is another key to the participants' learning. Classroom research highlights the benefits of the format: "They [students] were responsible for introducing ideas, clarifying one another's comments and questions, balancing talk among the participants, and so forth—behavior and activity that, within more traditional classrooms, lies primarily within the teacher's domain" (McMahon et al. 23).

10. Feeney-Wilfer observes that through the experience of Book Club "the offenders feel more confident and are willing to take the chance to share their values, their convictions and sometimes their innermost thoughts."

11. There are two main reasons for the repetition. First, we each use Book Club in one course per semester, and, since Mount Mercy's English program has only five full-time faculty members, students inevitably take a course that features Book Club most semesters. Second, and more important, Book Club is fun and rewarding.

Robin J. Barrow

Building Empathy through Service Learning and Narratives of Sexual Violence

Sexual violence is an undeniable fact of American life. According to the FBI's *Uniform Crime Report*, in 2010 there were 84,767 rapes reported and 20,088 arrests. There were an additional 72,628 arrests for sexual offenses ("Crime"). These numbers represent only cases determined to be "founded" by local officers and only acts against women. They exclude the many rapes that go unreported, as well as other acts along the continuum of sexual violence such as public indecency, voyeurism, verbal harassment, molestation, and sexual coercion (Kelly; Leidig). There are a myriad of ways to approach the problem of sexual violence: legal theorists tackle the definitions of rape, assault, and harassment; philosophers investigate the meaning of consent; psychologists study coping strategies in victims; sociologists examine group attitudes that condone or decry sexual violence; and cultural critics examine how ideology leads a society to accept sexual violence as the norm.

Representations of sexual violence in music, literature, and the visual arts can reflect social and political realities, and they can be used to communicate psychological or symbolic themes. In spring 2010, I taught an interdisciplinary seminar, Sexual Violence in Western Culture, which foregrounded stories of physical and emotional abuse in history, literature, and visual and audio arts to interrogate cultural attitudes about victims, perpetrators, sex, violence, and the individual. I assigned a service-learning project for several reasons: to satisfy the mission of a land-grant university to reach out to the community; to give students real-world experience with public service and professional responsibility; to build cultural diversity through exposure to local community organizations; and, most of all, to humanize sexual violence theory and statistics. Service learning and the discussion of literature functioned recursively to build students' empathy with both imaginary characters and real people, which contributed to students' desire for social change.

The Uses of Empathy

Though there is some disagreement about the exact definition of *empathy*, here I use the term to refer to the imaginative act of putting oneself into another's place to understand that person's emotions.[1] Empathy, compassion, sympathy, and altruism are vital elements of an egalitarian and democratic society. Martha Nussbaum explains, "Habits of empathy and conjecture conduce to a certain type of citizenship and a certain form of community: one that cultivates a sympathetic responsiveness to another's needs, and understands the way circumstances shape those needs, while respecting separateness and privacy" (*Not for Profit* 90). Empathy is also a vital element in Rogerian psychology, the dominant approach used in rape crisis centers. An empathetic listener acknowledges and accepts the survivor's feelings, whatever they may be. This perception of being understood is key to the recovery process. As Alice Sebold demonstrates in her memoir *Lucky*, survivors commonly feel alienated from their families and friends and believe that many people can no longer relate to them, that they are "other than" (20). Acceptance helps heal the rupture between survivors' former identities and their new conceptions of self. Empathy is an important element in rape *prevention*, as well. Empathy training is widely used in the rehabilitation of convicted sex offenders.[2] In a Canadian program, journal writing by participants combined with discussion of victim accounts "often elicits feelings of remorse from group participants and empathy for their victims" (Mamabolo 158). In the legal realm, jury members' empathy for victims correlates with harsher sentencing for the perpetrator (Deitz, Blackwell, Daley, and Bentley 382). These applications suggest the critical importance of empathy when investigating sexual violence.

The study of literature and the arts as the principal method of inculcating empathy, whether in rehabilitation programs or school curricula, is the subject of current debate among scholars. Nussbaum argues that schools "must give a central place in the curriculum to the humanities and the arts, cultivating a *participatory* type of education that activates and refines the capacity to see the world through another person's eyes" (*Not for Profit* 96; my emphasis). Suzanne Choo, in her argument for a Cosmopolitan Literature curriculum, asserts the importance of literature in the formation of responsible citizens "since, more than any art form, it provides access to the consciousness of another person or community" (61). But this pedagogical stance is not without its detractors. Susan Verducci laments the emphasis on aesthetic empathy over moral action. Suzanne Keen observes that there is no evidence that fantasy empathy, the type fostered by reading imaginative literature, will lead to altruistic action, although she concedes that the discussion of literature, as opposed to mere reading, can lead to altruism (91, 146). Lisa Taylor reminds educators of the self-centered possibilities of empathetic readings, "the desire for an apparently seamless psychic union with characters" without self-reflection (303). Megan Boler similarly cautions, "the social imagination reading model is a binary power relationship of self/other that threatens to consume and annihilate the very differences that permit empathy" (159); it can lead students to be content with passive empathy rather than active citizenship (156). While I concede these risks, a pedagogy that confronts assumptions and invites challenges holds the potential to improve students' critical thinking and to help them empathize in alternative contexts. Service learning constitutes a vital part of this oppositional pedagogy.

The Course

University Honors 257 provides students in the Chancellor's Honors Program at the University of Tennessee the opportunity to examine a particular topic in the arts and humanities from a multidisciplinary perspective. My course for the 2010 spring semester borrowed strategies not only from literature and the arts but also from history, economics, feminist studies, psychology, evolutionary biology, sociology, criminal justice, and media studies, although I emphasized cultural representations of sexual violence rather than statistics or legal debates. The readings included selections from Roman history, Greek mythology, the Bible, Harper Lee's *To Kill a Mockingbird*, Richard Wright's *Native Son*, Emily Brontë's *Wuthering Heights*, Alice Sebold's *Lucky*, and the films *Thelma and Louise* and *A Streetcar Named Desire*. Eighteen highly motivated students were enrolled in the course, most of them first-year students who had been involved in extracurricular high school programs like Jazz for Justice and Amnesty International. The students hailed from many majors and colleges: four were majoring in engineering, two in anthropology; three were nursing majors or premed; none were declared English majors. Sixteen were women, and two were men. Two were visible members of a minority group, which matched university demographics. One student self-identified as a survivor of sexual violence.

Service learning was fully integrated into the course. The class met twice each week for seventy-five minutes, and we usually spent fifteen minutes on discussion of service learning. One class session was substituted entirely with group planning. Each student dedicated twelve to fourteen hours to a community partner and reported his or her progress at three points during the term. For the final exam, each student submitted a time log and a final reflection, and each group created a presentation showcasing their work. The service-learning project, which was graded on effort and completion, counted for thirty percent of the course grade. Other related course requirements included weekly electronic journal entries, an annotated bibliography, and a literary synthesis paper.

Service Outcomes

The ideal of service learning is to benefit the students and community partners equally and significantly. My students worked in project groups with one of four partner organizations: Safe Haven Crisis and Recovery Center for Sexual Assault (the Sexual Assault Center of East Tennessee), the Knox County Health Department, CASA (Court Appointed Special Advocates), and the YWCA. Tasks were designed by the community partners in consultation with me.

The success of service learning often depends on factors both within and outside the educator's control. At Safe Haven, five students sorted through old records and created an index, discovering in the process that two of the original founders had been conflated because their first names were the same. They also conducted interviews by telephone and with a video camera at the founders' dinner. When two members of the group needed more hours, they created a mock-up of a publicity brochure. Students in this group worked independently and did not clearly communicate their schedule with the others; the two students who had planned to complete the bulk of their work later in the semester were left scrambling. This could have been prevented by my requiring a more detailed schedule of their plans and by contacting the staff at Safe Haven more frequently.

Five students worked with the health department's rape and violence prevention health educator, who wanted to institute a viral, online media campaign. The students researched qualities of effective public service announcements and used *iMovie* to produce two videos, one focused on bystander intervention and one on risk awareness. The products were intended to be spread through *YouTube*, *Facebook*, and *Twitter*, but because of turnover in the health department, neither product was used; the risk-awareness video may eventually be distributed by the new health educator.

Students working with CASA ran into difficulties when an event coordinator returned from leave and wanted to change the date of a ceremony they had already arranged. CASA, which works with children placed in foster care and often encounters cases of sexual abuse, was excited about forging ties with the university, though initially unsure how to employ the students since most of their volunteers were trained advocates. Four students assisted with CASA's 5K fund-raiser and helped arrange the annual candlelight ceremony. They recruited performers and advertised the event with flyers and on *Facebook*. After a series of e-mail negotiations, the ceremony was held as originally planned.

The four students partnered with the YWCA, which serves victims of domestic violence (sexual violence and domestic violence stem from similar drives and situations), wrote and performed skits on healthy relationship boundaries for the Y-Teens Real Talk Summit, an educational event for girls. Attendees noted these skits as their favorite part of the summit. The YWCA group was a model of good communication and clear expectations.

Despite and perhaps because of these challenges, students learned about our community and gained practical experience, such as the importance of clear communication and the difficulty of working through bureaucratic hurdles. Although only the YWCA group had direct contact with the population served by the partner organization, all students learned a great deal about sexual violence when being introduced to the organizations. At the start of the term, representatives from Safe Haven met with students to inform them about sexual violence on campus and in the local community. Most students had not previously realized the extent of the problem. In the second week of class, the county health educator spoke to the students about social norms that condone sexual violence and about her work trying to change those norms. From the earliest journal entries, students reported having their eyes opened and thinking about sexual violence in new ways. Discovering that there was a community need gave the academic subject relevance for the students. An obvious question is whether the same benefit could have been achieved without the service-learning requirement. The initial learning experience would have been almost the same, though it would have lacked the students' excitement about contributing to social change. Service learning also provided a catalyst for students to conceptualize survivors of sexual violence as individuals with distinct needs that the community organizations try to satisfy. Because few students had direct contact with survivors, this step toward empathy would have been incomplete without our discussion of literary texts.

Service Learning as Literature Pedagogy

The recursive relation of service learning and discussion of literature is traceable in students' service-learning reflections, their weekly journals, and their literary synthesis papers. For their weekly journals, students were asked to comment on some aspect of our class discussions, our readings, or their service-learning project.[3] I did not specifically direct students to discuss literary elements in this assignment, though many did. They analyzed the development of the theme of innocence in *To Kill a Mockingbird*, blindness as a symbol in *Native Son*, the applicability of Gustav Freytag's pyramid to Wright's novel,[4] the setting and Nelly Dean's unreliable narration in *Wuthering Heights*, and Blanche's illusion of youthfulness in *A Streetcar Named Desire*. More frequently, students used their journals to explore a text's personal or social relevance. They wrote about statistics; explanations of personal and interpersonal psychology, news stories and images in the media; and anecdotes about themselves, their families, or their communities. Statements about social conditions or needed changes to society were common. Empathetic reactions were apparent in hypothetical statements about what a student would do in a similar situation, questions about what an experience would feel like, and the use of feeling words or statements like "I identify with" and "this made me see." For the final synthesis paper, students were asked to use their service-learning experience to think through one of the course texts: their goals were to share what they had learned in their service-learning projects, to demonstrate close-reading skills, and to present a point of view supported with evidence and logical reasoning. To prepare students for this assignment, I incorporated comparisons between texts and our partner organizations throughout the semester.

Before reading *To Kill a Mockingbird*, students learned from Safe Haven about cultural attitudes of victim blaming and the revictimization that can occur during courtroom trials.[5] Using this information, the class examined Atticus Finch's behavior on the stand. Atticus seems a model of reason and empathy, which makes it difficult to criticize him. His statement to Scout could almost serve as an epigraph for this chapter: "You never really understand a person until you consider things from his point of view . . . until you climb into his skin and walk around in it" (33). Yet if one considers the possibility that Mayella Ewell might have been raped, Atticus's behavior in the courtroom demonstrates the revictimization that Safe Haven described. Here a community partner's information led to a more nuanced reading of character and narration. It highlighted Scout's limited point of view and revealed some of the ways that Mayella is a victim of her family, circumstances, and society. In the literary synthesis paper, four students stressed the filth the Ewells lived in, their poor nutrition, the father's alcoholism, and the family's isolation. They connected the novel to the preventative services offered by their community partners—the health department, CASA, and the YWCA—which, had they been available, would have improved the Ewells' living conditions and decreased their social ostracism. Exposure to groups like Safe Haven and the YWCA showed students that oppressions are interlocking rather than hierarchical.

Ethnic, racial, religious, class, and gender discriminations occur within the same social fabric, as evident in *Native Son*, which presents an ethical challenge to readers. Wright's vivid descriptions, presentation of an internal perspective, and detailed explanation of character motives encourage sympathetic identification with Bigger Thomas, but many readers initially reject this transfer because of their disapproval of Bigger's acts of murder and rape. Unsurprisingly, my students refused to say that they sympathized with Bigger, but after in-class discussion they conceded empathizing with him. Their sympathy was predicated on approval or perhaps pity, whereas empathy was perceived as neutral. Realizing that they could empathize with someone whose actions they could not condone, students became more open to empathy in general. They saw that although Bigger is a perpetrator, he is also a victim. They put themselves

into his place and acknowledged the influences that shaped his character: "Bigger had grown up caged like an animal"; "I wish I could see his
personality if he had been raised in a different time or under different circumstances, or even as a different race"; "He never had anyone to confide
in or to believe in him."

My students recognized that Wright's project was to horrify his audience to highlight the need for social change, and they observed that Bigger suffers not only from racism but also from poverty and neglect. Lisa
wrote:

> What would Bigger have become if just one person cared enough to sit
> down and talk to him as a human and not hound him about his responsi-
> bilities or remind him of the closed doors? This is my mission now. To be
> the one that listens to others who have no one else because it might save
> them from losing themselves like Bigger did.[6]

Recognizing Bigger as a person with feelings who is trapped by his social
situation led Lisa to make a commitment to social change, demonstrating the pedagogical dynamic among literary analysis, the development of
empathy, and the impulse toward social activism.

This interplay of service learning and literary analysis was further
demonstrated by the response to *Wuthering Heights*. In class and in journals, students noted the downward spiral of unhealthy relationships
and identified early warning signs, such as Heathcliff's calendar that reveals his obsession with how much time Cathy spends with him. Crystal,
a student in the YWCA group, remarked on the generational impact of
unhealthy boundaries in Linton's manipulation of young Cathy. Her perception that domestic violence operates in cycles was confirmed by a case
she witnessed at the local courthouse's Order of Protection Day. Crystal
and her group then applied their understanding to their service-learning
project. Their skits for the Y-Teens Real Talk Summit promoted healthy
relationships by illustrating negative behaviors, such as a girl constantly
texting her boyfriend and a boy pressuring his girlfriend to study in his
bedroom. Each skit ended at a crisis point, at which time the audience was
asked for possible solutions. Our classroom discussion of literature, driven
by the service-learning project, led to a direct benefit for the YWCA.

At times, the literature opened a new perspective on a community organization. Sebold's *Lucky* tells the first-person, true story of a first-year
college student who is raped. Students readily identified with Sebold and

felt outraged on her behalf. Service-learning students who partnered with Safe Haven compared our local facilities with the rape crisis center in Syracuse that had pressured Sebold to prosecute and to think of herself as a victim rather than a survivor. Among the Safe Haven team, Lily realized that factors such as aggressive politicization or a fear of stigma might alienate women like Sebold and prevent them from accepting the available advocacy and therapy. Lily's synthesis paper expressed her appreciation of Safe Haven's uniqueness in providing a sexual-assault nurse examiner and in supporting a survivor's decision to prosecute or not.

At other times, the community organization opened a new perspective on the text, such as when students working with the health department reflected on the difficulty of bystander intervention in the context of *Lucky* and their project. When passersby heard Sebold crying out, their investigation could have stopped the attack. Natasha asserted, "We, as a country, need to be more aware of what goes on around us, and we need to learn to step in if we think we are witnessing something peculiar." This is much easier said than done, as this group discovered. Their project was to create two video PSAs, one of which addressed bystander intervention. The five students struggled to develop a plausible scenario where they could imagine themselves intervening, finally settling on a party scene in which a drunken girl's friends prevent her from leaving with a new acquaintance. It was easy at first to criticize characters in a book but harder once students put themselves into their place. Ethan concluded, "[O]ne of the biggest challenges the Knox County Health Department faces is to give bystanders the courage to intervene in a potentially violent situation." These students would not have learned about bystander intervention without working with the community partner, nor would they have discovered the gap between theory and practice.

Reading the literary texts enriched the service-learning experience, and vice versa. Crystal commented, "I feel that through this service-learning project, I got the chance to see the material we studied in class become real." Hannah agreed: "I was able to connect fiction with reality through the experiences of others." Since most students did not have contact with victims, this transformation was largely conceptual. Service learning functioned as a pedagogical technique that granted a truth effect to the fictional stories and, by suggesting possibilities for social activism, prevented students from becoming too depressed by the emotionally challenging literature, which had been one of my concerns when designing the course. Conversely, reading literary characters' personal responses to sexual violence emphasized the need for services provided by our community partners.

Students in my course learned about rape trauma syndrome, the prejudices against rape victims within the legal system and their own social groups, the difficulties of victim advocacy, and the complexity of social change. They practiced critical thinking and empathizing with a variety of individuals—skills vital to active and engaged citizenship. Though the contribution of service learning to the course cannot be precisely measured, the students on the whole believed that it was one of the core components. On the semester-end evaluations, six students specifically identified service learning as the aspect of class that most contributed to their learning; the remaining twelve mentioned class discussions or individual texts. Instead of merely developing fantasy empathy, students learned ways to transform empathy into altruistic action, and several students like Lisa expressed a desire to continue working with their partner agencies. Service learning helped bridge the gap between students and victims, whether in literature or real life.

In Elizabeth Barrett Browning's epic poem *Aurora Leigh* (a portion of which was assigned for the course), the poet Aurora asserts the power of the imagination to effect social change. When her cousin Romney, wary of what Lisa Taylor would consider self-centered altruism, offers to make poverty personal by enlisting Aurora in his socialist project, she counters by averring the need for

> a poet's individualism
> To work your universal. It takes a soul,
> To move a body . . .
> . . . .
> It takes the ideal, to blow a hair's-breadth off
> The dust of the actual.   (book 2, lines 478–83)

Though Aurora eventually wins this battle, with she and her cousin uniting to alter beliefs and social structures, in my class the ideal and the real complemented each other. The study of literature, combined with service learning, rallied the students to engage in moral education and to improve their ability to empathize in new contexts.

NOTES

1. *Empathy* was coined at the end of the nineteenth century. Earlier discussions refer to sympathy, compassion, or altruism, which today are often conflated with empathy. Gustav Jahoda provides a useful history of the term's development. For a theoretical discussion of the implication of divergent views of empathy, see Verducci.

2. Kurt M. Bumby notes that empathy training's efficacy depends on several variables, such as intimacy, self-esteem, and cultural pressures, whose interrelations are not fully understood.

3. Students had the option of keeping public journals on *Blackboard Learn* (a course management system) or maintaining private journals, which were not included in this study.

4. Freytag's 1863 study, *Die Technik des Dramas* (translated as *Freytag's Technique of the Drama* by Elias J. MacEwan), identified five divisions of the standard dramatic arc: exposition, rising action, climax, falling action, and denouement.

5. Susan Estrich claims that the legal system seeks to discredit women, enacting a second violation on the stand (42). Similarly, Susan Ehrlich's linguistic study notes that defending attorneys use language more appropriate to consensual sex and that the "frame of utmost resistance" (the idea that if a woman does not physically fight with every ounce of her strength then she has consented) continues to affect court judgments despite its no longer being law (118).

6. All student names are pseudonyms.

Sarah D. Wald

Sustainable Harvests: Food Justice, Service Learning, and Environmental Justice Pedagogy

In fall 2011, I revamped a previously taught course, Sustainable Harvests: Food Justice and U.S. Literature, to incorporate a service-learning experience. Sustainable Harvests uses food justice as a window into twentieth-century literature of the United States. The class explores the contemporary politics of food and encourages students to consider the relation of literature and society, including the relation of literature and social movements. The primary community partner for the class was El Comité de Apoyo a los Trabajadores Agrícolas (CATA; The Farmworker Support Committee), an organization advocating on behalf of and organizing farmworkers across the mid-Atlantic region of the United States. Teaching Sustainable Harvests as a service-learning course convinced me of the value of service learning not only for the ways it benefits local communities but also for the ways it can deepen students' understanding of the power of narratives to produce, counter, and transform social relations in the world around them.[1]

Students in my class learned to see both established literary texts and their own writing as public work with a social impact. They increased their understanding of environmental justice issues associated with food and farming while contributing to an organization that advocates the equal distribution of environmental privileges and burdens. They produced outreach materials for the organization that required them to think about their representations of farmworkers alongside the more well-known literary representations we interrogated in the classroom. They considered the interpretive act of literary analysis alongside the interpretive act of translation as they engaged Spanish-speaking farmworkers in conversation, with the help of translators. The experience of listening to, learning from, and representing the voices of those occupying some of the most vulnerable positions in our food system was the primary component of their service project; this activity developed student understanding of positionality, an insight necessary for students to engage with contemporary cultural studies, one of the learning objectives of service learning.

The Course in Context

I taught the course in the College of Liberal Arts at Drew University, a small private university located thirty miles from New York City, in Madison, New Jersey. Drew University enrolls around 2,100 full-time students, of which 1,700 are undergraduates. Sustainable Harvests serves as an elective course for both the Program in Environmental Studies and Sustainability and the Department of English. The students have varying levels of experience with reading and analyzing literature, a challenge interdisciplinary teaching frequently poses.

Sustainable Harvests pushes students to develop an environmental justice—not just environmentalist—consideration of food and farming. The environmental justice movement originated in the United States in the early 1980s in protest against the disproportionate number of environmental ills that burden communities of color and low-income communities (Di Chiro 301). An environmental justice perspective on food and farming includes a focus on the process through which food is produced and distributed and an analysis of politically disenfranchised communities' access to food. Accordingly, the thematic content of Sustainable Harvests moves from the politics of food consumption to the politics of food production and includes fictional and nonfictional literary works in each of the course's four units. The first unit of the course, "The Consumer," revolves around Michael Pollan's *Omnivore's Dilemma*. In the second portion of the class, "The Farmer," we engage American agrarian narratives. Building from our discussions of Pollan, we analyze Willa Cather's *O Pioneers!* and David Mas Masumoto's *Four Seasons in Five Senses: Things Worth Savoring* to develop a more complex understanding of race and gender in American farming narratives. The third section of the class, "The Farmworker," explores John Steinbeck's *The Grapes of Wrath* in the context of the food justice movement and farmworker organizing efforts from the United Farm Workers to the Coalition of Immokalee Workers. The final section of the class, "The Factory," considers food systems workers beyond the farm, and our readings include Upton Sinclair's *The Jungle* and Eric Schlosser's *Fast Food Nation*.

Working with CATA enhanced students' ability to place food justice literature and their writing in the framework of economic and social conditions. CATA focuses on educating and empowering farmworkers in the eastern United States. There are an estimated 2.5 million farmworkers in the United States and about 25,000 farmworkers in Drew University's home state of New Jersey. Most farmworkers are undocumented, and fewer than 50,000 farmworkers nationwide have union contracts (Carrasquillo 121). According to Nelson Carrasquillo, CATA's general coordinator, "The purpose of this [food] system is to maximize profit to the producers and the merchants who distribute the food to consumers. Underlying this is a system of racial privilege, for as the principal beneficiaries, farmers are in their vast majority white, and farm workers, the tool that enables the system to work, are generally people of color." Carrasquillo would like to see the food system shift to one that values "the Human Being as a whole" (131). Students are encouraged to see the unequal power relations among farm labor, racial privilege, immigration policy, and labor law through their course readings, their conversations with CATA staff members and CATA members, and their work to produce outreach materials for CATA.

By the end of the course, students understand the centrality of labor and immigration to food politics in the United States and have shifted their focus from consumer health to worker well-being. Students consider what it would mean to have a food movement focused not only on the power of consumers but also on the rights of workers to organize, as well as on immigration reform. Through their analysis of literary texts and their engagement with CATA, students reflect on their place in society and in relation to the community partners. I required a series of reflective essays throughout the class asking the students to draw connections between the literature we read and their service-learning experience. In these writing assignments, alongside our class discussions, students discussed the role of literature in both exposing power relations and seeking to transform those relations.

Most students found that literature enhanced their empathy for farmworkers and farmers, as well as provided a socioeconomic context for their work with CATA. As one student, Julie, explained, "The literature we read this semester effectively entitled us to information about what it was like for small farm families to own a farm, or what it takes to harvest and grow peaches. From these lessons, we could begin to understand and relate to the members of CATA, in a way."[2] Angela, another student, wrote, "The literature from this semester has provided a historical foundation for the CATA experience. Both *The Jungle* and *Grapes of Wrath* identify with the historical plight of immigrant workers in the food industry." For Courtney, reading and analyzing literature alongside her work with CATA transformed her view of the world:

> My interaction with CATA members altered my belief on industry. Seeing the faces of those marginalized in effort to create cheap industrial food illustrated that bigger does not mean better. As an economics major this concept was hard to wrap my head around. I had come to accept that people sometimes get hurt in making profits. Starting with Steinbeck's *Grapes of Wrath* and then in *Fast Food Nation* and *The Jungle*, I read about workers' rights and livelihood sacrificed for speed and profits. . . . I began to question the model for success that economics instilled in me. Surely fair labor should be a sign of a farm's success and not profits alone.

Literature helped the students imagine lives different from their own as well as deepened their understanding of the power relations that structure race, class, and immigration status in the United States.

Listening to Workers

Service learning provides an innovative means to alter the ways that students read, analyze, and respond to literature. As Kevin Guerrieri explains, "community engagement is aimed at helping students juxtapose multiple (con)texts, helping them develop the ability to critically create meanings—and simultaneously question notions of absolute meaning—localized in the interstices between word and world" (160). Service learning asks students to learn to read real-world situations and to consider the gaps between their reading of texts and their reading of community interactions. This juxtaposition helped students in my course develop an understanding of the politics of representation and recognize the assumptions that many students brought into the community setting as a result of the novels we read.

Most students testified in reflective writing assignments that meeting with farmworkers humanized agricultural laborers. One senior, Elaine, wrote, "One of the most interesting aspects of the CATA project was being able to speak to farm workers and understand their perspectives on their work. It is difficult to read a novel—or even a nonfiction book like Eric Schlosser's *Fast Food Nation*—and gain a true understanding of a population's lifestyle or general experience." Courtney explained the experience further: "Having the opportunity to meet and converse with the CATA members put a face behind the anonymous system." Stephanie echoed this line of thought: "Making the trip to work with CATA gave me something I would never have achieved in a classroom, perspective. It is easy to read accounts of workers, explaining what they do and why they do it; reading allows distancing. . . . The community based learning component of the course changed my perspective from a bystander to a participant." For many of the students, our meetings with CATA defied their expectations. After returning from our first visit to CATA early in the semester, several students expressed to me their disappointment that the farmworkers did not appear more oppressed. The students' surprise does not reflect improved working conditions for farm laborers. Rather, the farmworkers did not perform their oppression for the students in the ways that the documentaries and novels featured in the class prepared them to expect. As one student, Jeff, stated:

> I had expected to hear stories of abuse and exploitation, not unlike the horrors which prompted the formation of the Coalition of Immokalee Workers (CIW). Although some stories we did hear were quite striking— like that some families will eat pesticide-ridden tomatoes in the field because they have nothing else to eat, or that some packinghouses still make ground turkey sausages using meat with worms—overall, what impressed me more deeply was not the sheer difficulty of the work experience, but rather the silent courage and resilience of the workers.

Through reflection and continued discussion with CATA staff and members, many of the students came to view the workers not simply as less oppressed than they originally expected but as more accustomed to the difficulties of their jobs. Conditions that would have traumatized the students did not seem particularly atrocious to workers. Understanding the difference between student expectations and the realities farmworkers described required students to shift their perspectives. As Elaine stated, "After reading multiple articles and books about the overwhelming mistreatment of farm workers and their lack of ability to change the system, I was surprised to see that actual farm workers were happier to have jobs than horrified by the conditions." Chelsea elaborated: "We have a very different view of the lives of the members of CATA than the members see their lives. We are so privileged that much of what they have to endure on a day to day basis seems unbearable to any of us, yet to the members of CATA it is everyday life and better than what they have experienced in their past." Several students took from this interaction the importance of understanding worker experiences and listening to workers' voices first-hand. As Elaine stated, "True knowledge of how farm workers perceive themselves is essential to understanding their role in the food system and in society."

It also seems to me that some students entered the service-learning component of the course expecting to "save" farmworkers, similar to the way they envisioned themselves "saving" the planet. The farmworkers' refusal to perform victimization for the students stymied students' paternalistic expectations that they would be assisting an agentless group. Interactions with farmworkers directly countered the powerlessness that many students saw in Sinclair's *The Jungle* or Steinbeck's *The Grapes of Wrath*. The farmworkers presented themselves to the students not as victims but as knowledgeable members of the community educating New Jersey youth about farm labor conditions. Students engaged with individuals whose life stories complicated preconceived notions of powerlessness and unchallenged exploitation.

Working with CATA required students to see farmworkers as complex individuals and encouraged students to grapple with the politics of representations in the novels we read. Listening to the farmworkers' diverse perspectives was the first time many of the students considered that the texts representing farmworkers we had been reading did not provide unmediated access to farmworkers' voices or lives. When we returned to the classroom, they asked to what extent Sinclair's and Steinbeck's characters, from a different time and place, were humanized or accountable to the workers they represented. Did the novels engage students' sympathy or their empathy? What would it mean to see farmworkers as the organizers of change rather than as the victims uplifted by change brought by others? Can protest literature inadvertently reaffirm the very power dynamics it seeks to upend? Was it possible for literature to capture the diverse experiences and perspectives of marginalized people? As students raised these questions in class discussions, they began thinking about the novels they read as public works, texts with political consequences and cultural power.

Writing as Public Work

This lesson about literary texts as public work was reaffirmed by the writing assignment the students undertook as the core part of their service to CATA—working in groups to generate outreach materials for CATA. This assignment helped students think about their writing in relation to the literature we analyzed in class. It also helped them think about form, audience, and intent with complexity and flexibility. It assisted CATA by providing a series of materials, or drafts of those materials, to be used in their outreach efforts to supporters across the states. A member of CATA's staff also told me that it was useful for her to see how local college students responded to CATA's messaging and what the students, after studying CATA's existing outreach materials, perceived as the main points CATA hoped to convey. Thus my students unintentionally acted as a focus group for CATA, and, although their function as such was not a planned part of the class, it was a benefit for the organization.

In collaboration with CATA, students produced a variety of materials, from brochures to *PowerPoint* presentations for different audiences in the state of New Jersey. One student group created a presentation and script that could be used at local churches, youth organizations, and schools to gain public support for CATA's work. Another group created a guide to writing letters to the editors about farmworker issues that CATA could supply to volunteers. A third student group created a series of posters and brochures aimed at CATA members and their families to advertise a community garden CATA was beginning. The final group developed brochures aimed at local organic farmers to inform them of the benefits of becoming Food Justice Certified, an emerging domestic fair-trade label by the Agricultural Justice Project that extends organic standards to also ensure fair and just treatment for agricultural laborers.

Each of the writing projects required students to produce a narrative about the conditions facing New Jersey farmworkers and the solutions CATA sought to those problems. To do so, students needed to learn about CATA and its work. We attended an event during which CATA staff members used popular education techniques to engage students and CATA members in a conversation about immigration and farm labor. We also watched several of CATA's short films in class, explored their Web site, and examined their existing outreach materials.

The students needed to craft narratives that not only reiterated CATA's positions but also adapted their message to specific audiences. Students developed their understanding of the significance of rhetoric and the role of writing outside the classroom. As they revised their initial outreach materials, students began to think critically about language and form. Considering these critical issues helped make students stronger writers. It also helped students think about the novels they read as texts reflecting specific authorial choices and encouraged students to grapple with the political consequences, intended or not, of those authorial choices. In drafting the outreach pieces, students realized, for example, that they needed to explain the benefits of the Food Justice Certified standards differently to organic farmers and to consumers. They were writing both for CATA and for the audience CATA sought to reach. As Chelsea explained, "for over a decade I have been writing in order to please professors, and this project forced us students to write for a different audience than what we are used to." Julie, among other students, echoed this thought, stating, "I feel I was forced to move outside of the classroom, and create a professional product for CATA, which was exciting and made me feel very accomplished."

Many students found it unnerving to have to present their understanding of farmworkers to the farmworkers themselves. Having students tell a story about the conditions facing farmworkers in New Jersey to the farmworkers countered tendencies to patronize or even dehumanize the workers. As Chelsea reflected, "I found it difficult to not belittle the workers or sound condescending when talking about their working conditions." Placing farmworkers in the role of audience and evaluators further helped prevent students from seeing the workers as passive victims, transforming the power dynamics between themselves and the farmworkers.

Interpretation and Translation and the Creation of a Bilingual Space

One of the most surprising ways Sustainable Harvests revised students' understanding of the relation of literature and society was through the creation of a bilingual space. Most of the farmworkers the students met with did not speak English, and most of the students did not speak Spanish, so translation was necessary during our meetings. In considering the interpretive acts required by translation, students deepened their understanding of the interpretive possibilities for literature.

Sustainable Harvests posed the unique challenge of placing students with limited Spanish skills in predominately Spanish-speaking communities. Twice during the semester, I filled a fifteen-passenger van with students and drove two hours to southern New Jersey for community meetings that CATA organized. The Drew University Center for Civic Engagement provided funding so that several Spanish majors could accompany us as interpreters. The first time we went to southern New Jersey was the first time many of my students had participated in a bilingual space and the first time that the Spanish majors had acted as interpreters. The use of interpretation was a source of frustration for my students as language became an impediment to direct communication with the farmworkers. As Chelsea realized, "There is just no way that exactly what everyone was trying to say was translated exactly." Thomas, another student, explained:

> This kind of communicating in a group was a first for me and I found it both slow and awkward at times. It occurs to me though that being able to communicate intelligently and successfully through translators is a crucial part of agricultural justice projects. Without the ability to have an intelligible dialogue, migrant workers are less able to be taken seriously. I feel this is a large part of what CATA provides, a way for the disadvantaged workers to communicate and be heard.

The mediated aspect of the experience was obvious to all of us. My students decided that we were experiencing not translation but interpretation. The Spanish majors made choices about wording and sentence structure to convey what they found to be the primary sentiment of each farmworker's statement. Word-for-word translation could not satisfactorily capture tone and intent. My students felt that their inability to fully understand the nuances of the farmworkers' statements left them unable to fully learn from the farmworkers.

Yet the discussions on translation and interpretation that followed developed my conviction that working with Spanish-speaking communities encouraged my English-speaking students to engage critically and consciously with the English-language texts in our class, to think about the connotations of particular words and the value of tone and idioms.[3] That is, the conversations we had earlier in the classroom about the purpose of close readings informed the discussions we had about translation. In discussing Masumoto's *Four Seasons in Five Senses*, we looked at the way his syntax slowed the reader down, encouraging us to savor the descriptions. Students applied their understanding of the power of word choice and syntax in writing assignments and class discussions on Masumoto to interpret their experience of this bilingual space. When asking what might it mean for our Spanish interpreters to describe the work as hard rather than difficult, tedious, or exhausting, students were following the pattern of class discussions in analyzing Masumoto's sensory-laden language.

Several students, moreover, spoke of a strong desire to learn Spanish when they realized that their lack of fluency in Spanish prevented them from accessing the knowledge the farmworkers shared with them. For me, it was an incredibly powerful moment when the students recognized that they had much to learn from the farmworkers. The students expressed an implicit understanding of experience as a form of knowledge and recognized that the farmworkers had a valuable perspective and insight into the subject about which students wished to learn. They could use their difficulty in these scenarios to begin to understand some of the challenges farmworkers might face in a society in which English remains the dominant language.

Students' experiences with bilingual spaces reaffirmed their sense of the limitations of texts like *The Grapes of Wrath* and *The Jungle* in which workers are represented but do not speak. It helped students understand the ways literature can never offer a direct line of understanding into the minds of those it seeks to represent. Students left the course feeling that the literature and the service learning could never replace each other but instead could work in partnership to deepen and enhance their understanding of the agrarian experience in the United States.

According to the environmental philosopher Robert Figueroa, in "Teaching for Transformation: Lessons from Environmental Justice," environmental justice pedagogy in the humanities encourages students to extend their moral imagination and see themselves as engaged with and responsible for the dynamics they study (323, 325). In Sustainable Harvests, juxtaposing literary representations of food systems workers with service to farmworkers encouraged students to see the workers they met as individuals and to view their own perspectives as limited and partial. It asked them to reexamine their positions in society in relation to the farmworkers' positions in society. As they produced materials representing these farmworkers to various New Jersey audiences, students grappled with the politics of representation and the challenges of cultural translations of all kinds. This experience encouraged them not only to see their own writing as public work but to consider the novels, essays, and short stories we analyzed in class as writing with a social impact. Students felt complicit in the systems of power and privilege about which they were learning. As the class progressed, previously invisible power relations structuring the landscape around them became visible, and students saw the opportunity to alter them.

In their final reflective papers, students emphasized that they gained a sense of engagement in and responsibility for the world in which they lived. As Olivia explained, "The reactions that the members of CATA had towards our work made me feel like my studies were worthwhile and had an impact on someone else other than myself. . . . This experience has helped me to look beyond the classroom and community at Drew, and has enhanced my hopes in the possibilities of . . . changing our food system." Incorporating service learning into the interdisciplinary literature class empowered students to see themselves as part of a socioeconomic system, and they came to consider their position in society in a web of uneven power relations. Through the juxtaposition of literature and service learning, students learned to see the acts of writing and reading as urgent and directly related to understanding and transforming the world in which they live.

NOTES

1. Thank you to the CATA staff members and CATA members, especially Nelson Carrasquillo and Alexa Malishchak for their work with students; to the students, all of whom allowed me to quote from their essays, for engaging in this semester-long adventure with me; and to Drew University's Center for Civic Engagement, and especially Amy Koritz, for financial and logistical support. Conversations with and suggestions from Eric Larson, Jessica Johnson, Elise Dubord, and Christina Ocampo also informed my thinking and writing.

2. To retain anonymity, I have used pseudonyms for students' names.

3. Guerrieri makes a somewhat similar point in *"Leer y Escribir"*: "As language students in a literature course read these phrases they are reminded of the differences between the two Spanish verbs translated as *to be* in English: *estar* and *ser*. . . . As language students work through [a] short story, learning to read in Spanish, they are also learning to read literature" (154–55).

Part VI

Selected Resources

Roberta Rosenberg

Selected Resources for Research and Teaching in Service Learning and Literature

The following is a selected list of the key resources available to faculty members, students, and administrators interested in service learning and literary studies. Because service learning expands the reach of literary studies to public and social issues, the opportunities for publishing, seeking grant opportunities, and attending interdisciplinary conferences are numerous and new for some.

Those interested in service learning and literature should consider joining the *MLA Commons* group Service Learning in Literature, Language and Composition by going to http://commons.mla.org/groups/service-learning-in-literature-language-and-composition.

Scholarly Publishing Opportunities in Service Learning

With the increased acceptance of service learning as an academic pedagogy in literary studies, many traditional literary journals (e.g., *Early American Literature, College English, Pedagogy, Profession, PMLA*) are now publishing articles on service learning and literary studies. Scholars and practitioners may also consider publishing in the following journals focused on civic engagement, experiential education, and academic innovation in higher education. All descriptions are from the mission statements of the journals and note a formal peer-review policy when applicable. Additional information on editorial policy and publishing guidelines and interests can be found on each journal's Web site.

> *Active Learning in Higher Education.*   Publishes peer-reviewed articles on higher education teaching and learning with an emphasis on innovation and best practices.

Change: The Magazine of Higher Learning. Publishes peer-reviewed essays on innovative pedagogies, trends, and programs in higher education.

College Teaching. Provides instructors in a variety of academic disciplines with peer-reviewed essays on innovative pedagogies to improve student learning.

Compact Current (Campus Compact's newsletter). Provides the latest information for educational institutions and not-for-profit organizations involved in community and public service.

Education Resources Information Center (ERIC). An online digital library of education research and information available free of charge.

Engaged Scholar Magazine. Focuses on collaborative partnerships of mutual benefit between Michigan State University and its external constituencies.

Equity and Excellence in Education. A peer-reviewed journal focused on K–16 educators, administrators, and researchers interested in multicultural education and issues of equality, social justice, and human rights.

International Journal for the Scholarship of Teaching and Learning. Publishes peer-reviewed scholarship on teaching and learning in higher education.

International Journal of Education and the Arts. An open-access platform; publishes literary studies that integrate several fields in the arts.

International Journal of Teaching and Learning in Higher Education. A peer-reviewed forum for higher education faculty members, staff, administrators, researchers, and students who are interested in improving postsecondary instruction.

Journal of College and Character. Publishes peer-reviewed research and information about educational programs related to moral and civic learning.

Journal of Community Engagement and Scholarship. Emphasizes peer-reviewed research that focuses on how communities identify critical problems through a process of collaboration.

Journal of Curriculum Studies. Publishes articles on all aspects of curriculum studies, including teaching education, service learning, and pedagogical theories.

Journal of Democracy.   Engages academics, intellectuals, and activists in discussions about both the problems and future of democracy in the world.

Journal of Experiential Education.   Provides a wide-ranging selection of peer-reviewed articles on service-learning research and theory, including environmental education, the creative arts, and other topics.

Journal of Higher Education Outreach and Engagement.   An interdisciplinary peer-reviewed journal devoted to advancing the theory and practice of outreach and engagement in higher education.

Journal of Public Scholarship in Higher Education.   Publishes peer-reviewed articles on the ways in which higher education faculty and administrators work in the field of community engagement.

Journal of Social Change.   Publishes interdisciplinary research on social change that improves the future for individuals, communities, and society in general.

Journal of the Scholarship of Teaching and Learning.   Publishes peer-reviewed articles on the scholarship of teaching and learning, including reflective essays, literature reviews, and data-driven research projects.

Journal on Excellence in College Teaching.   Publishes peer-reviewed articles on teaching pedagogies that increase student learning and facilitate positive classroom experiences.

Liberal Education.   Publishes articles on liberal learning as it is translated into practice at colleges and universities.

Michigan Journal of Community Service Learning.   Publishes peer-reviewed essays on current research, theory, pedagogy, and issues in service learning, with an emphasis on engaged scholarship and campus-community partnerships.

Mobilization.   Emphasizes interdisciplinary perspectives on social change and social movements in public life.

New Directions for Teaching and Learning.   Publishes new pedagogical techniques for improving college teaching as well as the latest research on higher education teaching. Each issue has a specific editor who selects a topic and solicits essays.

Partnerships: A Journal of Service-Learning and Civic Engagement.   Publishes articles on the theory and practice of service-learning partnerships, connections, and collaborations between colleges and their communities.

Public: A Journal of Imagining America.   Publishes publicly engaged peer-reviewed articles on scholarship and practice in a wide variety of humanistic fields including the arts, humanities, and design, in terms of literary texts, video, photography, performance, sound, historical representation, and interactive media.

Reflections: A Journal of Public Rhetoric, Civic Writing, and Service Learning.   Publishes faculty as well as student work, including peer-reviewed essays on empirical studies, interviews, and reviews in the fields of community-based writing and civic engagement.

Undergraduate Journal of Service Learning and Community-Based Research. A multidisciplinary online undergraduate journal; publishes intellectual and reflective work on service learning and community-based research and is open to undergraduate students in the United States and around the globe.

VA Engage Journal.   Publishes community-based research, reflective essays, book reviews, and case studies on civic engagement written by undergraduates of Virginia colleges and universities.

Professional Organizations that Provide Online Resources in Service Learning

Many governmental and private not-for-profit organizations provide online resources — including syllabi, programs, tool kits, and publications — for novice and experienced instructors.

American Association of Higher Education (AAHE). Published the twenty-one-volume series Service-Learning in the Disciplines, edited by Edward Zlotkowski. The series is now published by Stylus Publishing.

American Democracy Project (ADP).   Sponsored by the American Association of State Colleges and Universities in partnership with the *New York Times.* ADP focuses on creating the next generation of informed citizens through its multicampus initiative in higher education.

Animating Democracy.   A not-for-profit organization that connects the arts and culture to further social change in communities.

Art in the Public Interest. Formerly the Community Arts Network. Provides information and assistance to artists and organizations that are culturally engaged.

Campus Compact. A national not-for-profit organization providing service-learning resources for faculty members, staff members, and administrators as well as links to Web sites, information about conferences, funding opportunities, and publications.

Carnegie Foundation for the Advancement of Teaching. Its Community Engagement Classification system provides, among other things, guidance in formulating service-learning programs in English and foreign language study. For more information, see Amy Driscoll's *Carnegie's Community-Engagement Classification: Intentions and Insights*, on the foundation Web site.

Center for Information and Research on Civic Learning and Engagement (CIRCLE). Sponsored by Tufts University. Conducts research on student service and activism in schools, colleges, and communities.

Civic Practices Network. A collaborative and nonpartisan project bringing together a diverse group of scholars and community organizations interested in the new civic renewal movement.

CIVNET. Provides a Web site for teachers, scholars, policymakers, journalists, and nongovernmental organizations promoting civic education all over the world.

Community College National Center for Community Engagement. Lists events, conferences, syllabi, awards, and publications related to service learning.

Corporation for National and Community Service (CNCS). A federal agency providing information about and funding for its programs: Senior Corps, AmeriCorps, and the Social Innovation Fund. It also sponsors the National Service-Learning Clearinghouse and awards grants (see below).

Imagining America. A nationwide consortium of colleges, universities, and their community partners that fosters new educational initiatives between the university and the public. Imagining America hosts workshops and conferences and sponsors research initiatives, publications, and grants.

Institute for Global Education and Service Learning (IGESL).   A not-for-profit organization that provides resources, service-learning trainers' tool kits, and various programs in literacy in collaboration with schools and communities around the world.

International Association for Research on Service-Learning and Community Engagement (IARSLCE).   An international not-for-profit organization promoting research and discussion about service learning and community engagement. IARSLCE develops and disseminates research on service learning, posts job opportunities, sponsors conferences, and makes awards.

International Coalition of Sites of Conscience.   Includes a worldwide network of historic sites, museums, and artists involved in cultural memory, social justice, human rights, and peace activism.

National Collaborative for the Study of University Engagement (NCSUE).   Builds collaborative relationships among the faculty, the academy, and the community. NCSUE supports research studies and disseminates information through conferences, workshops, research studies, and a newsletter.

National Council of Teachers of English (NCTE).   Publishes books and articles on service learning in composition and literature and hosts a series of conferences at all educational levels.

National Forum on Higher Education for the Public Good.   Affiliated with the Center for the Study of Higher and Postsecondary Education at the University of Michigan. The forum focuses on higher education and its relation to public, private, and philanthropic sectors committed to an educated and just society.

National Service-Learning Clearinghouse (NSLC).   Funded by the federal agency Learn and Serve America through the Corporation for National and Community Service; the clearinghouse provides the world's largest database of service-learning materials, electronic resources, and job listings.

National Service-Learning Partnership.   A national network of states dedicated to advancing service learning.

National Society for Experiential Education.   Posts conference information, publications, resources, and membership information on experiential education.

Network for Good.   Includes information about corporate giving, fund-raising, and outreach for not-for-profit organizations and funders.

New England Resource Center for Higher Education (NERCHE).   Sponsored by the University of Massachusetts, Boston. Focuses on three areas of interest: reflective inquiry into practice, the scholarship of engagement, and transitions in higher education.

Points of Light Foundation.   A not-for-profit, nonpartisan organization that promotes volunteerism and community service nationwide.

Grants Support for Service-Learning Projects

The following organizations provide information about service-learning programs and funding opportunities. Foundation priorities change constantly; consult organizations' Web sites for current and upcoming grant cycles.

Campus Compact.   Provides a variety of fund-raising resources, including links to state Campus Compacts, other major funders, and publications.

Chronicle of Philanthropy.   Publishes information about grant writing and fund-raising and contains a searchable database of corporate and foundation grants.

Community-Campus Partnerships for Health (CCPH).   The organization's Web site includes links to funders that relate to health, higher education, service learning, civic engagement, and partnerships.

Council on Foundations.   Provides information on national, state, and local foundations that award grants for national and community service efforts.

Foundation Center.   Supports an international Web site of funders and funding opportunities as well as information about the grant application process. The center publishes *The Foundation Directory, Guide to Funding for International and Foreign Programs, Foundation Grants to Individuals,* and *National Directory of Corporate Giving and Philanthropy News Digest.* It also sponsors free tutorials and paid seminars in grant proposal writing and fund-raising.

Grantmaker Forum on Community and National Service (GFCNS; the publication division of Philanthropy for Active Civil Engagement

[PACE]).   Provides information on foundations and corporations as well as individual donors.

HandsNet.   A national not-for-profit organization that provides news and collaborative opportunities for individuals interested in public issues and funding.

Idealist.   Provides national resources on funding related to youth leadership and community involvement as well as volunteer opportunities and jobs in not-for-profit organizations.

National Committee for Responsive Philanthropy (NCRP).   Provides information on the current trends for not-for-profit organizations and funders.

National Network of Grantmakers (NNG).   Includes information for individuals seeking funding for projects on social and economic justice among other topics.

National Youth Leadership Council (NYLC).   Supports national conferences, publications, and information on funding awards for service-learning practitioners.

VolunteerMatch.   Acts as an intermediary between potential volunteers and not-for-profit organizations in need of help.

Youth Service America.   Provides information about grants, resources, and events available for youth (ages 5–25) who are interested in improving their communities through service projects.

International Service Learning, Study Abroad, and Service Learning in Non-English Languages and Literatures

The International Partnership for Service-Learning and Leadership (IPSL) is a not-for-profit organization dedicated to providing students with international service-learning experiences and publishing theoretical books and articles. Among its many publications is Humphrey Tonkin's *Service-Learning across Cultures: Promise and Achievement*, a report to the Ford Foundation. For general information about international service learning, see *International Service Learning: Conceptual Frameworks and Research*, edited by Robert Bringle, Julie Hatcher, and Steven Jones.

Although service learning is primarily represented in American and British literatures, the field has expanded to include other languages with an emphasis in Spanish classes. For a further discussion of models of service learning in modern languages other than English, see the many articles in the journal *Hispania*. In addition, two sources for service learning and foreign language study are Adrian J. Wurr and Josef Hellebrandt's edited volume *Learning the Language of Global Citizenship: Service-Learning in Applied Linguistics* and Hellebrandt and Lucía Varona's edited collection *Construyendo Puentes (Building Bridges): Concepts and Models for Service Learning in Spanish.*

Service Learning and New Media

An increasing number of literary projects in service learning use digital storytelling to involve students in the multimedia, multimodal composing of literary texts, and there are now workshops and organizations that train faculty members in this process. The Web sites listed below offer online training resources and information.

> *Prairienet: Community Connections through Technology Tools.* Sponsored by the University of Illinois. Offers online tutorials, including a resources section linking to organizations, articles, and materials on digital storytelling.
>
> *Center for Digital Storytelling.* Provides online tutorials and workshops for higher education faculty and staff members interested in digital storytelling.
>
> *The National Clearinghouse on Service-Learning.* Includes a tool kit on digital storytelling in Native American communities entitled *Carrying Your Story in the Four Directions: Using Technology to Support and Sustain Indian Tribes' and U.S. Territories' Service-Learning Programs.*

Private Foundations and Corporations that Fund Service-Learning Projects

The following is a selective list of private foundations and corporations that may provide direct funding of service-learning projects: Adobe Systems, Aetna Foundation, American Express, Andrew W. Mellon Foundation, AT&T Foundation, the Ben & Jerry's Foundation, Bill & Melinda Gates Foundation, Carnegie Corporation of New York, the Case Foundation, Charles Stewart Mott Foundation, Common Counsel Foundation, the Dana Foundation, Do Something Seed Grants, Ewing Marion Kauff-man Foundation, Ford Foundation, the George Gund Foundation, the Henry Luce Foundation, John D. and Catherine T. MacArthur Founda-tion, John Simon Guggenheim Memorial Foundation, John S. & James L. Knight Foundation, Nathan Cummings Foundation, New World Founda-tion, Nippon Foundation, Open Society Foundations, Paul G. Allen Family Foundation, the Pew Charitable Trusts, Philanthropic Ventures, the Spen-cer Foundation, State Farm Companies Foundation, Teagle Foundation, Weingart Foundation, William T. Grant Foundation, William and Flora Hewlett Foundation, W. K. Kellogg Foundation, the Z. Smith Reynolds Foundation. Since deadlines, funding priorities, and programs change constantly, consult specific Web sites when seeking financial support for service-learning projects.

Federal Agencies that Fund Service-Learning Projects

The following is a selective list of federal agencies that may provide direct funding of service-learning projects: Community Outreach Partnerships Centers Program (US Dept. of Housing and Urban Development), Corpo-ration for National and Community Service, Fund for the Improvement of Postsecondary Education (FIPSE) (US Dept. of Educ.), National Endow-ment for the Arts, National Endowment for the Humanities, National In-stitute of Child Health and Human Development, National Institute of Justice, National Institute of Mental Health, National Institute on Drug Abuse. Many of these agencies (e.g., NEH and NEA) also have state-based agencies that may offer support for service-learning projects. Since dead-lines, priorities, and programs change constantly, consult specific Web sites when seeking financial support for service-learning projects. For general information about new funding cycles, new grants opportunities, and current deadlines, see the federal Web site grants.gov.

Conferences on Service Learning

Most of these conferences are held yearly, and many move around the United States: America Democracy Project and the Democracy Commit-ment National Meeting; American Education Research Association An-nual Meeting, which includes sessions organized by the Service-Learning and Experiential Education Special Interest Group; Community College

National Center for Community Engagement Annual Conference; Conference on Volunteering and Service; Continuums of Service Conference; Gulf South Summit on Service-Learning and Civic Engagement through Higher Education Annual Conference; Imagining America National Conference; IMPACT National Conference; International Association for Research on Service-Learning and Community Engagement Conference; National Outreach Scholarship Conference; National Service-Learning Conference; National Society of Experiential Education Annual Conference; Service-Learning World Forum. Some conferences also hold regional meetings, webinars, and workshops. Consult the individual conference Web sites for detailed, current information.

Notes on Contributors

Diana C. Archibald, associate professor of English at the University of Massachusetts, Lowell, specializes in Dickens, the Victorian novel, and Anglo-American transatlantic studies. She is the author of *Domesticity, Imperialism, and Emigration in the Victorian Novel* and guest editor of three journal special issues on Dickens and on transatlanticism. In addition, she has contributed to the *Dickens Studies Annual* and was cocurator of the 2012 exhibition *Dickens and Massachusetts* (library.uml.edu/dickens). She remains committed to supporting public humanities and digital humanities projects.

Robin J. Barrow is senior lecturer at the University of Tennessee, Knoxville. She specializes in British Victorian literature and has published on the sensation writer Mary Braddon. She is currently completing revisions of her book manuscript, "Narratives of Outrage: Rape in Victorian Fiction." Her research interests include railways, popular fiction, and the periodical press.

Ann Marie Fallon is professor of humanities and international studies and director of the University Honors College at Portland State University. She is the author of *Global Crusoe: Comparative Literature, Postcolonial Theory and Transnational Aesthetics* and the coeditor of *Community Based Learning and the Work of Literature* and *Rebels without a Cause? Renegotiating the American 1950s*. Her current book project, a comparative study on the early novel in the Americas, is titled "The Novel in the New World."

Elizabeth K. Goodhue is assistant director of the Center for Community Learning at UCLA, where she develops and maintains academic civic engagement programs. As part of her work, she teaches undergraduate service-learning courses in the arts and humanities and leads workshops for faculty members and graduate students interested in developing community-based courses. She is the author of articles on eighteenth-century British literature and, with colleagues from Imagining America, of an essay on the role of academic administrators as intermediaries between campus and community stakeholders.

Laurie Grobman is professor of English and women's studies at Penn State University, Berks. Her teaching, research, and service interests center on service learning and community-based research. She is the author of *Multicultural Hybridity: Transforming American Literary Scholarship and Pedagogy* and *Teaching at the Crossroads: Cultures and Critical Perspectives in Literature by Women of Color* and the coeditor of *Undergraduate Research in English Studies* and *On Location: Theory and Practice in Classroom-Based Writing Tutoring*. She was the 2012 recipient of Penn State University President's Award for Excellence in Academic Integration.

Matthew C. Hansen, associate professor of English at Boise State University, researches and publishes on Shakespeare, the teaching of Shakespeare, and early modern English drama and poetry. Also an actor and director, he has most recently directed productions of Shakespeare's *The Taming of the Shrew* and Austen's *Pride and Prejudice* and appeared onstage as Mozart. He is working on a project on memory, materiality, and English Renaissance revenge tragedy.

Scott Hicks is associate professor of English at the University of North Carolina, Pembroke. He teaches classes in African American and environmental literatures and first-year composition, and his research appears in *Arizona Quarterly, Callaloo, Environmental Humanities,* and *ISLE: Interdisciplinary Studies in Literature and Environment*.

Jennifer Leeman is associate professor of Spanish at George Mason University and research sociolinguist at the United States Census Bureau. Recent publications have analyzed the racialization of Spanish in the United States Census, accent discrimination in Arizona, language ideologies in Spanish heritage language instruction, and evidence in United States language policy. She is the editor (with Manel Lacorte) of *Spanish in the US and Other Contact Environments: Sociolinguistics, Ideology and Pedagogy*.

Kristina Lucenko is associate director of the Program in Writing and Rhetoric at Stony Brook University. Her research and teaching interests include autobiography, composition pedagogy, women's writing, early modern literature and culture, and digital storytelling.

Claudia Monpere McIsaac, senior lecturer of English at Santa Clara University, has written many poems and short stories that appear in such literary journals as the *Kenyon Review, Nimrod, Prairie Schooner,* the *Massachusetts Review,* and the *Cincinnati Review.* She is currently working on a poetry manuscript, "Person in Water," and a novel.

Elizabeth Parfitt is lecturer in the Writing, Literature and Publishing Department at Emerson College. Her nonfiction has appeared in *The Chronicle of Higher Education, Inside Higher Ed,* and *The Writing Lab Newsletter.* Her research interests include the connections between service learning, creative writing, and composition, and she is working on "Our World, Our View," an English composition textbook focusing on the choices writers make in local and global contexts.

Lisa Rabin is associate professor of Spanish at George Mason University, where she teaches literary, film, and cultural studies in Spanish and is an active member of the cultural studies program. Her current research concerns film and its reception in the Progressive and Cold War eras. Her recent publications include articles on the history of heritage language education at East Harlem's Benjamin Franklin High School, early-twentieth-century teen moviegoing, and radical film education in 1930s and 1940s New York City.

Kathleen Béres Rogers, assistant professor of English at the College of Charleston, is the author of articles about British Romantic-era writing and medicine, published in such venues as *Women's Writing, Essays in Romanticism, Romanticism and Victorianism on the Net,* and *Prose Studies.* She has written about published illness narratives, and her continuing research concerns obsession and the Romantic-era imagination.

Roberta Rosenberg, professor of English and director of an interdisciplinary minor in civic engagement and social entrepreneurship at Christopher Newport University, teaches courses in multicultural American literature, women's studies, and the writing of civic engagement. She is the author of three books and of numerous articles on American literature and culture that have appeared in *MELUS, Pedagogy, Studies in American Indian Literatures,* and *Studies in Jewish American Literature,* among others. In addition, she was the editor of *DoubleTake Magazine* (with Robert Coles and Terry Lee). Her community work includes consulting with federal, state, and local governmental agencies and many arts and cultural not-for-profit organizations.

Ivy Schweitzer, professor of English and women's and gender studies at Dartmouth College, is the author of *The Work of Self-Representation: Lyric Poetry in Colonial New England* and *Perfecting Friendship: Politics and Affiliation in Early American Literature* and is on the editorial board of the *Heath Anthology of American Literature*. Her current projects include *The Occom Circle*, a scholarly digital edition of documents by and about Samson Occom; a study of American women writers from 1650 to 1990; and a documentary film about a course she coteaches in prisons.

Carol Tyx, professor of American literature and creative writing at Mount Mercy University, writes creative nonfiction and poetry. Her latest poetry collection is *Rising to the Rim*. Her teaching interests include African American literature, Latino literature, and the personal essay.

Emily VanDette is associate professor of English at the State University of New York College, Fredonia, where she teaches undergraduate and graduate courses in American literature and women's literature, as well as the undergraduate capstone and graduate research courses. She is the author of *Sibling Romance in American Fiction, 1835–1900* and several articles on nineteenth-century American literature. Her current research project focuses on the reception history of antebellum women writers.

Mary Vermillion is professor of English at Mount Mercy University, where she teaches a range of courses, including creative writing, Shakespeare, and law and literature. She is the author of three mystery novels and, with her husband, Benjamin Thiel, is working on a joint memoir about his gender transition.

Joan Wagner is director of the Center for Community-Engaged Learning at St. Michael's College in Colchester, Vermont, where she has also taught undergraduate and graduate writing courses. Drawing from her pedagogical experience, she works with faculty members across the disciplines to design and implement courses that integrate community-engaged learning. She is particularly interested in the power of memoir to nurture understanding within and among communities. She is pursuing a doctorate in educational leadership and policy at the University of Vermont.

Sarah D. Wald is assistant professor of English and environmental studies at the University of Oregon. She is completing a book on race, citizenship, and nature in representations of California agricultural labor. She is also the author of articles in *Western American Literature* and *Food, Culture, and Society* and in the anthologies *American Studies, Ecocriticism, and Citizenship: Thinking and Acting in the Local and Global Commons* and The Grapes of Wrath: *A Reconsideration*. Her research interests include ecocriticism, critical race theory, Asian American literature, and Latina/o literature.

Works Cited

"About the Life Story Commons." *University of Southern Maine.* U of Maine, n.d. Web. 28 Aug. 2012.

Acosta, Andres, Jordan Drutman, Jessica Hiestand, Gabrielle Nunez, and Chelsea Williams. "Imagine." Parfitt 32.

Adler-Kassner, Linda, Robert Crooks, and Ann Watters. "Service-Learning and Composition at the Crossroads." Adler-Kassner, Crooks, and Watters, *Writing* 1–17.

———, eds. *Writing the Community: Concepts and Models for Service Learning in Composition.* Washington: Amer. Assn. for Higher Educ., 1997. Print.

Ahmed, Sara. *Strange Encounters: Embodied Others in Post-coloniality.* London: Routledge, 2000. Print.

Alexander, Bryan. *The New Digital Storytelling: Creating Narratives with New Media.* Santa Barbara: ABC-CLIO, 2011. Print.

Alexander, Buzz. "Smitty, Prayer, Astronomy, 'Y2K and the Wicked Stepmother,' and Asia Romero: Dimensions in the Work of the Prison Creative Arts Project." *Teaching the Arts behind Bars.* Ed. Rachel Marie-Crane Williams. Boston: Northeastern UP, 2003. 125–37. Print.

Allen, Ashley, Sosha McAllister, Bernise Moody, and Patricia Taylor. *Crisis!* Pembroke: Print Services, U of North Carolina, Pembroke, 2011. Print.

Allison, Dorothy. "A Question of Class." *Skin: Talking about Sex, Class, and Literature.* Ithaca: Firebrand, 1994. 13–36. Print.

———. *Two or Three Things I Know for Sure.* New York: Dutton, 1995. Print.

Allison, Jay, and Dan Gediman, eds. *This I Believe: The Personal Philosophies of Remarkable Men and Women.* New York: Holt, 2007. Print.

Anderson, Benedict R. *Imagined Communities: Reflections on the Origin and Spread of Nationalism.* 1983. London: Verso, 1991. Print.

Arnold, Matthew. *Culture and Anarchy: An Essay in Political and Social Criticism.* 1869. *Project Gutenberg.* Project Gutenberg, n.d. Web. 7 Sept. 2012.

Astin, Alexander W., and Lori J. Vogelgesang. *Understanding the Effects of Service-Learning: A Study of Students and Faculty. The Higher Education Research Insti-*

tute. Higher Educ. Research Inst., U of California, Los Angeles, 2006. Web. 30 Oct. 2012.

Baker, Katie, Renae Eades, Lewis Edwards, and Jovita Vereen. *Dreams, Actions, Resolve, Evolve: Those Who Dare to Grow Become Leaders in Life's Undertow.* Pembroke: Print Services, U of North Carolina, Pembroke, 2011. Print.

Bakhtin, Mikhail. *The Dialogic Imagination: Four Essays.* Trans. Caryl Emerson and Michael Holquist. Ed. Holquist. Austin: U of Texas P, 1981. Print.

Ball, Kevin, and Amy M. Goodburn. "Composition Studies and Service Learning: Appealing to Communities?" *Composition Studies* 28.1 (2000): 79–94. Print.

Barney, Steve T., Grant C. Corser, and Lynn H. White. "Service-Learning with the Mentally Ill: Softening the Stigma." *Michigan Journal of Community Service Learning* 16.2 (2010): 66–77. Print.

Bartel, Anna Sims. "Talking and Walking: Literary Work as Public Work." Danielson and Fallon 81–102.

Bauby, Jean-Dominique. *The Diving Bell and the Butterfly: A Memoir of Life in Death.* 1997. Trans. Jeremy Leggatt. New York: Vintage, 1998. Print.

Bawarshi, Anis. *Genre and the Invention of the Writer: Reconsidering the Place of Invention in Composition.* Logan: Utah State UP, 2003. Print.

———. "Genres as Forms of In(ter)vention." *Originality, Imitation, and Plagiarism: Teaching Writing in the Digital Age.* Ed. Caroline Eisner and Martha Vicinus. Ann Arbor: U of Michigan P, 2008. 79–89. Print.

Baym, Nina, et al., eds. *The Norton Anthology of American Literature.* 7th ed. Vol C. New York: Norton, 2007. Print.

Bechdel, Alison. *Fun Home: A Family Tragicomic.* Boston: Houghton, 2006. Print.

Bennett, Gwendolyn. "Hatred." Patton and Honey 509.

———. "Heritage." Patton and Honey 510.

Bérubé, Michael. *The Employment of English: Theory, Jobs, and the Future of Literary Studies.* New York: New York UP, 1998. Print.

Bérubé, Michael, Hester Blum, Christopher Castiglia, and Julia Spicher Kasdorf. "Community Reading and Social Imagination." *PMLA* 125.2 (2010): 418–25. Print.

Bigelow, Martha, Robert Delmas, Kit Hansen, and Elaine Tarone. "Literacy and the Processing of Oral Recasts in SLA." *TESOL Quarterly* 40 (2006): 665–89. Print.

The Big Read. Natl. Endowment for the Arts, n.d. Web. 4 Sept. 2012.

"Big Read-ing in Brocton." *My Antonia—The Big Read Program of Chautaqua and Cattaraugus Counties.* N.p., 25 Feb. 2010. Web. 4 Sept. 2012.

Blake, William. *Songs of Innocence. The Complete Poetry and Prose of William Blake.* Ed. David V. Erdman. Berkeley: U of California P, 1982. 7–17. Print.

Bloom, Lynn Z. "American Autobiography and the Politics of Genre." *Genre and Writing: Issues, Arguments, Alternatives.* Ed. Wendy Bishop and Hans Ostrom. Portsmouth: Boynton, 1997. 151–59. Print.

Bloom, Lynn Z., and Edward M. White. *Inquiry: Questioning, Reading, Writing.* 2nd ed. Upper Saddle River: Prentice, 2004. Print.

Boger, Matthew, and Tim Zaal. "From Hate to Hope." Museum of Tolerance, Los Angeles. 2007. Lecture.

Boggis, JerriAnne, Eve Allegra Raimon, and Barbara W. White, eds. *Harriet Wilson's New England: Race, Writing, and Region.* Durham: U of New Hampshire P, 2007. Print.

Bolaños, Roberto. *2666.* New York: Vintage Español, 2009. Print.

Boler, Megan. *Feeling Power: Emotions and Education.* New York: Routledge, 1999. Print.

Booth, Wayne C. *The Company We Keep: An Ethics of Fiction.* Berkeley: U of California P, 1988. Print.

Bourdieu, Pierre. "For a Scholarship with Commitment." *Profession* (2000): 40–45. Print.

Boyer, Ernest L. "The Scholarship of Engagement." *Journal of Public Service and Outreach* 1.1 (1996): 11–12. Print.

———. *Scholarship Reconsidered: Priorities of the Professoriate.* Princeton: Carnegie Foundation for the Advancement of Teaching, 1990. Print.

Brampton, Sally. *Shoot the Damn Dog: A Memoir of Depression.* New York: Norton, 2008. Print.

Brattin, Joel J. "Constancy, Change, and the Dust Mounds of *Our Mutual Friend.*" *Dickens Quarterly* 19.1 (2002): 23–30. Print.

Breen, Tom. "Pat Robertson: Alzheimer's Justifies Divorce." *The Huffington Post.* Huffington Post, 14 Sept. 2011. Web. 6 Mar. 2012.

Brewster, Larry. *A Qualitative Evaluation of the California Arts-in-Corrections Program. USF Scholarship Repository.* Public and Nonprofit Administration, School of Management, U of San Francisco, 2010. Web. 15 Oct. 2013.

Bringle, Robert, Julie Hatcher, and Steven Jones, eds. *International Service Learning: Conceptual Frameworks and Research.* Sterling: Stylus, 2011. Print.

Brontë, Emily. *Wuthering Heights.* 1847. London: Penguin, 2003.Print.

Brother to Brother. Screenplay by Rodney Evans. Dir. Evans. Wolfe Releasing, 2004. Film.

Brown, Sylvia A. "Scripting Wholeness in Lucy Grealy's *Autobiography of a Face.*" *Criticism: A Quarterly for Literature and the Arts* 48.3 (2006): 297–322. Print.

Browning, Elizabeth Barrett. *Aurora Leigh*. 1864. Ed. Margaret Reynolds. New York: Norton, 1996. Print.

Bruner, Jerome. "Life as Narrative." *Social Research* 54.1 (1987): 11–32. Web. 3 Sept. 2011.

Buber, Martin. *I and Thou*. Trans. Walter Kaufman. New York: Scribner, 1970. Print.

Bumby, Kurt M. "Empathy Inhibition, Intimacy Deficits, and Attachment Difficulties in Sex Offenders." *Remaking Relapse Prevention with Sex Offenders: A Sourcebook*. Ed. D. Richard Laws, Stephen M. Hudson, and Tony Ward. Thousand Oaks: Sage, 2000. 143–66. *Google Books*. Web. 30 May 2012.

Burney, Frances. "Olde Tyme Mastectomy." *JonahWorld!*. Wes Clark, n.d. Web. 30 May 2012. <http://wesclark.com/jw/mastectomy.html>.

Butin, Dan. "Service Learning as Postmodern Pedagogy." *Service Learning in Higher Education: Critical Issues and Directions*. Ed. Butin. New York: Palgrave, 2005. 89–104. Print.

Butler, Johnnella E. "Democracy, Diversity, and Civic Engagement." *Academe* 86.4 (2000): 52–55. Print.

Calderón, José. "Organizing Immigrant Workers: Action Research and Strategies in the Pomona Day Labor Center." *Latino Los Angeles: Transformations, Communities, and Activism*. Ed. Enrique C. Ochoa and Gilda L. Ochoa. Tucson: U of Arizona P, 2008. 278–79. Print.

Carrasquillo, Nelson. "Race and Ethnicity from the Point of View of Farm Workers in the Food System." *Race/Ethnicity: Multidisciplinary Global Contexts* 5.1 (2011): 121–31. Print.

Cather, Willa. *My Ántonia*. 1918. New York: Barnes, 2003. Print.

———. *O Pioneers!* 1913. New York: Dover, 1993. Print.

Chambers, Tony, and Bryan Gopaul. "Decoding the Public Good of Higher Education." *Journal of Higher Education Outreach and Engagement* 12.4 (2008): 59–91. Print.

Changing Lives through Literature: An Alternative Sentencing Project. U of Massachusetts, Dartmouth, 2003. Web. 12 June 2012.

"Charleston (City), South Carolina." *United States Census Bureau*. US Dept. of Commerce, 7 Jan. 2014. Web. 7 Mar. 2014. <http://quickfacts.census.gov/qfd/states/45/4513330.html>.

Charon, Rita. *Narrative Medicine: Honoring the Stories of Illness*. Cary: Oxford UP, 2006. Print.

Chase, Darren. *Digital Storytelling: Research and Subject Guide. Stony Brook University*. Stony Brook U Libs., 22 May 2013. Web. 27 May 2013.

Choo, Suzanne S. "On Literature's Use(ful/less)ness: Reconceptualizing the Literature Curriculum in the Age of Globalization." *Journal of Curriculum Studies* 43.1 (2011): 47–67. Print.

Chun, Justin. "Boston ReStore Warehouse Renovation Reflection." *Digication. Emerson College.* Emerson Coll., 2010. Web. 3 Oct. 2012.

———. "Commentary: Boston Cares: An Education in Civic Engagement." *Digication. Emerson College.* Emerson Coll., 2010. Web. 3 Oct. 2012.

Chun, Terrilyn. Message to Ann Marie Fallon. 4 June 2012. E-mail.

Cisneros, Sandra. *Caramelo.* New York: Vintage, 2003. Print.

Clark, Lorna J. "The Diarist as Novelist: Narrative Strategies in the Journals and Letters of Frances Burney." *English Studies in Canada* 27.3 (2001): 283–302. Print.

Clark, Trevor. "Poetry and Self Recovery." *Australasian Psychiatry* 15 supp. (2007): S104–06. Print.

Clayton, Patti, Robert Bringle, Bryanne Senor, Jenny Huq, and Mary Morrison. "Differentiating and Assessing Relationships in Service-Learning and Civic Engagement." *Michigan Journal of Community Service Learning* 16.2 (2010): 5–22. Print.

"Climate Survey Summaries." *Emerson College.* Office of Diversity and Inclusion, Emerson Coll., 2009. Web. 3 Oct. 2012.

Cohen, David Elliot. *What Matters: The World's Preeminent Photojournalists and Thinkers Depict Essential Issues of Our Time.* New York: Sterling, 2008. Print.

Cohen, Jeremy, and Rosa Eberly. "Higher Education, Democratic Capacity, and Public Scholarship." *Campus Compact.* Campus Compact, 2006. Web. 15 Oct. 2013.

Collins, Courtney, Katherine Laws, Brittany Morales, and Meeko Simpson, eds. *I Dream.* Pembroke: Print Services, U of North Carolina, Pembroke, 2011. Print.

Comstock, Cathy. "Literature and Service Learning: Not Strange Bedfellows." *Building Community: Service Learning in the Academic Disciplines.* Ed. Richard Kraft and Marc Swadener. Denver: Colorado Campus Compact, 1994. 83–90. Print.

Cooper, David D. "Can Civic Engagement Rescue the Humanities?" Danielson and Fallon 1–25.

Couser, G. Thomas. *Signifying Bodies: Disability in Contemporary Life Writing.* Ann Arbor: U of Michigan P, 2009. Print.

Crassons, Kate. "Poverty, Representation, and the Expanded English Classroom." *English Language Notes* 47.1 (2009): 95–103. Print.

"Creating a Culture of Inclusion: A Strategic Plan for Racial and Ethnic Diversity." *Emerson College.* Office of Diversity and Inclusion, Emerson Coll., Nov. 2011. Web. 3 Oct. 2012.

Cress, Christine M., and David M. Donahue. Introduction. *Democratic Dilemmas of Teaching Service-Learning: Curricular Strategies for Success.* By Cress, Donahue, and associates. Sterling: Stylus, 2011. 1–13. Print.

"Crime in the United States 2010." *Federal Bureau of Investigation.* US Dept. of Justice, n.d. Web. 23 May 2012.

Cushman, Ellen. "Opinion: Public Intellectuals, Service Learning and Activist Research." *College English* 61.3 (1999): 328–66. Print.

———. "The Rhetorician as an Agent of Social Change." *College Composition and Communication* 47.1 (1996): 7–28. Print.

———. "Service Learning as the New English Studies." *Beyond English Inc.: Curricular Reform in a Global Economy.* Ed. David Downing, Claudia Hurlbert, and Paula Mathieu. Portsmouth: Boynton, 2002. 201–18. Print.

———. "Sustainable Service Learning Programs." *College Composition and Communication* 54.1 (2002): 40–63. Web. 13 Jan. 2012.

Danielson, Susan. "Reconnecting the Disconnect: Exploring the Links between Literary Studies and Community Service." Danielson and Fallon 231–41.

Danielson, Susan, and Ann Marie Fallon, eds. *Community-Based Learning and the Work of Literature.* Bolton: Anker, 2007. Print.

Danticat, Edwidge. *Brother, I'm Dying.* New York: Vintage, 2008. Print.

Davidson, Cathy N. "Humanities 2.0: Promise, Perils, Predilictions." *PMLA* 123.3 (2008): 707–18. Print.

Davis, Tamera. "Pay It Forward: Sustaining University-Community Projects." Imagining America: Artists and Scholars in Public Life National Conference. U of Minnesota, Minneapolis. 22 Sept. 2011. Address.

Deans, Thomas. *Writing Partnerships: Service-Learning in Composition.* Urbana: NCTE, 2000. Print.

Deans, Thomas, Barbara Roswell, and Adrian J. Wurr, eds. *Writing and Community Engagement: A Critical Sourcebook.* Boston: Bedford, 2010. Print.

Deepening the Roots of Civic Engagement: 2011 Annual Membership Survey: Executive Summary. Campus Compact. Campus Compact, 2011. Web. 3 Oct. 2012.

Deitz, Sheila R., Karen Tiemann Blackwell, Paul C. Daley, and Brenda J. Bentley. "Measurement of Empathy toward Rape Victims and Rapists." *Journal of Personality and Social Psychology* 43.2 (1982): 372–84. Print.

Derrida, Jacques. "Structure, Sign, and Play in the Discourse of the Human Sciences." *The Structuralist Controversy: The Languages of Criticism and the Sci-*

ences of Man. Ed. Richard Macksey and Eugenio Donato. Baltimore: Johns Hopkins UP, 2007. 247–72. Print.

Dewey, John. *Democracy and Education.* 1916. New York: Free, 1997. Print.

Díaz, Junot. *The Brief Wondrous Life of Oscar Wao.* New York: Riverhead, 2007. Print.

Di Chiro, Giovanna. "Nature as Community: The Convergence of Environment and Social Justice." *Uncommon Ground: Rethinking the Human Place in Nature.* Ed. William Cronon. New York: Norton, 1996. 298–320. Print.

Dickens, Charles. *American Notes for General Circulation.* 1842. New York: Penguin, 2001. Print.

———. *A Christmas Carol.* 1843. New York: Penguin, 2012. Print.

———. *Our Mutual Friend.* 1864–65. New York: Penguin, 1997. Print.

DiPardo, Anne. "Narrative Knowers, Expository Knowledge: Discourse as a Dialectic." *National Writing Project.* Natl. Writing Project, Jan. 1989. Web. 18 Mar. 2014. Natl. Center for the Study of Writing and Literacy Occasional Paper 6.

Disraeli, Benjamin. *Sybil; or, The Two Nations.* 1845. Oxford: Oxford UP, 1998. Print.

"Doing Time, and Doing Good, in La.'s Angola Prison." *WBUR Boston.* NPR, 26 Apr. 2010. Web. 20 June 2013.

Draxler, Bridget. "Adaptation as Interpretation: Teaching Gothic Literature to Non-majors." American Society for Eighteenth-Century Studies Annual Meeting. Sheraton Vancouver Wall Centre, Vancouver. 18 Mar. 2011. Address.

Driscoll, Amy. *Carnegie's Community-Engagement Classification: Intentions and Insights. Change* Jan.-Feb. (2008): 39–41. *Carnegie Foundation for the Advancement of Teaching.* Web. 24 Oct. 2014.

Driscoll, Frances. "Difficult Word." F. Driscoll, *Rape Poems* 12–13.

———. "Island of the Raped Women." F. Driscoll, *Rape Poems* 75–76.

———. "Page 134." F. Driscoll, *Rape Poems* 58.

———. *The Rape Poems.* Port Angeles: Pleasure Boat Studios, 1997. Print.

———. "That She May." F. Driscoll, *Rape Poems* 64–68.

Durrow, Heidi. *The Girl Who Fell from the Sky.* New York: Algonquin, 2010. Print.

Eagleton, Terry. *Literary Theory: An Introduction.* Minneapolis: U of Minnesota P, 1983. Print.

Eberly, Rosa A. *Citizen Critics: Literary Public Spheres.* Urbana: U of Illinois P, 2000. Print.

Ehrenreich, Barbara. *Nickel and Dimed: On (Not) Getting By in America.* New York: Metropolitan, 2001. Print.

———. "Welcome to Cancerland." *Harper's Magazine* Nov. 2001: 43–53. Web. 30 Aug. 2012.

Ehrlich, Susan. *Representing Rape: Language and Sexual Consent.* London: Routledge, 2001. Print.

Ehrlich, Thomas. Preface. *Civic Responsibility and Higher Education.* Ed. Ehrlich. Westport: Amer. Council on Educ.; Oryx, 2000. v–x. Print.

Ellison, Julie. "The New Humanists." *PMLA* 128.2 (2013): 289–98. Print.

"ELSJ Course Design." *Santa Clara University.* Santa Clara U, 2014. Web. 24 Oct. 2014.

Epstein, Julia L. "Writing the Unspeakable: Fanny Burney's Mastectomy and the Fictive Body." *Representations* 16 (1986): 131–66. Print.

Estrich, Susan. *Real Rape.* Cambridge: Harvard UP, 1987. Print.

Evans, Stephanie Y. "Preface: Using History, Experience, and Theory to Balance Relationships in Community Engagement." Evans, Taylor, Dunlap, and Miller xi–xx.

Evans, Stephanie Y., Colette M. Taylor, Michelle R. Dunlap, and DeMond S. Miller, eds. *African Americans and Community Engagement in Higher Education Community Service, Service-Learning, and Community-Based Research.* Albany: State U of New York P, 2009. Print.

"Everybody Reads 2012." *Multnomah County Library.* Multnomah County Lib., n.d. Web. 18 July 2012.

Eyler, Janet. "Creating Your Reflection Map." *New Directions for Higher Education* 114 (2001): 35–43. Rpt. in *Developing and Implementing Service-Learning Programs.* Ed. Mark Canada and Bruce W. Speck. San Francisco: Jossey, 2001. 35–44. Print.

Eyler, Janet, and Dwight E. Giles, Jr. *Where's the Learning in Service-Learning?* San Francisco: Jossey, 1999. Print.

Eyler, Janet S., Dwight E. Giles, Jr., Christine M. Stenson, and Charlene J. Gray. *At A Glance: What We Know about the Effects of Service-Learning on College Students, Faculty, Institutions, and Communities, 1993–2000.* 3rd ed. Corp. for Natl. and Community Service, 2001. Web. 12 Oct. 2012.

"Facts about Prisons and Prisoners." *The Sentencing Project.* Sentencing Project, June 2011. Web. 7 June 2012.

Fallon, Ann Marie. Preface. Danielson and Fallon xv–xxii.

Feeney-Wilfer, Mary. Letter to Carol Tyx. 18 July 2012. TS.

Felski, Rita. "'Context Stinks!'" *New Literary History* 42.4 (2011): 573–91. Print.

———. *Uses of Literature.* Malden: Blackwell, 2008. Print.

Fies, Brian. *Mom's Cancer*. New York: Abrams, 2006. Print.

Figueroa, Robert. "Teaching for Transformation: Lessons from Environmental Justice." *Environmental Justice Reader: Politics, Poetics, Pedagogy*. Ed. Joni Adamson, Mei Mei Evans, and Rachel Stein. Tucson: U of Arizona P, 2002. 311–30. Print.

Fish, Stanley. "Aim Low." *Chronicle of Higher Education*. Chronicle of Higher Educ., 16 May 2003. Web. 23 Apr. 2012.

———. *Is There a Text in This Class? The Authority of Interpretive Communities*. Cambridge: Harvard UP, 1980. Print.

———. "Profession Despise Thyself: Fear and Self-Loathing in Literary Studies." *Critical Inquiry* 10.2 (1983): 349–64. Print.

———. *Save the World on Your Own Time*. New York: Oxford UP, 2008. Print.

Fisher, Rudolph. "The City of Refuge." Patton and Honey 388–99.

Fitzgerald, F. Scott. "Babylon Revisited." 1931. Baym et al. 1839–53.

Fix, Michael, Jeffrey Passel, and Kenneth Sucher. *Trends in Naturalization. Urban Institute*. Urban Inst., 17 Sept. 2003. Web. 16 Oct. 2013.

Fleming, Dolly. Message to Joan Wagner. 21 Aug. 2012. E-mail.

Floyd, Antoinette. "Back Then." Collins, Laws, Morales, and Simpson 5.

Foucault, Michel. *Discipline and Punish: The Birth of the Prison*. Trans. Alan Sheridan. New York: Pantheon, 1977. Print.

Frank, Arthur W. *The Wounded Storyteller*. Chicago: U of Chicago P, 1995. Print.

Freire, Paolo. *Education for Critical Consciousness*. London: Continuum, 1974. Print.

———. *Pedagogy of the Oppressed*. New York: Seabury, 1970. Print.

Freytag, Gustav. *Freytag's Technique of the Drama: An Exposition of Dramatic Composition and Art*. 1863. Trans. Elias J. MacEwan. 3rd ed. Chicago: Scott, Foresman, 1900. *Open Library*. Web. 16 Oct. 2012.

Frost, Robert. "Mending Wall." *The Civically Engaged Reader*. Ed. Adam Davis and Elizabeth Lynn. Chicago: Great Books Foundation, 2006. 81–82. Print.

"FY 2012 Adopted Budget." *Multnomah County Library*. Multnomah County Lib., n.d. Web. 18 July 2012.

Gallegos, Rómulo. *Doña Bárbara*. Trans. Robert Malloy. New York: Smith, 1948. Print.

Garbus, Julia. "Service-Learning, 1902." *College English* 64.5 (2002): 547–65. Print.

Garden, Rebecca. "Telling Stories about Illness and Disability: The Limits of Narrative." *Perspectives in Biology and Medicine* 53.1 (2010): 121–35. Print.

Gardner, Howard. *The Unschooled Mind: How Children Think and How Schools Should Teach*. New York: Basic, 1995. Print.

Garland-Thomson, Rosemarie. *Extraordinary Bodies: Figuring Physical Disability in American Culture and Literature*. New York: Columbia UP, 1997. Print.

Gaskell, Elizabeth. *Mary Barton: A Tale of Manchester Life*. 1848. New York: Penguin, 1996. Print.

Gates, Henry Louis, Jr., and Nellie Y. McKay. "Harlem Renaissance, 1919–1940." Gates and McKay, *Norton Anthology* 953–62.

———, eds. *The Norton Anthology of African American Literature*. 2nd ed. New York: Norton, 2004. Print.

Gerard, Philip. *Creative Nonfiction: Researching and Crafting Stories of Real Life*. Long Grove: Waveland, 1996. Print.

Glaspell, Susan. *Trifles*. 1916. Baym et al. 1412–21.

Goldstein, Gary, and Peter Fernald. "Humanistic Education in a Capstone Course." *College Teaching* 57 (2009): 27–36. Print.

Goodman, Amy. "Democracy Now." Saint Michael's Coll. Oct. 2011. Address.

Gouws, Dennis S. "Boys and Men Reading Shakespeare's *1 Henry 4*: Using Service Learning Strategies to Accommodate Male Learners and Disseminate Male-Positive Literacy." *International Journal of Learning* 16.10 (2009): 483–96. Print.

Graff, Gerald. Foreword. Danielson and Fallon vii–x.

———. "Hidden Intellectualism." *Pedagogy: Critical Approaches to Teaching Literature, Languages, Composition and Culture* 1.1 (2001): 21–36. Print.

Graff, Gerald, et al. "Today, Tomorrow: The Intellectual in the Academy and in Society." *PMLA* 112.5 (1997): 1132–41. Print.

Graham, Natalie, and Pat Crawford. "Instructor-Led Engagement and Immersion Programs: Transformative Experiences of Study Abroad." *Journal of Higher Education Outreach and Engagement* 16.3 (2012): 107–10. Print.

Grealy, Lucy. *Autobiography of a Face*. New York: Harper, 2003. Print.

Gregory, Marshall. *Shaped by Stories: The Ethical Power of Narratives*. Notre Dame: U of Notre Dame P, 2009. Print.

Grimké, Angelina. *Rachel*. 1916. Patton and Honey 189–226.

Grobman, Laurie. "Is There a Place for Service Learning in Literary Studies?" *Profession* (2005): 129–40. Print.

———. "Service-Learning and Literature: Initiating Conversations." *Journal on Excellence in College Teaching* 18.1 (2007): 79–95. Print.

———. "Thinking Differently about Difference: Multicultural Literature and

Service-Learning." *Teaching English in the Two-Year College* 31 (2004): 347–57. Print.

Guaman Poma de Ayala, Felipe. *El primer nueva corónica y buen gobierno* [The First New Chronicle and Good Government]. 1615. Ed. John V. Murra, Rolena Adorno, and Jorge L. Urioste. Madrid: Historia 16, 1987. *El sitio de Guaman Poma / The Guaman Poma Website*. Det Kongelige Bibliotek, Sept. 2004. Web. 20 Nov. 2012.

Guerrieri, Kevin. *"Leer y Escribir La Frontera*: Language, Literature, and Community Engagement in the San Diego–Tijuana Borderlands." Danielson and Fallon 154–79.

Guillory, John. *Cultural Capital: The Problem of Literary Canon Formation*. Chicago: U of Chicago P, 1993. Print.

Guthrie, Kathy L., and Holly McCracken. "Making a Difference Online: Facilitating Service-Learning through Distance Education." *Internet and Higher Education* 13 (2010): 153–57. Print.

———. "Teaching and Learning Social Justice through Online Service-Learning Courses." *International Review of Research in Open and Distance Learning* 11.3 (2010): 78–94. Print.

Hadford, Andrew, Dominic Rainsford, and Tim Woods. "Introduction: Literature and the Return to Ethics." *The Ethics in Literature*. Ed. Hadfield, Rainsford, and Woods. New York: St. Martin's, 1999. 1–14. Print.

Halberstam, Judith. *The Queer Art of Failure*. Durham: Duke UP, 2011. Print.

Hall, Geoff. *Literature in Language Education*. New York: Palgrave, 2005. Print.

Hampl, Patricia. "Memory and Imagination." *Fields of Reading*. 9th ed. Ed. Nancy R. Comley et al. New York: Bedford, 2009. 782–91. Print.

Hansen, Matthew C. "Learning to Read Shakespeare: Using Read-Throughs as a Teaching and Learning Strategy." *Working Papers on the Web 4: Teaching Renaissance Texts* (2002): n. pag. Web. 14 Aug. 2012.

———. "'O Brave New World': Service-Learning and Shakespeare." *Pedagogy: Critical Approaches to Teaching Literature, Language, Composition, and Culture* 11.1 (2011): 177–97. Print.

Hardison, O. B. "The MLA and Social Activism." *PMLA* 83.4 (1968): 985–87. Print.

Hawkins, Anne Hunsaker. *Reconstructing Illness: Studies in Pathography*. West Lafayette: Purdue UP, 1999. Print.

Heard, Sarah, Desirée Manello, Keon Pacheco, and Stephanie Tillman, eds. *Inspiration of Talented Youth*. Pembroke: Print Services, U of North Carolina, Pembroke, 2011. Print.

Hellebrandt, Josef, and Lucía T. Varona, eds. *Construyendo puentes (Building Bridges): Concepts and Models for Service-Learning in Spanish*. Washington: Amer. Assn. for Higher Educ., 1999. Print.

Hernandez, Pati. *Telling My Story*. Hernandez, 2009. Web. 27 Nov. 2012.

Herzberg, Bruce. "Community Service and Critical Teaching." *College Composition and Communication* 45.3 (1994): 307–19. Print.

Himley, Margaret. "Facing (Up to) the Stranger in Community Service-Learning." *College Composition and Communication* 55.3 (2004): 416–38. Print.

Hjortshoj, Keith. *The Transition to College Writing*. Boston: Bedford, 2001. Print.

Holcroft, Thomas. "The Dying Prostitute: An Elegy." 1785. *The New Oxford Book of Eighteenth Century Verse*. Ed. Roger Lonsdale. Oxford: Oxford UP, 1984. 683. Print.

Honnet, Ellen Porter, and Susan J. Poulsen. *Principles of Good Practice for Combining Service and Learning: A Wingspread Special Report*. Racine: Johnson Foundation, 1989. *National Service Knowledge Network*. Web. 9 Nov. 2012. <https://www.nationalserviceresources.gov/files/r4174-principles-of -good-practice-for-combining-service-and-learning.pdf>.

Hosseini, Khaled. *The Kite Runner*. New York: Riverhead, 2003. Print.

Howe, Florence. "Why Teach Poetry?—An Experiment." Kampf and Lauter, *Politics* 259–307.

Hudson, Patricia, and Simogne Hudson. "Arts and Life: Everybody Reads 2012: Patricia and Simogne Hudson." *YouTube*. Oregon Public Broadcasting; YouTube, 8 Mar. 2012. Web. 28 July 2014. <https://www.youtube.com/ watch?v=UlpBRbNa7kY>.

Hughes, Langston. *Mulatto: A Tragedy of the Deep South*. 1935. Patton and Honey 476–505.

———. "The Negro Artist and the Racial Mountain." 1926. Gates and McKay, *Norton Anthology* 1311–14.

Hull, Glynda A., and Mira-Lisa Katz. "Crafting an Agentive Self: Case Studies of Digital Storytelling." *Research in the Teaching of English* 41.1 (2006): 43–81. Print.

Hurston, Zora Neale. "The Gilded Six-Bits." 1933. Baym et al. 1713–21.

———. "Passion." Patton and Honey 324–25.

———. "Sweat." Patton and Honey 331–37.

Irvine, Judith T. "When Talk Isn't Cheap: Language and Political Economy." *American Ethnologist* 16.2 (1989): 248–67. Print.

Jackson, Spoon. "On Prison Reform." *SFGate*. Hearst Corp., 14 July 2006. Web. 7 June 2012.

Jacoby, Barbara. "Civic Engagement in Today's Higher Education: An Overview." Jacoby and associates, *Civic Engagement* 5–30.

Jacoby, Barbara, and associates, eds. *Building Partnerships for Service-Learning*. San Francisco: Jossey, 2003. Print.

———. *Civic Engagement in Higher Education: Concepts and Practices*. San Francisco: Wiley, 2009. Print.

Jahoda, Gustav. "Theodor Lipps and the Shift from 'Sympathy' to 'Empathy.'" *Journal of the History of the Behavioral Sciences* 41.2 (2005): 151–63. Print.

James, Jayson, Ashley Maietta, Chris Peck, and Maggie Sinkiewicz. "Reflect." Parfitt 24–25.

Jay, Gregory. "The Engaged Humanities: Principles and Practices of Public Scholarship and Teaching." *Journal of Community Engagement and Scholarship* 3.1 (2010): 51–63. Web. 19 Nov. 2013.

———. "Service Learning, Multiculturalism, and the Pedagogies of Difference." *Pedagogy: Critical Approaches to Teaching Literature, Languages, Composition and Culture* 8.2 (2008): 255–81. Print.

Kalu, Uchechi. "Autobiographical Reflection." *Days I Moved through Ordinary Sounds*. Ed. Chad Sweeney. San Francisco: City Lights Foundation, 2009. 155–56. Print.

Kamen, Henry. "The Myth of a Universal Language." *Imagining Spain*. New Haven: Yale UP, 2008. 150–71. Print.

Kampf, Louis, and Paul Lauter. Introduction. Kampf and Lauter, *Politics* 3–54.

———, eds. *The Politics of Literature: Dissenting Essays on the Teaching of English*. New York: Pantheon, 1972. Print.

Kaplan, Carey, and Ellen Cronan Rose. *The Canon and the Common Reader*. Knoxville: U of Tennessee P, 1990. Print.

Keen, Suzanne. *Empathy and the Novel*. Oxford: Oxford UP, 2007. Print.

Kelly, Liz. "The Continuum of Sexual Violence." 1987. *Sexualities: Critical Concepts in Sociology*. Ed. Ken Plummer. New York: Routledge, 2002. 127–39. *Google Books*. Web. 23 May 2012.

Kenyon, Jane. "Having It Out with Melancholy." *Poets.org*. Acad. of Amer. Poets, 1993. Web. 2 Dec. 2012.

Kessler, Lauren. *Finding Life in the Land of Alzheimer's*. New York: Penguin, 2008. Print.

Kezar, Adrianna J., Tony C. Chambers, and John C. Burkhardt, eds. *Higher Education for the Public Good: Emerging Voices from a National Movement*. San Francisco: Jossey, 2005. Print.

Kidd, Lori I., Jaclene A. Zauszniewski, and Diana L. Morris. "Benefits of a Poetry

Writing Intervention for Family Caregivers of Elders with Dementia." *Issues in Mental Health Nursing* 32.9 (2011): 598–604. Print.

King, Martin Luther, Jr. "Where Do We Go from Here?" 11th Annual SCLC Convention. Atlanta. 16 Aug. 1967. *The Martin Luther King, Jr., Research and Education Institute at Stanford University.* Web. 29 Aug. 2012.

Kirby, Dan, Dawn Kirby, and Tom Liner. *Inside Out: Strategies for Teaching Writing.* 3rd ed. Portsmouth: Heinemann, 2004. Print.

Kirby, Katherine E. "Encountering and Understanding Suffering: The Need for Service Learning in Ethical Education." *Teaching Philosophy* 32.2 (2009): 153–76. Print.

Koritz, Amy. "Beyond Teaching Tolerance: Literary Studies in a Democracy." *Profession* (2005): 80–91. Print.

Koritz, Amy, and George J. Sanchez, eds. *Civic Engagement in the Wake of Katrina.* Ann Arbor: U of Michigan P, 2009. Print.

Kristof, Nicholas D., and Sheryl WuDunn. *Half the Sky: Turning Oppression into Opportunity for Women Worldwide.* New York: Vintage, 2009. Print.

Kuh, George D. *High-Impact Educational Practices: What They Are, Who Has Access to Them, and Why They Matter.* Washington: Assn. of Amer. Colls. and Univs., 2008. Print.

"Lakewood Library—Discussion: On Individuality." *My Antonia—The Big Read Program of Chautauqua and Cattaraugus Counties.* N.p., 24 Feb. 2010. Web. 4 Sept. 2012.

Lang-Peralta, Linda. "'Clandestine Delight': Frances Burney's Life-Writing." *Women's Life-Writing: Finding Voice / Building Community.* Bowling Green: Popular, 1997. 23–41. Print.

Langstraat, Lisa, and Melody Bowdon. "Service-Learning and Critical Emotion Studies: On the Perils of Empathy and the Politics of Compassion." *Michigan Journal of Community Service Learning* 17.2 (2011): 5–14. Print.

Larsen, Nella. *Quicksand.* 1928. Mineola: Dover, 2006. Print.

Latour, Bruno. *Reassembling the Social: An Introduction to Actor-Network Theory.* Oxford: Oxford UP, 2005. Print.

Lee, Harper. *To Kill a Mockingbird.* 1960. New York: Harper, 2002. Print.

Leeman, Jennifer. "Engaging Critical Pedagogy: Spanish for Native Speakers." *Foreign Language Annals* 38.1 (2005): 35–45. Print.

———. "The Value of Spanish: Shifting Ideologies in US Language Teaching." *ADFL Bulletin* 38.1–2 (2007): 32–39. Print.

Leeman, Jennifer, and Glenn Martínez. "From Identity to Commodity: Discourses of Spanish in Heritage Language Textbooks." *Critical Inquiry in Language Studies* 4.1 (2007): 35–65. Print.

Leeman, Jennifer, and Lisa Rabin. "Reading Language: Critical Perspectives for the Literature Classroom." *Hispania* 90.2 (2007): 304–15. Print.

Leeman, Jennifer, Lisa Rabin, and Esperanza Román-Mendoza. "Critical Pedagogy beyond the Classroom Walls: Community Service-Learning and Spanish Heritage Language Education." *Heritage Language Journal* 8.3 (2011): 1–22. Web. 31 May 2012.

———. "La Web 2.0 al servicio de la comunidad en un programa de español como lengua de herencia en Estados Unidos." *Teoría de la Educación: Educación y Cultura en la Sociedad de la Información* 12.3 (2011): 118–40. Web. 31 May 2012.

Leidig, Marjorie Whittaker. "The Continuum of Violence against Women: Psychological and Physical Consequences." *Journal of American College Health* 40.4 (1992): 149–55. Print.

Levinson, Brett. *The Ends of Literature: The Latin American "Boom" in the Neoliberal Marketplace.* Stanford: Stanford UP, 2002. Print.

"Liberal Arts in Prison." *Grinnell College.* Grinnell Coll., n.d. Web. 26 June 2012.

"Life Story Commons." *University of Southern Maine.* U of Maine, n.d. Web. 28 Aug 2012.

"Literature Course Guidelines and Objectives." *University of North Carolina at Pembroke.* U of North Carolina, Pembroke, 5 May 2011. Web. 6 Jan. 2014.

Long, Adam, Daniel Singer, and Jess Winfield. *The Complete Works of William Shakespeare (Abridged).* New York: Applause, 1987. Print.

Lopate, Phillip. *The Art of the Personal Essay: An Anthology from the Classical Era to the Present.* New York: Anchor, 1995. Print.

Lynch, Cara R., Elizabeth E. Henry, Lisa V. Bardwell, and Jennifer A. Richter. "Utilizing Social Media for Democratic Service-Learning Practice: A Framework and Guide for Educators." *Designing Problem-Driven Instruction with Online Social Media.* Ed. Kay Kyeong-Ju Seo, Debra A. Pellegrino, and Chalee Engelhard. Charlotte: Information Age, 2012. 127–46. Print.

Lynn, Steven. *Texts and Contexts: Writing about Literature with Critical Theory.* 5th ed. New York: Pearson, 2008. Print.

Lyon, George Ella. *George Ella Lyon: Writer and Teacher.* N.p., n.d. Web. June 2012.

MacDonald, Michael Patrick. *All Souls.* Boston: Beacon, 1999. Print.

MacLachlan, Patricia. *Sarah, Plain and Tall.* New York: Harper, 1985. Print.

Madanski, Dana. Message to Kathleen Béres Rogers. 23 Aug. 2012. E-mail.

Mairs, Nancy. "On Being a Cripple." Bloom and White, *Inquiry* 24–34.

Malachuk, Daniel S. "Cultural Studies, Compassion, and the Promise of Community-Based Learning." Danielson and Fallon 26–45.

Malone, Eileen. *Letters with Taloned Claws*. San Francisco: Bedlam, 2005. Print.

———. "Outdoor Sky." Malone, *Letters* 21.

———. "The Visit Secured." Malone, *Letters* 16.

Mamabolo, Lott M. "Group Treatment Program for Sexually and Physically Assaultive Young Offenders in a Secure Custody Facility." *Canadian Psychology / Psychologie canadienne* 37.3 (1996): 154–60. *CSA PsycArticles*. Web. 6 Jan. 2010.

Mangum, Teresa. "Going Public: From the Perspective of the Classroom." *Pedagogy: Critical Approaches to Teaching Literature, Languages, Composition and Culture* 12.1 (2012): 5–18. Print.

———. "The Many Lives of Victorian Fiction." *Romanticism and Victorianism on the Net* 55 (2009): n. pag. Web. 13 Jan. 2012.

Martínez, Glenn. "Classroom Based Dialect Awareness in Heritage Language Instruction: A Critical Applied Linguistic Approach." *Heritage Language Journal* 1.1 (2003): n. pag. Web. 31 May 2012.

Marullo, Sam. "Sociology's Essential Role: Promoting Critical Analysis in Service-Learning." *Cultivating the Sociological Imagination: Concepts and Models for Service Learning in Sociology*. Ed. James Ostrow, Garry Hesser, and Sandra Enos. Washington: Amer. Assn. for Higher Educ., 1999. 10–27. Print.

Masumoto, David Mas. *Four Seasons in Five Senses: Things Worth Savoring*. New York: Norton, 2004. Print.

Mauer, Marc, and Ryan S. King. "Uneven Justice: State Rates of Incarceration by Race and Ethnicity." *The Sentencing Project*. Sentencing Project, July 2007. Web. 7 June 2012.

McBride, James. *The Color of Water: A Black Man's Tribute to His White Mother*. New York: Penguin, 1996. Print.

McCabe, Ronald B. *Civic Librarianship: Renewing the Social Mission of the Public Library*. Lanham: Scarecrow, 2001. Print.

McCall, Lisa. "Arts and Life: Everybody Reads 2012: Lisa McCall." *YouTube*. Oregon Public Broadcasting; YouTube, 21 Mar. 2012. Web. 28 July 2014. <http://www.youtube.com/watch?v=QMx3zoDf36o>.

McCarty, Heather Jane. "Educating Felons: Reflections on Higher Education in Prison." *Radical History Review* 96 (2006): 87–94. Print.

McLaughlin, Meghan, Jean Trounstine, and Robert P. Waxler. *Success Stories: Life Skills through Literature*. *Ed.gov*. US Dept. of Educ., Jan. 1997. Web. 7 June 2012.

McMahon, Susan I., et al. *The Book Club Connection: Literacy Learning and Classroom Talk*. New York: Teachers Coll., 1997. Print.

Mehaffy, George. "Preparing Undergraduates to Be Citizens: The Critical Role of the First Year of College." *First Year Civic Engagement: Sound Foundations for College, Citizenship, and Democracy*. Ed. Martha LaBare. New York: New York Times Knowledge Network, 2008. 5–8. Print.

Melville, Herman. *Billy Budd*. 1962. New York: Simon, 2006. Print.

Miller, Carolyn R. "Genre as Social Action." *Quarterly Journal of Speech* 70 (1984): 151–67. Print.

Miller, J. Hillis. "Today, Tomorrow: The Intellectual in the Academy and in Society." *PMLA* 112.5 (1997): 1137–38. Print.

Mintz, Susannah B. "Writing as Refiguration: Lucy Grealy's *Autobiography of a Face*." *Biography: An Interdisciplinary Quarterly* 24.1 (2001): 172–84. Print.

Misook, H. "Digital Storytelling: An Empirical Study of the Impact of Digital Storytelling on Pre-service Teachers' Self-Efficacy and Dispositions towards Educational Technology." *Journal of Educational Multimedia and Hypermedia* 18.4 (2009): 405–28. Print.

Mitchell, Tania. "Traditional vs. Critical Service-Learning: Engaging the Literature to Differentiate Two Models." *Michigan Journal of Community Service-Learning* 14.2 (2008): 50–65. Print.

Moll, Luis. "Captives of Words: Challenging the Pedagogy of Control." AERA Distinguished Lecture, Montreal. 1999. Address.

Mollis, Kara. "Servicing Reading: Community Work and the Revaluation of Literary Study." Danielson and Fallon 46–62.

Moody, Bernise. "I Am an Overcomer." Allen, McAllister, Moody, and Taylor 7.

Morton, Keith. "The Irony of Service: Charity, Project, and Social Change in Service Learning." *Michigan Journal of Community Service Learning* 2 (1995): 19–32. Print.

Mueller, Isolde. "Rewriting the Egg: Community-Based Learning, German Literature, and Intercultural Competence." Danielson and Fallon 180–95.

"Municipal Solid Waste." *United States Environmental Protection Agency*. US Environmental Protection Agency, 3 Apr. 2012. Web. 28 June 2012.

"My Interpretation of ME." Collins, Laws, Morales, and Simpson 4.

Noddings, Nel. "Care, Justice, and Equity." *Justice and Caring: The Search for Common Ground in Education*. Ed. Michael Katz, Noddings, and Kenneth Strike. New York: Teachers Coll., 1999. 7–20. Print.

Nussbaum, Martha C. *Not for Profit: Why Democracy Needs the Humanities*. Princeton: Princeton UP, 2010. Print.

———. *Poetic Justice: The Literary Imagination and Public Life*. Boston: Beacon, 1995. Print.

Ochoa, Gloria L., and Enrique R. Ochoa. "Education for Social Transformation: Chicana/o and Latin American Studies and Community Struggles." *Latin American Perspectives* 31.1 (2004): 59–80. Print.

"Official Student Enrollment." *George Mason University*. Institutional Research and Printing, George Mason U, n.d. Web. 28 July 2014. <http://irr.gmu.edu/off_enrl/>.

Olsen, Tillie. "I Stand Here Ironing." 1953. *The Seagull Reader: Stories*. Ed. Joseph Kelly. 2nd ed. New York: Norton, 2008. 402–10. Print.

Oppermann, Matthias, and Michael Coventry. *Digital Storytelling Multimedia Archive and Website. Georgetown University*. Georgetown U, 2012. Web. 27 May 2013.

"Our Mission, Vision and Values." *Mount Mercy University*. Mount Mercy U, 17 Aug. 2010. Web. 12 June 2012.

"Our Network." *HandsOn Network*. Points of Light Inst., 2013. Web. 18 Mar. 2014.

Palmer, Parker. *The Courage to Teach: Exploring the Inner Landscape of a Teacher's Life*. San Francisco: Jossey, 2007. Print.

Pannapacker, William. "The MLA and the Digital Humanities." *Chronicle of Higher Education*. Chronicle of Higher Educ., 28 Dec. 2009. Web. 16 Oct. 2013.

Parfitt, Elizabeth, ed. *The Sky Is Wicked Huge*. Emerson Coll., Apr. 2010. Web. 3 Oct. 2012.

Patton, Venetria K., and Maureen Honey, eds. *Double-Take: A Revisionist Harlem Renaissance Anthology*. 2nd ed. New Brunswick: Rutgers UP, 2006. Print.

Paulson, William. *Literary Culture in a World Transformed: A Future for the Humanities*. Ithaca: Cornell UP, 2001. Print.

Peck, Chris. "The Art of Experience." *Digication*. Emerson Coll., 2010. Web. 3 Oct. 2012.

Perloff, Marjorie, et al. "The Intellectual, the Artist, and the Reader." *PMLA* 112.5 (1997): 1129–32. Print.

Poe, Edgar Allan. "The Purloined Letter." *"The Fall of the House of Usher" and Other Writings: Poems, Tales, Essays and Reviews*. Ed. David Galloway. London: Penguin, 2003. 281–300. Print.

Poindexter, Sandra, Pamela Arnold, and Christopher Osterhout. "Service-Learning from a Distance: Partnering Multiple Universities and Local Governments in a Large Scale Initiative." *Michigan Journal of Community Service Learning* 15.2 (2009): 56–67. Print.

Pollan, Michael. *Omnivore's Dilemma: A Natural History of Four Meals*. New York: Penguin, 2007. Print.

Pomerantz, Anne. "Language Ideologies and the Production of Identities: Spanish as a Resource for Participation in a Global Marketplace." *Multilingua* 21.2–3 (2002): 275–302. Print.

Porter, Rachel. "Arts and Life: Everybody Reads 2012: Rachel Porter." *YouTube*. Oregon Public Broadcasting; YouTube, 21 Mar. 2012. Web. 28 July 2014. <https://www.youtube.com/watch?v=zAFmM3_rHvI&feature=relmfu>.

"The Power of SUNY." *The State University of New York*. State U of New York, 2012. Web. 4 June 2012.

Prins, Esther, and Nicole Webster. "Student Identities and the Tourist Gaze in International Service-Learning: A University Project in Belize." *Journal of Higher Education Outreach and Engagement* 14.1 (2010): 5–32. Print.

"Prison Book Club." *Mount Mercy University*. Mount Mercy U, n.d. Web. 1 Apr. 2014. <http://www.mtmercy.edu/prison-book-club>.

Rabin, Lisa. "The Culmore Bilingual ESL and Popular Education Project: Coming to Consciousness on Labor, Literacy, and Community." *Radical Teacher* 91 (2011): 58–67. Print.

———. "Literacy Narratives for Social Change: Making Connections between Service-Learning and Literature Education." *Enculturation* 6.1 (2008): n. pag. Web. 27 July 2008.

Rabkin, Eric. "Real Work Is Better Than Homework." U of Michigan, Ann Arbor. 19 Nov. 2008. Address.

Rae'Kwon. "Theme for English B." Heard, Manello, Pacheco, and Tillman 7.

"Randolph Library—Discussion Part 1." *My Antonia—The Big Read Program of Chautauqua and Cattaraugus Counties*. N.p., 3 Mar. 2010. Web. 4 Sept. 2012.

"Randolph Site—Part 2." *My Antonia—The Big Read Program of Chautauqua and Cattaraugus Counties*. N.p., 10 Mar. 2010. Web. 4 Sept. 2012.

Rickett, Carolyn, Cedric Greive, and Jill Gordon. "Something to Hang My Life On: The Health Benefits of Writing Poetry for People with Serious Illnesses." *Australasian Psychiatry* 19.3 (2011): 265–68. Print.

Rideau, Wilbert. *In the Place of Justice: A Story of Punishment and Deliverance*. New York: Vintage, 2011. Print.

Riggio, Milla C., ed. *Teaching Shakespeare through Performance*. New York: MLA, 1999. Print.

Rimmon-Kenan, Shlomith. "The Story of 'I': Illness and Narrative Identity." *Narrative* 10.0 (2002): 9–27. Web. 15 July 2014.

Robin, Bernard. *The Educational Uses of Digital Storytelling. University of Houston.* U of Houston, 2013. Web. 27 May 2013.

Robinson, Mary. "London's Summer Morning." 1800. *Poems (Continued).* Ed. Daniel Robinson. London: Pickering, 2009. 117–18. Print.

Rocklin, Edward I. *Performance Approaches to Teaching Shakespeare.* Urbana: NCTE, 2005. Print.

Rockwell, Geoffrey. "On the Evaluation of Digital Media as Scholarship." *Profession* (2011): 152–68. Print.

Roorbach, Bill. *Writing Life Stories: How to Make Memories into Memoirs, Ideas into Essays, and Life into Literature.* Cincinnati: Writer's Digest, 2008. Print.

Said, Edward W. "Opponents, Audiences, Constituencies and Community." *Critical Inquiry* 9.1 (1982): 1–26. Print.

Sanders, Scott Russell. "The Inheritance of Tools." Bloom and White, *Inquiry* 503–10.

———. "Under the Influence: Paying the Price of My Father's Booze." Bloom and White, *Inquiry* 521–33.

Sandy, Marie, and Barbara A. Holland. "Different Worlds and Common Ground: Community Partner Perspectives on Campus-Community Partnerships." *Michigan Journal of Community Service Learning* 13.1 (2006): 30–43. Print.

Sarmiento, Domingo Faustino. *Facundo: Civilization and Barbarism.* Trans. Kathleen Ross. Berkeley: U of California P, 2003. Print.

Scarry, Elaine. *The Body in Pain: The Making and Unmaking of the World.* Oxford: Oxford UP, 1985. Print.

Schlosser, Eric. *Fast Food Nation: The Dark Side of the All-American Meal.* New York: Harper, 2001. Print.

Schneider, Pat. *Writing Alone and with Others.* New York: Oxford UP, 2003. Print.

Scholes, Robert. "Presidential Address 2004: The Humanities in a Posthumanist World." *PMLA* 120.3 (2005): 724–33. Print.

Schreibman, Susan, Laura Mandell, and Stephen Olsen. Introduction to "Evaluating Digital Scholarship." *Profession* (2011): 123–36. Print.

Schutz, Aaron, and Anne Ruggles Gere. "Service Learning and English Studies: Rethinking 'Public' Service." *College English* 60.2 (1998): 129–49. Print.

Schuyler, George S. *Black No More: A Novel.* 1931. New York: Mod. Lib., 1999. Print.

Schwartz, Marcy. "Public Stakes, Public Stories: Service Learning in Literary Studies." *PMLA* 127.4 (2012): 987–93. Print.

———. "The Right to Imagine: Reading in Community with People and Stories / Gente y Cuentos." *PMLA* 126.3 (2011): 746–52. Print.

Sebold, Alice. *Lucky*. Boston: Little, 2002. Print.

Seider, Scott, James Huguley, and Sarah Novick. "College Students, Diversity, and Community Service Learning." *Teachers College Record* 115.3 (2013): 1–44. Print.

Seifer, Sarena D., and Kara Conners, eds. *Faculty Toolkit for Service-Learning in Higher Education. National Service-Learning Clearinghouse*. NCLS, 2007. Web. 19 Nov. 2013.

Seiter, Bill, and Ellen Seiter. *The Creative Artist's Legal Guide: Copyright, Trademark, and Contracts in Film and Digital Media Production*. New Haven: Yale UP, 2012. Print.

Sennett, Richard. *The Fall of Public Man*. New York: Norton, 1974. Print.

Shakespeare, William. *The Complete Works of Shakespeare*. Ed. David Bevington. 6th ed. New York: Pearson, 2009. Print.

———. *Macbeth*. Shakespeare, *Norton Shakespeare* 2555–618.

———. *The Norton Shakespeare*. Ed. Stephen Greenblatt et al. New York: Norton, 1997. Print.

———. *Othello*. Shakespeare, *Norton Shakespeare* 2091–174.

Shelley, Mary. *Frankenstein*. 1831. Ed. Johanna M. Smith. 2nd ed. Boston: Bedford–St. Martin's, 2000. Print. Case Studies in Contemporary Criticism.

Simon, Leslie. "*Bleak House, Our Mutual Friend*, and the Aesthetics of Dust." *Dickens Studies Annual: Essays on Victorian Fiction* 42 (2011): 217–26. Print.

Simons, Judy. "The Unfixed Text: Narrative and Identity in Women's Private Writings." *The Representation of the Self in Women's Autobiography*. Bologna: U of Bologna, 1993. 1–16. Print.

Sinclair, Upton. *The Jungle*. 1906. New York: Bedford, 2005. Print.

Smith, M. Cecil. "Does Service Learning Promote Adult Development? Theoretical Perspectives." *New Directions for Adult and Continuing Education* 118 (2008): 5–15. Print.

Smith, Sidonie. "The English Major as Social Action." *Profession* (2010): 196–206. Print.

Smith, Sidonie, and Julia Watson. *Reading Autobiography: A Guide for Interpreting Life Narratives*. 2nd ed. Minneapolis: U of Minnesota P, 2010. Print.

Sommer, Doris. *Foundational Fictions*. Berkeley: U of California P, 1993. Print.

Steinbeck, John. *The Grapes of Wrath*. New York: Viking, 1939. Print.

Steinberg, Kathryn S., Robert D. Bringle, and Matthew J. Williams. *Service-Learning Research Primer. National Service-Learning Clearinghouse*. NCLS, 2010. Web. 19 Nov. 2013.

Stevenson, Robert Louis. *Dr. Jekyll and Mr. Hyde.* 1886. New York: Signet, 2003. Print.

Stoecker, Randy, and Elizabeth Tryon, eds. *The Unheard Voices: Community Organizations and Service Learning.* Philadelphia: Temple UP, 2009. Print.

———. "Unheard Voices: Community Organizations and Service Learning." Stoecker and Tryan, *Unheard Voices* 1–18.

Strage, Amy. "Long-Term Academic Benefits of Service Learning: When and Where Do They Manifest Themselves?" *College Student Journal* 38.2 (2004): 257–62. Print.

Strait, Jean, and Tim Sauer. "Constructing Experiential Learning for Online Courses: The Birth of E-service." *Educause Quarterly* 27.1 (2004): 62–65. Web. 16 Oct. 2013.

Strand, Kerry J. "Community-Based Research as Pedagogy." *Michigan Journal of Community Service Learning* 7 (2000): 85–96. Print.

A Streetcar Named Desire. Dir. Elia Kazan. Perf. Vivien Leigh, Marlon Brando, and Kim Hunter. 1951. Warner Home Video, 1997. DVD.

Tannenbaum, Judith. *Disguised as a Poem: My Years Teaching Poetry at San Quentin.* Boston: Northeastern UP, 2000. Print.

———. *Teeth, Wiggly as Earthquakes: Writing Poetry in the Primary Grades.* Portland: Stenhouse, 2000. Print.

Taylor, Lisa K. "Reading Desire: From Empathy to Estrangement, from Enlightenment to Implication." *Intercultural Education* 18.4 (2007): 297–316. Web. 23 May 2012.

Taylor, Signe, dir. *Telling My Story: Movie.* Taylor, 2011. Web. 27 Nov. 2012. <http://tellingmystorymovie.com>.

Teres, Harvey. *The Word on the Street: Linking the Academy and the Common Reader.* Ann Arbor: U of Michigan P, 2011. Print.

Thelma and Louise. Dir. Ridley Scott. Perf. Susan Sarandon and Geena Davis. 1991. MGM Home Entertainment, 2004. DVD.

Thurman, Wallace. "Emma Lou." Patton and Honey 526–37.

———. *Infants of the Spring.* 1932. Boston: Northeastern UP, 1992. Print.

Todd, Stephanie. "The Broken Mirror of Identity in Lucy Grealy's *Autobiography of a Face.*" *New Essays on Life Writing and the Body.* Newcastle upon Tyne: Cambridge Scholars, 2009. 207–22. Print.

Todorov, Tzvetan, et al. "The Genealogy of the Intellectual since the French Enlightenment." *PMLA* 112.5 (1997): 1121–28. Print.

Toker, Leona. "Decadence and Renewal in Dickens's *Our Mutual Friend.*" *Connotations: A Journal for Critical Debate* 16.1–3 (2006–07): 47–59. Print.

Tonkin, Humphrey. *Service-Learning across Cultures: Promise and Achievement.* Portland: Intl. Partnership for Service-Learning and Leadership, 2004. Print.

Toomer, Jean. *Cane.* Ed. Rudolph P. Byrd and Henry Louis Gates, Jr. New York: Norton, 2011. Print.

Trounstine, Jean, and Robert P. Waxler. *Finding a Voice: The Practice of Changing Lives through Literature.* Ann Arbor: U of Michigan P, 2005. Print.

Verducci, Susan. "A Conceptual History of Empathy and a Question It Raises for Moral Education." *Educational Theory* 50.1 (2000): 63–81. Print.

Waldner, Leora S., Sue Y. McGorry, and Murray C. Widener. "E-Service-Learning: The Evolution of Service-Learning to Engage a Growing Online Student Population." *Journal of Higher Education Outreach and Engagement* 16.2 (2012): 123–50. Print.

———. "Extreme E-service Learning (XE-SL): E-service Learning in the 100% Online Course." *MERLOT Journal of Online Learning and Teaching* 6.4 (2010): 839–51. Web. 28 July 2014.

Welch, Marshall. "Moving from Service-Learning to Civic Engagement." Jacoby and associates, *Civic Engagement* 174–95.

Williams, Raymond. *Marxism and Literature.* Oxford: Oxford UP, 1977. Print.

Williams, Tennessee. *A Streetcar Named Desire.* 1947. New York: Signet-Penguin, 1974. Print.

Willis, Deborah. "'The Gnawing Vulture': Revenge, Trauma Theory, and *Titus Andronicus.*" *Shakespeare Quarterly* 53.1 (2002): 21–52. Print.

Woodward, Kathleen. "The Future of the Humanities—in the Present and in Public." *Daedalus* 138.1 (2009): 110–23. Print.

Woolf, Michael. "Not Serious Stuff? Service-Learning in Context: An International Perspective." *Frontiers: The Interdisciplinary Journal of Study Abroad* 17 (2008): 21–32. Print.

Wordsworth, William. *The Thirteen-Book Prelude.* 1805. Ed. Mark L. Reed. 2 vols. Ithaca: Cornell UP, 1991. Print.

Wright, Richard. *Native Son.* 1940. New York: Harper, 2005. Print.

Wrigley, Heide, and Jim Powrie. *Meeting the Challenge on the Border: A Report on Language and Literacy on the U.S.-Mexico Border.* Washington: US Dept. of Labor, 2003. Print.

WritersCorps, Judith Tannenbaum, and Valerie Chow Bush. *Jump Write In! Creative Writing Exercises for Diverse Communities, Grades 6–12.* San Francisco: Jossey, 2005. Print.

Wurr, Adrian J., and Josef Hellebrandt, eds. *Learning the Language of Global Citizenship: Service-Learning in Applied Linguistics.* Bolton: Anker, 2007. Print.

Zengerski, Ashley. Message to Emily VanDette. 25 Sept. 2012. E-mail.

Ziemianski, Jillian. "The Criticisms of Both Public and Academic Workshops." *A Writer and a Piece of Mind*. N.p., 6 May 2010. Web. 4 Sept. 2012.

———. "Exploring the Creative Writing Community." *A Writer and a Piece of Mind*. N.p., 6 May 2010. Web. 4 Sept. 2012.

Zlotkowski, Edward. Introduction. Danielson and Fallon xi–xiv.

Zlotkowski, Edward, and Donna Duffy. "Two Decades of Community-Based Learning." *New Directions for Teaching and Learning* 123 (2010): 33–43. Print.

Index